CW01631648

HOUSEQUAKE

Is this the right time to buy a house?

Is this the right time to own a house?

Also by Robert Beckman

Supertiming
(1979)

The Downwave
(1982)

Into The Upwave
(1987)

Crashes
(1988)

Powertiming
(1992)

* * * * *

This book is dedicated to all homeless people, many of whom would now have homes if it were not for the unconscionable and irrational forces of the pseudo-market economies that turned precious nests into pernicious nest-eggs.

HOUSEQUAKE

Is this the right time to buy a house?

Is this the right time to own a house?

ROBERT BECKMAN

Rushmere Wynne

Published 1996

© Robert Beckman

All rights reserved. No part of this publication may be reproduced, stored in a retrieval system, or transmitted, in any form or by any means, electronic, mechanical, photocopying, recording or otherwise, without the prior permission of the publishers.

The right of Robert Beckman to be identified as the author of this work has been asserted by him in accordance with the Copyright, Designs and Patents Act 1988.

British Library Cataloguing in Publication Data. A catalogue record for this book is available from the British Library.

ISBN 0 948035 46 3

Designed and typeset by:
MacWing

Cover Design by:
Lee Gibbons

Published by:
Rushmere Wynne Limited
4-5 Harmill, Grovebury Road,
Leighton Buzzard, Bedfordshire LU7 8FF
Tel: 01525 853726
Fax: 01525 852037

Printed by:
BOOKCRAFT Book Printers & Binders
First Avenue, Westfield Trading Estate,
Midsomer Norton, Bath, Avon BA3 4BS

CONTENTS

ACKNOWLEDGEMENTS

NO WORK of the size and scope of this book could ever be attributed to any one person. I may have put the words on paper but the influences and assistance that are responsible for the final outcome, and which should be acknowledged, are very far reaching. If it was not for my grandfather and my father, both of whom taught me to think for myself from a very early age, this book certainly would never have come to being, nor would I have had the courage to question the conventional wisdom of my teachers and professors during the formative years of my education. Dumb is dumb. A lot of them were really, really dumb. Thanks, Grandpa! Thanks Pop! I think both of you did a great job on me, something that you can be proud of. This book is an example, as were my other books.

A great deal of the research that went into the compilation of *Housequake* was undertaken when I was writing *The Downwave*, *Into the Upwave* and *Crashes*. I will be eternally grateful to Nicholas Pine of Milestone Publications for his untiring efforts in ensuring that these books achieved the success and exposure which we felt they deserved. I am equally indebted to Lord Rees-Mogg for encouraging me to take matters one step further in *Crashes*.

I can tell you, it was an uphill battle all the way when it came to publishing my research on the long-term history of house prices and the future implications. There were no shortage of dissenters who would have preferred that my research was kept under wraps, locked away in some archive in perpetuity. I was banned from Capital Radio in London for voicing my views on the housing market. The City Editor of *The Mail on Sunday* physically descended upon the offices of LBC to insist I be taken off the air because of my reference to the prospects for house prices. Then there was the continuing battles with Marc Boleat, Secretary General of the Building Societies Association, who attempted to counter everything I said at every opportunity, and others who would habitually denigrate and deride anything in contravention of the populist stance. But, thanks to Doug Moffatt, Financial Editor of LBC, who defended my right to provide what I considered to be an objective view, the subject of house prices received a balanced hearing and the views I expressed at the time are now embodied in this work.

It has been said that one man with the truth is an army. For a time I felt like David fighting a battalion of self-interest Goliaths, but not for long. Thankfully, there remains journalistic integrity in some quarters. In my battle to bring the truth about the residential housing market to the public, one brave lady writing for the *Evening Standard* in London, published an interview where I gave my prognosis for house prices. The day after the paper was inundated with letters and telephone calls from estate agents and others who were regular advertisers on property-related matters. In concert, the vultures threatened to cancel their advertising unless a complete retraction was made regarding my opinions on the residential property market. There was no retraction. One journalist single-handedly fought and won the battle for objective and balanced reporting. Other journalists writing for the *Investors Chronicle*, *Financial Times*, *The Times* and *The Guardian* picked up the gauntlet and joined the battle against those in the media who use their position to mislead and misguide in the sole interest of satisfying managing editors who are unable to see beyond the week's advertising revenue. I certainly owe a debt of gratitude to those journalists who have put their careers on the line in their battle to protect members of the public and who continue to do so. Without them this book would not have a market and would not have been worth writing.

I am beholden to my editor Bob Finigan, formerly with the BBC who once again was able to make the unreadable readable, while rendering the confused absurdity of my prose lucidly absurd. Bob also helped me to avoid some very dumb mistakes, like treating the bowel movements of indigenous butterflies as analogous to the manner in which the gyrations in house prices might unfold, and helped me turn what could have been a paralysingly boring subject into something quite interesting and entertaining.

Then there are the unsung heroes, who may not have been directly involved in the editorial content of this book, but without whose efforts there would be no book. Once again I am indebted to Nick Stabler and John Lawlee who, in spite of their burgeoning task of producing *Investors Bulletin* every week, always managed to find time to support my research by pouring over material that I might not ordinarily have access to and passing it on to me.

There is also the lynch-pin of *Investors Bulletin*, Betty Stabler, to whom eating, sleeping and leading a normal life never seems to have been a high priority. Betty was once again landed with the awesome task of re-typing and correcting my manuscripts while at the same time attending to the needs of the several thousand people who have come to rely on the *Investors Bulletin*.

I certainly owe a debt of gratitude to Tony Drury and Sue Gibbons of my new publishers, Rushmere Wynne. It was just like the movies. As soon as Tony read the manuscript of *Housequake*, he hopped on the next jet to Nice, then took a helicopter to Monte Carlo to sign a deal and get the project on the road as soon as possible. Sue took impeccable care of all the organisation.

Thanks heaps.....all of you!

Robert Beckman

September 1996

PREFACE

ECONOMICS has long been called the dismal science and professional practitioners have never failed to live down that depressing reputation. One of their more esteemed members, John Maynard Keynes, summed it up concisely in his General Theory of Employment: "Practical men are usually the slaves of some defunct economist".

Keynes highlighted the frightening impact of the economist's art. The people who run our lives are deeply fearful of innovative thinking and distrust the future perspective. If economists are seen as the high priests of government, future-thinkers are dismissed as the witch-doctors. Thus, for generations, we have been ruled by the tyranny of received wisdom and the short-term view.

My years at the Hudson Institute under its director Herman Kahn — nutty, iconoclastic but always original — taught me a powerful lesson. Received wisdom is always dangerously out of date, invariably by ten years at least. Take a look at just one example from recent economic history. After the oil shock of the early 1970s, when crude prices quadrupled, we were told the era of cheap petroleum was over. Yet, even then, closer scrutiny of the numbers for oil reserves and potential production pointed to a longer-term scenario of plenty and hence a downward pressure on oil prices. A few lone voices, including my own, forecast a return to affordable oil within a matter of years. We were widely ridiculed for our efforts to second guess the future. Yet, today, oil prices are lower, in real terms, than they were before those crisis-ridden months two decades ago.

Unimaginative, short-term, thinking is the biggest problem of our age. At a time when traditional answers to vital economic questions no longer make sense, we shelter behind outmoded theories and irrelevant philosophies. Governments struggle to stimulate growth, reduce debt and create jobs but events are directed by forces they no longer control. Above all, the financial system that shapes our future prosperity now serves only itself. National economies are swayed by vast, invisible movements of monetary resources. Individual savings — the nest-eggs of countless millions — are victims of a frenzy of marketing hype, bloated costs and conflicts of interest.

We need new ideas to explain our predicament, offer solutions and provide new tools for managing our economic future. The start point is to jettison the baggage of a generation of views about how the world works — views that are many years past their sell-by date. Brave new thinking. Radical analysis. A long, hard look at the facts and influences that rule our lives and put our wealth at risk. This book is part of that new start.

Dr James Bellini

INTRODUCTION

IT OFTEN appears that we live in an era when change is so rapid, total and unprecedented that the most useful advice that anyone can give about the future is “expect the unexpected”. It may be a useful generalisation, but not a helpful one. It does nothing to alter the dangerous paradigm harboured by most individuals who believe the future will merely be a semi-predictable extension of the past, interspersed by random events. Although startling at times, these unexpected events will not necessarily alter the manner in which we will be able to live our lives in the future. While most people have become accustomed to change — and expect change — those that have been taking place in our contemporary environment bear no resemblance to those previously experienced by the present generation. The changes that are taking place, and have already done so as we approach the millennium, will alter the lifestyles of most human beings on this planet; especially in the industrialised nations. They will do so in a manner unlike anything seen before.

Just as animals sense something strange before an earthquake, most people have developed an inchoate sense that the particular historic dividing line we are approaching — the turn of the century and the dawn of a new millennium — signifies fundamental changes in the way we live and the world as we know it. Yet most lack certitude about such basic issues as whether the future will be brighter or darker than the past or present; whether we will all be richer or poorer. Most important of all is, the extent to which the vast changes to come will affect our style of living; and how we may have to adjust to the economic and social changes that could otherwise disrupt the plans we may have made for our future.

There is little doubt that a seismic shift is occurring in the composition of personal wealth. It is convulsing the structure of personal relationships and personal finances, and changing the rules of personal financial planning. Future planning has now been torn up. This seismic shift has changed the lives of thousands of people, some beyond redemption. Many who planned a tranquil retirement will have to extend their working years for longer than they had anticipated. Many individuals who had always paid their bills regularly, and been prudent in their credit management, now find themselves technically bankrupt. I see the phenomenon that has caused such massive personal dislocations as a Housequake!

So far, we've felt an initial movement that at the epicentre might measure about five on the financial Richter scale. We've also had a few after-shocks, interspersed with meagre attempts at reconstruction. Whether or not what has happened so far in the residential housing market will be the precursor to another major volcanic eruption — and a shock of greater magnitude — is the subject of this book. So too are the measures that should be taken by the individual to mitigate the problems currently associated with the Housequake; along with the type of planning needed in the light of the future of the residential housing market in most major industrialised countries.

There are a number of ways of coping with the Housequake — besides being shocked into a state of mental and financial inertia by it. There are also a number of ways in which the average individual can cope with this phenomenon and possibly profit by it in the years ahead. These strategies involve selecting areas likely to be the most resilient to any future shock waves and avoiding areas likely to be the most vulnerable to future Housequake tremors. They also include arranging a purchase on the best possible terms and the use of creative financing where applicable. If you are forced to sell, a number of tactics can be employed to help you unload your house quickly and at the best possible price. There are also many pitfalls to be avoided. This could make the difference between a quick sale at a favourable price as opposed to having a property sitting on the market for years, only to be disposed of in the end at a forced-sale price. I have attempted to deal with all these problems — and future considerations — in a practical manner, one which can be applied by any individual who has been, or may be affected, by the likely trends in residential property.

It should also be recognised that owner-occupation, while seemingly a good proposition, is not viable for all and sundry. There are special situations where mobility, occupation, age, marital status and prospective marital status, future employment prospects and a wide variety of reasons can make owner-occupation the worst possible move an individual could consider. I have compiled guidelines which I hope will assist those individuals for whom home ownership is not a viable proposition. Remember — individuals in the categories for whom owning a home was always inadvisable have been the worst hit by the Housequake we are still experiencing.

It was back in the early 1980s that I began to feel the tremors of an approaching Housequake. It was a time when virtually the whole of the community was convinced that house prices could only rise and never fall. I questioned this belief. One thing I learned over many years as an economist and financial commentator is that if everyone believes something to be true, it's time to take another look. There is usually an implicit guarantee that the most widely accepted beliefs are never true.

EARLY WARNING IN THE 1980s

THE TREMORS I was beginning to feel back in the 1980s involved the escalation of personal debt, the relaxation of credit, the political sponsorship of the residential housing market and other factors. None of them it seemed could be sustained for very long. Obviously, if the forces behind the residential property boom were unlikely to hold, then the boom itself could not be sustained in perpetuity as so many had been led to believe.

At about the time the residential property boom was approaching its peak, I had employed a secretary on a part-time basis. Her skills were adequate but her stability and creditworthiness fell short of the desirable. In addition, she appeared to be congenitally economical with the truth. Her husband was unemployed; reputedly on drugs. She had no permanent residence, nor had she ever held a permanent job. Yet she managed to find a mortgage broker who was able to arrange a 100% endowment mortgage with a building society, while securing an additional loan for the payment of legal fees. These were connected with the purchase of a grotesquely overpriced, converted apartment on a lease. She came to me one morning to ask for an advance on her salary. I asked why. She said she didn't have any money to pay the first monthly premium on the endowment policy which secured the new mortgage; while the rent on the apartment she lived in at the time was six months in arrears.

Subsequently it seemed that the monthly payments on the endowment policy and the interest payments due to the building society were the furthest from her mind. She seemed to be under the illusion that a mortgage was some kind of Government grant; the inalienable right of all those living in Britain, regardless of race, colour, creed, religion or financial status. The fact that money borrowed on a mortgage represented a debt that must be repaid, did not occupy even the most remote recesses of her mind. I came to the ultimate conclusion that housing credit had become maniacal. This poor young lady had become a building society number in the actuarial trade-off between potential defaulters and market share. I had noted this phenomenon at work many times in other markets. For example, back in the 16th century, people in Holland were granted vast loans to purchase investment tulip bulbs so they could buy more investment tulip bulbs. How all such affairs end has been written about many times. It is the history of fiat credit. Thus, back in the 1980s, I felt the end of an era had arrived and the tremors of the Housequake, now beneath my feet, were vibrating through the floorboards of my office.

This time around the host of the credit mania was residential housing in the UK. Although a similar mania occurred in the UK during the early 1970s, when the host was commercial property and second-line banking operations, it appeared to be the first time that residential housing in the UK had become the vehicle of a popular credit mania. I began to investigate the history of residential housing in Britain to determine if there had ever been a similar occasion in British history during which some precedents had been established. Much to my surprise, I could find little solid information on the subject. So I decided to turn my attention to other areas in order to seek examples. In Germany, which has always had a penchant for record-keeping, I found a plethora of data, going back nearly two centuries for the German residential housing market. Germany was certainly no stranger to the Housequake. There had been several. The most notable was during the German hyperinflation of the 1920s. Here I ran across a story of a woman who had sold her apartment during the hyperinflation of 1926. Over the two months it took to complete the legal work for the sale, German property prices had continued to fall, with inflation rising at an even faster pace. The result was that the proceeds of the property sale left her little more than the price of a collar for her dog. She didn't have enough left over to pay for a lead. So she was forced to make do with a discarded piece of rope tied to the new collar.

I investigated long-term property trends in France, Italy, Spain, Switzerland, Australia, New Zealand, Japan, Canada and the United States. In some cases, my research took me up a blind-alley, but in others, the data was formidable and conclusive. I could see that a Housequake was on the way — not only in Britain, but in many other areas where there had been a housing boom of like proportions; a boom fuelled by an apparently unlimited availability of credit for all and sundry, regardless of their ability to repay. The housing boom of the 1980s seemed to be a global phenomenon. So too, I concluded, would be the global Housequake.

I have to say that as my investigations proceeded, I found myself confronted with ignorance, indifference and a considerable amount of hostility. There was not, as I had supposed, any co-ordinated strategy — at any level — to counter the burgeoning mountain of residential housing debt and the threat of the Housequake made inevitable by this debt mountain. **There was no single body responsible for preparing to react to this potentially catastrophic event.** Meanwhile the warning voices of respected economists and analysts were being totally ignored; apparently overshadowed by a wealth of commonly shared, erroneous perceptions relating to the factors that influence residential property prices. Nearly all of these, to be honest, were completely spurious. The boom in the 1980s residential property market was the biggest ever witnessed in any of the industrialised countries. Indeed, for residential housing, the boom was without precedent. Hitherto, a property boom of that magnitude would normally be confined to speculative development and commercial property. Now billions upon billions were being splurged all over the world on housing and housing construction as private home ownership became the fashion of the age, totally unrelated to the obligations that home ownership entails.

THROUGH THE ROOF

INVESTMENT in residential property by the Americans, British, Japanese and Dutch reached the highest level in the history of all four nations. The price of residential property was pushed up beyond levels never seen before. The effect of this has been reverberating on the downside of the residential property market ever since, as the sting in the tail has continued to reveal a severity which has been building in intensity since the beginning of the 1990s.

Through my studies on the inner working of the global residential housing market, I found that the most comprehensive and reliable statistics on housing trends available were those applicable to the United States. It would appear that — like the Germans — the Americans also consider their residential housing market important enough to justify the compilation and maintenance of particularly exhaustive data. My investigation into the international residential property markets, the determinants of price levels and underlying influences have also revealed very close parallels in the relationship between the determinants and pricing structure of the US residential housing market and housing markets elsewhere. As a consequence, those statistics currently available for the US residential housing market — not available for other residential housing markets — provide extremely vital clues as to what may be taking place in the housing markets of other major industrialised countries. This particularly applies to those which have experienced a credit boom and attendant housing boom similar to that which the United States experienced in the 1980s.

According to current estimates, there are 3.2 million homes on the market in the United States at this time. This happens to be 33% more than the 1982-1988 average of 2.4 million. That oversupply certainly isn't limited to the United States alone; nor do those statistics represent a worst-case picture. Virtually all European markets are suffering a residential property slump due to oversupply. The situation is similar in the Far East, Australia and all of North America from Dallas, Texas to Montreal. Given the relationship between credit expansion and supply levels in the

United States, it would not be unreasonable to assume that the very worst of the oversupply problem at this time is probably in Britain. **Britain has been experiencing the most serious residential property crisis in its history due to the volume of unserviceable mortgage debt,** the product of the previously unregulated housing credit expansion which has led to a ballooning oversupply. Unfortunately for UK home owners, the debt overhang is only one of many problems now coming home to roost.

In my book, *Into The Upwave* published in 1987, I touched on the subject of residential property prices. I said in no uncertain terms that residential property prices would fall further and faster, and for much longer, than anybody believed possible. This has already happened. Donald Trump is history; Olympia and York — the world's largest conglomerate — has defaulted on billions in real estate debt; home ownership has led to penury and homelessness for thousands. A home, once the foundation of wealth for many people, has become a pool of illiquidity. The debt-induced growth of the residential property market during the Thatcher Administration in Britain and the Reagan-Bush Administrations of the 1980s has now fizzled in the 1990s into an era of self-feeding debt liquidation, debt consolidation and debt reduction.

MORE TO COME

BUT THE story certainly does not end there. It is possible that we may not yet have experienced the epicentre of the Housequake. The future holds several possibilities and overriding probabilities. The multitudes remain enmeshed in a Housequake which shows no sign of abatement. For the majority, what happens next is what counts. It is true that opportunities may now exist for the cash-rich to exploit the demise of the residential property market to their own advantage. Yet the cash-rich in our society are unlikely to part with their cash until they feel certain that the decline in house prices has spent its force. Bargains may seem to abound for first-time buyers who have in the past been frightened out of the housing market by over-inflated prices and a lack of capital for a downpayment. For these innocents, there is the vague notion that there exists some sort of intrinsic value in a home. On the flip-side, there are now fewer people who would qualify as first-time buyers than during the 1980s, and with far more reason to be scared of the residential housing market and the burden of debt than ever before. For the innocents who are in a position to buy a home for the first time, and who believe there is some kind of mystical intrinsic value in a home, the realisation that a house is only worth what someone else is willing to pay for it, could come all too quickly.

For the most part, people — rich and poor — continue to suffer through a residential housing crunch that has yet to show the slightest sign of approaching its terminal juncture. Until there is a sustainable upturn in the housing market, mountains of prospective wealth-producing capital — that could be deployed profitably for retirement and other purposes — will be finding its way to money heaven; the home of all ill-advised transactions that turn sour.

Financial advice can represent the lowest common denominator of intellectual achievement, combined with the highest possible common factor of vested interest. In the field of investment, it would seem that the media have selected stockbrokers as the only group of seers capable of throwing light on the future of the economy. There are in fact many skilled economists, far more qualified to undertake this important function than any stockbroker. But you will rarely find an independent, highly skilled economist enlightening you on the future of the nation. The risk to the TV stations is that the economists are prone to tell the truth. A stockbroker, on the other hand, may generally be relied upon to foster the best interests of the firm which employs him. This usually involves acquiescence to the political views of the Establishment, whatever they may be at the time; and almost always involves the desire to peddle investments. These can only be successfully peddled if an impression is given that the future is all polkadots, moonbeams and candy-floss.

Recently, forecasting trends in residential housing appear to have become big media news. Those selected by the media to predict the future of the housing market — on radio or the boob tube — fall into a similar category to those chosen to provide information to serve the vested interests in economics and investment. In the housing market, the hearty breeds who have been selected to do this in this particular area of endeavour tend to be chosen from the ranks of building society managers, estate agents and mortgage brokers. They then spew forth their pseudo-expertise, unencumbered by any special qualifications that might give their commentary credibility. **We live in a world where marketing has been substituted for advice, and where sales literature is treated as objective information.** This applies to housing as much as anything else.

Not surprisingly, objective commentary from qualified economists, experienced in the determinants of property values, are conspicuous by their absence on radio and television. The same people who were sounding the alarm when this irresponsible, credit-induced mania was sucking the innocents into a whirlpool of self-destruction — who were being ignored then — are once again voiceless as the Housequake rumbles on. The risk for those in the media, where advertising revenue spells the difference between extinction and survival, is always the same. Those who tell it the way it is might upset those advertisers who are seeking to sell houses and get their market share of debt peddling. The consequence is that members of the public are left with the burden of distinguishing information from disinformation. This can be quite a prodigious task, since there is so much of the latter and so little of the former.

This book, then, is a straightforward attempt to look at the problem of this Housequake in a detailed, unbiased manner, providing all the facts that are relevant, while exploding a large number of myths promoted by vested interests. These, I must say, are misleading, erroneous, spurious, inconsequential and totally irrelevant. Frankly, I have no axe to grind. There are no properties I want to buy. Nor have I any property to sell. I have no interest in any estate agency or any business related to the housing market. I do not even need to sell my books. I must confess, however, that from the top of my head to the depths of my psyche, there is a desire to contribute something to the society of which I am a part; and hopefully to provide some help for the many people who are so desperately in need of it.

This book is not aimed at economists, academics or intellectuals; and I hope that the concepts it embraces will be easily understood by anyone — anyone who already owns a home, who is thinking of purchasing a home, or who has once owned a home and would never consider doing it again. It will also, I trust, illuminate to some extent the workings of the domestic property market and global property market, with a view to the avoidance of pitfalls and the exploitation of opportunities that are still possible among private individuals. I am thankful that in the past I have been able to assist a number of people to avoid the potentially financially fatal problems they may have encountered when embarking upon home ownership. I now hope to help many more.

Above all, this book should encourage further research by pundits and practitioners responsible for contributing to the plight of those so cruelly victimised by home ownership. It is my wish that those who fall into this category — through ignorance, or possibly design — will be more sympathetic and understanding, not only in respect of the risks associated with a Housequake and the hardship it brings to so many, but also of the fact that under certain conditions it is inevitable.

Surviving the Quake

- *How is this book designed to help you? First, by removing several layers of myth and propaganda. Second, by introducing you to the concerns and opportunities of the recent past. Last, by enabling you to view past disasters in a new light. This should make it easier for you to prosper at the present time.*

- *The property market is a sophisticated one, dominated by greedy professionals. Don't expect a free lunch. What looks like a bargain can turn into the most costly undertaking you could imagine.*

- *The recent fall in property values was no accident. The residential property bubble made it inescapable.*

- *Rental values and the market for rented accommodation are likely to prove the most important factors in determining when the fall in house prices has actually ended and the next boom is about to begin.*

- *A home is a nest. It is rarely a nest-egg.*

CHAPTER ONE

WHEN A HOUSE WAS NOT A HOME

"A house is not an investment. It's merchandise, like a car, a washing machine or a toothbrush. Its only real value is its utility value."

From: *The Downwave*
by **R.C. Beckman**

IT IS difficult to pinpoint the precise timing of the collapse in house prices. In real terms, taking inflation into account, house prices have been falling since the late 1980s. In absolute terms, in round numbers, it would appear that prices began falling in early 1990. What we do know is that the residential housing markets have been in recession. It has been a long recession and its extent and duration still remains highly uncertain. The uncertainty, which is heightened by the absence of complete and reliable statistics, has led to conflicting interpretations and forecasts. Many of these interpretations and forecasts can be misleading and actually dangerous. Most of the forecasts which are currently produced are prepared by those whose interests lie less in the direction of accurate forecasting than in making a sales presentation, or vehicle for the sequestration of political capital.

Some see in the present difficulties a necessary — and perhaps "moral" transitional phase — to correct past speculative excesses. That seems to be the attitude of the Government. It also seems to be the paradigm of estate agents, building societies and others who see in every minor upswing in the property market, no matter how transient, fresh evidence of a sustained recovery and a return to "normality". Others, however, see the fall in residential property prices as the consequence of profound and enduring structural changes. Consequently, they expect the difficulties to continue. Those personally afflicted by the residential property crisis — many of whom have been immobilised and shocked into a state of inertia — have little truck with philosophising. They still feel bludgeoned by problems of a more pressing nature.

For instance, Sally always believed that owning a home was sound practice; and, until the late 1980s, that seemed an unassailable view to most people. After all, house prices in most places had never declined. Moreover, journalists writing in the quality papers said that house prices could only rise and would never fall.

For much of the 1970s and 1980s appraisals soared in most areas, impelled by a demographic bulge of baby boomers buying their first house, as lending policies became more lenient. Tax incentives also proliferated and the persuasive theme of Governments was the virtue of private home ownership. It was clearly recognised that this was one of the greatest vote-gathering moves ever devised.

But to return to Sally! The situation has changed dramatically for her. She is now one of tens of thousands of recent home buyers — many of them young professionals — who occupy homes that have declined in value. Often they have declined to the point where the home is worth less than the outstanding mortgage. This is the all too familiar condition known as negative equity. Financiers refer to it as being "underwater".

Sally now has a big problem. With little hope of selling at a profit — or even refinancing to lower the monthly mortgage repayments — the only chance for her and others like her, is a slender one. Many who have outgrown their homes are taking a substantial loss; staying put and paying off the mortgage until it is at least smaller than the home's appraised value. Others are renting out the home and risking not covering the mortgage repayments. Many are still walking away from the problem, inviting the prospect that they will never again be able to qualify for a mortgage.

Sally's total assets exceed the level of negative equity in her home. In this she is very lucky. In many cases, the difference between the value of the home and the amount of debt outstanding on the mortgage exceeds the total net worth of the individuals involved. If those who are in such a position are unable to maintain mortgage repayments, the only available option is personal bankruptcy. Many foreclosures have been postponed because of the large number of individuals in such a position.

Financiers have a name for those who are drowning in debt. They call them Nebbies — negative equity baby boomers.

In Sally's case, with a £7,000 deposit — her entire life savings — she bought a converted flat on a 45-year lease in south-east London at a price of £70,000. That flat is now worth half the price she paid for it in 1987. Even if she found a buyer willing to pay £35,000, she would still have to hand over to the building society the entire proceeds of sale plus an additional £22,000 to clear the mortgage. There remains a debt of £57,000 outstanding. Since 1987, only £6,000 of her payments have been used to amortise the debt of £63,000. Sally says:

"I bought the property because I was sure it would be a good investment. It was for a while. I never thought the value of the property would fall. I was told that property prices never fall. I'm hoping there will be a miracle, perhaps some sort of semi-recovery". Then she added, "Almost everyone I know tells me I should let the building society foreclose and take it back."

The story of Sally is an interesting one, offering a number of lessons; some subtle, some glaringly obvious. It might be assumed that Sally would know better than most. She happens to be a mortgage broker. However, assuming a mortgage broker knows any more about property values than a migratory fruit-picker is only a self-deluding assumption.

While the credibility of Sally in her chosen profession may be wanting, she intends to protect her credit rating. She refuses to allow the building society to foreclose on her mortgage. Instead, Sally rents out the flat that she purchased and pays the difference between the rent she collects and the combination of her mortgage payments and monthly maintenance charges on the property. That sets her back about £400 a month. She also pays £800 a month in rent for her apartment in the West End of London.

"I didn't expect to make a fortune", she concluded, "But now I have learned that you only buy things that you want to live in and you are committed to."

Sally has finally learned that a residential property is intended to be a home. In 1982, when my book *The Downwave* was published, I stated in no uncertain terms that a house is a home. It is merchandise — like an automobile, washing machine or toothbrush. You pay for its utility value. A home is no more an investment than a dishwasher or stereo equipment. Throughout history, rising house prices have been extremely transient occurrences. This would appear to be the financial wisdom spread by bankers and estate agents these days: that a house is not an investment — it is your home. Better late than too late!

"When you purchase a home, you should be evaluating what you are willing to pay for where you want to live", said Patricia Niemas, President of the Mortgage Bankers Association of New York, a trade association. "You do not gain or lose money until you decide to sell. Unfortunately", she added, "purchasing a home in recent years has been proclaimed as a short-term investment. And this is not so."

That was precisely the message I was trying to deliver 14 years ago — as a lone voice. **Unfortunately, it took about 14 years, a housing crisis and hardship for millions all over the world to grasp the reality — to which virtually the entire community had turned a deaf ear.** While certain lessons may have been learned, there are so many more to be learned. The nadir of the number of pitfalls to be encountered in the residential housing market has certainly not passed. In order to arrive at an evaluation of the extent to which the fall in property prices will continue — its possible duration and the financial strategy to adopt — calls for a precise long-term evaluation of the inner mechanism of the residential property market. This, and an appreciation of its price determinants, are still lacking. This may be due to apathy or design — on which I am not prepared to specify.

BODY OF INFLATION

WHEN the perceived determinants of property values are considered, it can readily be seen that those concerned are still way off-base. One reason why residential property was considered to be a good investment during the 1970s and 1980s was the inflationary nature of the global economy. Many believed that rising inflation was a permanent way of life. The fact was that the rate of inflation fell from a peak of 26% in Britain in 1976 to a low of 8% in the early 1980s, yet many continued to believe that inflation was still a permanent way of life. 20 years later, with inflation among the G-7 nations in the 2.5% to 3.5% range, rising inflation still remains a major fear. The aspect of deflation and falling prices never seemed to have entered the global vocabulary. Yet we find deflation affecting all goods and services — especially housing.

The period from the late 1940s through the mid-1970s produced steadily rising inflation and steadily rising house prices. It is not unreasonable for the ordinary member of the public to assume that a trend that has been in motion for 30 years will continue in perpetuity. That is what most people believed when they were rushing to buy houses. It is what many still believe. Real assets, like residential property and property in general, almost always do well in inflationary times. But, as I demonstrated in my book *The Downwave*, inflation is not a permanent way of life and has never continued in perpetuity in any nation. At sometime inflation is always followed by deflation. This phenomenon can be traced back to the 15th century. The problem for most people is to recognise the existence of these very long cycles. Normally, an inflationary cycle can run from 25 to 40 years and a deflationary cycle from 15 to 25 years. These long-term trends are outside the frame of reference of most people who are unaware of their existence. Others have gone further and have chosen to deny their existence.

In spite of the number of temporary inflationary fears that have emerged in recent years, inflation has been benign and under control for quite some time. Moreover there are strong indications that we will not see inflation resurfacing for many years. There are some good reasons for this. They include — in technical terms — the slowdown in the growth of the monetary aggregates, illiquidity and the low level of food and energy prices. The recessions that have punctuated economic activity over the last 20 years are additional factors, leading to lower interest rates and reduced consumption. There remains a strong likelihood that zero inflation will become a reality before the end of this decade. We may even see price attrition at the turn of the millennium.

Deflation has a tremendous impact on residential property prices in inverse proportion to high inflation. Here we have a market that is besieged with oversupply. In the period ahead, those who are cash-rich will be in a position to select houses for pennies in the pound as an increasing number of distressed home owners, developers, building societies and banks try to unload property at or below cost or borrowing levels in order to restore liquidity. In the future, for some who buy select properties in areas that are artificially depressed, this could mean the beginning of a great new cycle of property values.

It is quintessential that those contemplating purchasing a property should be acutely aware of the cyclical nature of property prices. It is vital that people understand that property values follow cycles like the economy and most other values. You must expect to see — time and time again in the years ahead — an incessant flow of reports claiming a new property boom is about to begin. It will not happen. There will certainly not be a property boom during the 1990s of any sort. To help you ignore the type of literature you are likely to be bombarded with — and to help you appreciate the factors that are needed to produce such a boom — an acquaintance with the elements that will influence future residential property values is necessary.

COUNTING HEADS

DEMOGRAPHY is an important factor in future property values. For those anxious to buy a home (still harbouring the hope that their home will rise in value) the shifting patterns of demographics do not bode well for the future. In the light of the two major recessions since the 1980s, many baby-boomers — the foundation of the post-war expansion of wealth in the industrialised nations — have received the first real wake-up call in their working lives. The professional working group, the so-called middle and upper classes, have felt the wrath of a downturn in the long-term economic cycle. It has been unlike anything seen in the post-war era. Unlike the recessions that punctuated the growth period from the late 1940s through the 1970s, the recessions that have caused the contractions of the past 15 years have turned the baby-boomers into the victims of their own consumption. Job losses may have affected the white-collar worker more than the blue-collar one during this contraction, but the work force is in the process of being decimated across an unprecedently wide spectrum.

The numbers involved are enormous, but they pale into insignificance when compared to their economic impact. In the US, the demographic statistics are amazing. So are their implications. These statistics are equally applicable to all of the other industrialised nations. The numbers may differ, but the ratios and the relationships are as applicable to Tokyo as they are to New York.

Fully one-third of all Americans — 76 million people — were born between 1946 and 1965. This phenomenon was due partly to the soaring and widespread feeling of hope brought by the war's ending; and partly by the fact that when the boys returned home, couples made up for lost time on romance. In most countries, while prodigious, the birth spurt lasted for three to six years. But in the United States, Britain, Canada, Australia, New Zealand and Japan — for reasons that demographers still debate — the boom lasted for nearly two decades. Likened by demographers to a "pig moving through a python", this generation has dominated the cultures and business environments of those countries for nearly four decades. To the extent that the US and Britain have been leaders in global culture and business during this period, the boom generations have enormously influenced life on the rest of this planet as well.

At each stage of their lives, the needs and desires of the baby-boomers have become the dominant concern of business. During the last 40 years, the shifting patterns of populations have created some of the most potent driving forces in social, political and economic developments in the United States and elsewhere. Most of the influences were of a positive nature — in terms of demand for goods and services in a variety of areas. Many influences have now turned negative, with the demand from this group diminishing at an accelerating rate. Among the negative forces this group will now exert, involves the greater presence of women in the work force and the ageing of baby-boomers.

The fact that more women in the industrialised nations are seeking careers in the work force, and have been postponing marriage until their late twenties or early thirties, is a negative factor for the residential property market. Moreover, since most working singles have fewer tax deductions as a result of having fewer dependants, many buy — or already have bought — houses to qualify for the mortgage interest deduction. The consequence of this particular demographic aspect could easily be millions of new houses with "For Sale" signs as the previously singles begin completing their pair-bonding in the years ahead.

A veritable time bomb for the residential property market is the likelihood that most of the baby-boomers who will ever buy a house have already done so. The backbone of the residential housing market has always been the demand from first-time buyers. There can be little question that even without a housing crisis, the number of first-time buyers in the years ahead will be vastly lower than when these baby-boomers reached the age when they would buy a house during the 1980s. The housing crisis has exacerbated an already potentially disastrous equation.

According to the National Bureau of Economic Research investigators, Gregory Manike and David Weil, the baby-bust following the baby-boom will cause real home prices to fall by about 3% a year during the next 14 years — following their 1992 estimate of a cumulative total of 42% by the year 2007. Last year, house prices in Britain fell by 5%. The 3% figure could well be an extremely conservative estimate.

One of the most negative factors of all is the strong chance that a glut of houses will hit the market early in the next century. That will be when the baby-boomers reach retirement age, en masse. Then they will begin to sell their existing properties, seeking smaller retirement homes outside the areas where property values have been artificially influenced by them. The oldest of the boomers are now in their fifth decade, with grown-up children whose proclivity for house buying is a mere fraction of that of their baby-boomer parents. This forties-plus group, whose children have embarked upon their own lives outside the family residence, now have more accommodation than they require. This is also eating into capital that could be employed for producing an income at retirement. Authoritative estimates suggest that the over-65 group will soar to 22% of the total population in the decade beginning 2010. These people will need capital to provide for their retirement, not a depreciating asset that is surplus to their needs. If you think house prices are already under pressure, just wait until those baby-boomers — who counted on the appreciation in the value of their homes to finance their retirement — all start trying to sell at the same time.

It was the American humorist and philosopher Will Rogers who said, "You have to invest in land because they ain't makin' any more". Obviously, Will Rogers was a Malthusian who believed that the population would continue to expand while real estate was a finite asset, supply of which would diminish as demand increased. While the notion advanced by the humorist may have appeared attractive to would-be house buyers seeking something more than a home — and was a useful phrase for estate agents — this simple, appealing dogma is belied by fact. Population growth is no longer expanding, in fact it is now contracting markedly. The supply of residential property vastly exceeds demand; and the excess in supply is likely to increase well into the next century. **The amount of land available for housing is more than sufficient to meet the needs of the population of this planet for the next 5,000 years.**

The subject of density clearly demonstrates the fallacy of the argument that land for housing may one day be in short supply. As with the demographic trends, arguments about population lend themselves to fun with numbers. In this they provide a further example of how figures can't lie, but liars sure as hell can figure.

So, how many people are in the world — breathing today — really? If you try to count heads in the Black Hole of Calcutta, or even in your own house for that matter, when your teenagers are having a party, you'll probably miss a few. There will always be those two or three teenagers with illicit motives who confine their activities to the garage or utility closet. The 1992 revision of the *UN World Population Prospects* says 5,295,300,000 people were breathing at the time of the report. The Comparative International Statistics section of the 1991 *Statistical Abstract of the United States* says 5,318,013,000. And *Information Please* says 5,321,000,000. An entire country's worth of people — maybe two — representing 25.7 million have gone missing in the count. Another peculiarity is that the sum total of the population of individual countries added together comes to a lower level than the estimate for the total world population.

But all of that is minutiae and trivia. You may be interested in what the world population is now, but if you are hoping that an expansion in the world population is going to help push the value of your property any higher, then you should be far more interested in what the world population is likely to be several years hence, when you're going to have to sell your property and live off the proceeds during retirement.

The 1993 Information Please Almanac claims population will grow from the current level of 5.3 billion or so to 8.2 billion by the year 2020. US Vice President Al Gore, in his study *Earth in the Balance* says the number of living humans will reach 14 billion someday, but doesn't tell us precisely when. Charles C. Mann, in a very long and serious article about population (published in February 1993 in *Atlantic Monthly Magazine*), points out that world fertility rates peaked quite some time ago in the developed countries. But, even in the very poor countries, with the highest baby production, fertility rates dropped by 20% between the late sixties and early eighties. According to Mann, if this trend continues, world population growth could reach replacement levels by 2005, when the UN estimates there will be 6.7 billion people. (Actually, the population would keep growing because of something called "demographic lag"). On the other hand, the fertility-rate decrease could start increasing for a number of reasons. But, you don't want to concern yourself too much with that. Remember! It's the future value of your house that you're really interested in.

With that in mind, let's return to basics. Take the figure of 5.3 billion as a fair estimate of the number of people breathing on this planet at the moment. Now ask yourself, how crowded does this make the world? A little crowded? A lot crowded?

Very, very crowded? So crowded that all of the people in the world may soon have to stand up all of the time? Your answer might be somewhat vague since the subject is also a bit vague. Let me see if I can come closer to providing something approximating to a logical answer; one which will help you determine the extent to which population growth is likely to exert an influence on future residential housing prices.

Let us exclude Antarctica — assuming that it is unlikely to be a particularly popular place for house building or home buying in the years ahead. Then a figure of 5.3 billion people in the world gives the earth's land surface a population density of 101 people per square mile. That means that each person on the planet can have a plot of land for himself, or herself, of about 1/100th of a square mile to live in and build a home. That also includes the Chinese. It must never be forgotten that one in every five persons in the world is Chinese. If we put this into a real world perspective, this would give every person in the world a bit more space than the sparsely populated state of Tennessee where there are 118 people per square mile.

I might now be accused of being unfair. Included in my calculation of land masse divided by population is the Sahara desert, the Amazon Basin, the Bronx and Brixton along with a lot of the earth's land surface that is not very habitable. But then neither is a lot of Tennessee for that matter. Nor is sparsely populated Northern Ireland. The point is, if the 6.7 billion population peak comes true, we'll have 128 people per square mile. If *Information Please* is right, by the time I am ready for a terminal experience, there will be 156 people per square mile. If Al Gore has accurately frightened himself, we would eventually wind up with 267 people per square mile. Once again, putting the matter into perspective, the City of New York has a density of 52,415 people per square mile, which is only slightly more than the density of London and Paris and appreciably less than the density of Tokyo!

The State of New Hampshire has a density of 124 people per square mile and is obviously sparsely populated with room for plenty more homes. The State of Indiana has 154; Pennsylvania 265. We are thus moving from a world as congested as Tennessee towards a world at least as thronged as New Hampshire, possibly as teaming as Indiana and maybe even as jam-packed as the State of Pennsylvania that has nearly two million acres of state forest and nine million acres of farms.

At present, if the world wants to live in Freemont, California, or a Milton Keynes-type of new-town sprawl — and a lot of the world seems to — then everyone of us on the globe can have a single family home in Europe, with most of Russia west of the Urals left over for land fill. If we'd prefer a more cosmopolitan environment — such as San Francisco, with its density of 15,502 people per square mile — then all of the 5.3 billion of us could fit into the states of Texas and

Oklahoma, with a few million left over to keep the planet's bird-feeders full — and rake and weed the rain forests. If we want a more down-market zip code, then — at the Manhattan population density of 52,415 per square mile — the entire population of the world could be squeezed into the former Yugoslavia. If we want to act like New Yorkers, the former Yugoslavia is really what we deserve.

There is a message in all of this madness. The message is that if you believe that demographics or population growth in your country is going to have other than a negative influence on the future value of your home, you'd better hitch your property wagon to a star with a bit more sparkle. Harbouring mythical dogma of that nature can be dangerous to your wealth and financial planning.

So far, I have gone into detail on two factors which many thought would exert a positive influence on property values in the future, but are actually more likely to exert a negative influence. These two factors are demographics and population; along with the manner in which these two influences impact supply conditions. The residential property market is like any other auction market whose price levels are determined by supply and demand. When supply exceeds demand, prices fall. It is only when demand exceeds supply that prices can rise. Demand must not be confused with desire. Assume that the 5.3 billion people in the world wish to own their own home, unless those 5.3 billion people have the wherewithal to purchase those homes, the desire for 5.3 billion houses is not going to be translated into demand. Currently, the number of people able and willing to buy houses is fewer than the supply of houses.

Demographics and population are just the tip of the iceberg. Many other elements will have a serious impact on residential property values in the future. These include debt overhang, immobility, the growing market in rented accommodation, interest rates, inflation, credit availability, employment trends, changes in work patterns along with other seemingly subtle but compelling forces.

While what I have outlined until now applies to the residential housing market in general, there are a number of preponderances that will hit various classes of property, depending on region. Changing demographic patterns will be accompanied by a change in migration patterns. This shift could be catastrophic for some, while offering opportunities for others; just like other great economic upheavals in the past.

On January 3, 1930, the following advertisement ran in the town paper of Greenwich, Connecticut, a fashionable suburb that had long been favoured by the well-to-do. "Invest in Greenwich Real Estate Instead of Stock", said the advertisement. "The town of Greenwich 'market' never hits the toboggan. In 50 years, there has never been a decrease in value, but in 50 years, assessed value has increased 50-fold."

As it happened, the newspaper ran that advertisement at the early stage of the Great Depression in the US when most people continued to hold the view that optimism was enough to support the residential property market. It wasn't enough. As it turned out, some estates that had sold for $1 million in 1929 subsequently sold for as little as $75,000 by the mid-1930s. Greenwich, Connecticut was considered as recession proof then as Orange County, California and Hemel Hempstead, England were in the late 1980s. New York was expanding fast at the time and Greenwich, Connecticut represented a slice of suburbia close to the mainstream where a lot of rich folks wanted to live.

If we now substitute Orange County, California for the Greenwich, Connecticut, of the 1930s, we have a clear picture of what the US residential property market looks like in the 1990s. The way that upper-end of the perceived-to-be recession-proof residential property market behaved during the period of the Great Depression in the US provides an ideal object lesson for anyone owning a home, especially an expensive home in suburbia.

A precipitous decline in the value of the upper end of the housing market in areas falling into the category of the affluent suburbs like Orange County, California, or the stockbroker belt in Surrey, England (where the bulk of middle-class savings have been invested) will cause the most grief during this Housequake. In these areas, more so than others, are housed the greatest number of those who were convinced that property values would fall elsewhere, but never on their patch. Those who live in these areas, conditioned by a lifetime of rising values, are probably still looking at past property values rather than contemporary fundamental influences. Most will probably attempt to ride the slide in property values down to its bitter end. Assuming they will be able to do so, they will continue until they see the extent to which valuable, potentially income producing capital has been whittled away to almost nothing. Many, who think about it, will probably conclude that the decline in property values is no more than another shakeout of the kind that normally occurs during a recession. It could be a costly error. The evidence indicating that the 1990s is likely to be very different from previous decades is overwhelming. Those who fail to accept to the realities of the slump in property values — and the future prospects, particularly in expensive homes in suburbia — could be facing extremely serious financial consequences. Or at best they risk a nasty shrinkage of their net worth.

BACK TO TOWN

ALREADY underway is a nationwide migration away from suburbia. It is a grave development for the upper-end of the residential housing market, which I had forecast would be the hardest hit by the Housequake. One of the very few positive aspects of the housing boom was that people were able to live in more expensive neighbourhoods without changing homes. This will now pass. There are few, if any, positive aspects left.

Rising and falling residential property prices on a regional basis are characteristic of the type of migration we are now witnessing. Prices soften and plummet in regions of exodus as they have done in Orange County, California; and as they are about to do in areas such as Jersey in the Channel Islands, suburban areas close to London and other affluent zones in the South East and South West. The softening process has been underway for quite some time in England.

People normally move to the suburbs to escape the evils of the inner cities, which is logical. The more convenient the escape route, the higher the price of the home. But, in recent years, the problems these people have hoped to escape from have arrived on their doorstep — congested traffic, unreliable commuter transportation, an escalating crime rate, air pollution — all are now beginning to foul that suburban paradise in a way that will not be reversed quickly. The residential property fortunes of the 1980s seem destined to turn to ashes within a few years. For most of the middle classes, such a development will be a catastrophe on a scale which will make the stockmarket crash of 1987 look like a honeymoon in Tahiti.

Expensive housing in inner-cities will present special problems, possibly of an even more financially debilitating nature than those which confront the high-class properties in suburbia. Not only are the inner-cities regions of slow economic growth and continuing urban decay, but they have a neglected infrastructure which will require billions in new spending. This will mean the threat of tremendous legislative burdens by local and national government for those who live there.

The reasons for the current migration away from areas that are potentially problematical, and the manner in which residential property values will be affected in these areas, should by now be obvious. Of course, in areas that are the beneficiaries of a population influx, the reverse of what can be anticipated for properties in suburbia and the inner cities, is the normal expectation. The depressed state of property values in some regions — like those of the new towns — have already begun to stir the interest of speculators with a taste for bottom fishing. In some cases, it is now possible to purchase properties for less than the cost of construction. But attempting to pick the bottom of the residential property markets is not for those of a weak disposition; for widows and orphans or those simply seeking a home. This is not a strategy I would recommend at this time. Though the time will come. It is my belief that those who profit most will conduct their affairs on the well-defined lines I will be recommending.

In sum, for now — quite simply — mortgages are defaulting, personal bankruptcies are sky rocketing, consumption has decreased, and the crowd at the local county building permit office is much smaller than the crowd on the courthouse steps.

NO END IN SIGHT

THE RESIDENTIAL housing cycle has certainly not ended. A trough isn't even close. The downturn of the cycle may still be in its incipient stages. As the face of the population changes in industrialised nations all over the world, so will the face of the residential property market. Increasing crime. Higher taxes. Reductions in tax relief on the expenses involved in home ownership. A rotting inner-city infrastructure. Unbearable traffic. Air pollution. The decline of the educational system in large cities — and even some suburbs. This is the multifarious confluence of the forces that are descending on property values in all of the nations of Europe, the Far East and North America. They are doing so with a vengeance.

Oversupply, deflation, the tax structure, high unemployment and shifting demographic patterns are key factors that will create a wholly new residential property landscape as the Housequake proceeds to its ultimate conclusion. Understanding the manner in which the residential property market functions — and the elements that determine residential property values — will provide you with a game plan for success.

I am fully aware that most people do not want to hear a negative argument about residential property; understandable, since by far their largest asset is their home. But for the average person, a home is much more than a home. It is a combination of investment, savings programme, tax shelter, and retirement programme. A home is something you make a part of yourself, and perhaps pass on to your children. Home ownership is more the stuff of the British middle-class than motherhood, public schools, football and roast beef with Yorkshire pudding. It pushes a psychological hot button in most people to be told that the one asset they have been counting on to bail them out of all their other financial problems is just not going to make it.

We must all now face the facts. Unfortunately, your home may still be many of the things that I have made reference to. It is also no longer a large number of those things. If you become like an ostrich and stick your head in the sand, your tail will become the target. The fact that the residential property market is in for hard times, doesn't mean we are all going to become a nation of cave dwellers. For some people, it makes a lot of sense to sit tight. For others, it will even make more sense to be a first-time buyer. Just make sure you've done your homework.

This is your homework. Now for lesson two!

◆◆◆

CHAPTER TWO

FAIR WARNING

"The residential property market has become a balloon looking for a pin."

From: *Crashes* by **R.C. Beckman**

ON MY desk as I write there lies a cutting from the *Financial Times* dated 6 December 1989. It reads:

"House price inflation last month slowed to its lowest level since 1982 as prices continued to fall in many areas of the country, Halifax Building Society said yesterday...the average price of a UK home of £60,837 in November 1989 was only 4.5 per cent higher than in the corresponding month last year...

"At the end of last year, house prices were rising at an annual rate of more than 34 per cent".

In no time at all, the press and vested interests began chanting their litany: "The market is on the turn. Recovery is on the way. Now is the time to borrow and to spend."

But how many of those offering an opinion were prepared to stand up and say - "Wait! It's not over yet. It's going to take a couple of years before the present situation is cleared up."

Very few, I can tell you. Even when the collapse of the speculative joyride was staring them in the face. Ask what they were doing to warn the public in the early eighties of the dangers that lay ahead. I'll tell you - precious little! I personally knew of no one willing to stand up...let alone be counted.

I can say that because I believe I was the first and only analyst to anticipate the collapse in UK residential property in Britain; while, at the same time, singling out the debt relationship as the factor most likely to lead to the collapse. Moreover that cutting reminds me that I did get it right.

It was in the early 1980s that I recognised the storm signals at a time when the euphoria over residential property was mounting. I outlined these warning signs in my book *The Downwave*. Later, I pointed to the rapid collapse of property prices in Aberdeen; and in my next book I referred to the unthinkability of middle class folk being dispossessed and put into a bed and breakfast establishment. That was before the actual problems had begun to register. It was also before the advent of Cardboard City under the arches beneath Waterloo Bridge. Such a thing had not been seen since the turn of the century. But there were growing signs that the market was about to take that inevitable dive.

The fact is that it has always been my aim to anticipate important terminal junctures before they occurred, rather than recommend remedial action after the damage had been done. I felt this approach was vital in the case of the snail's pace residential property market, where it takes a considerable amount of time to sell a single property. Moreover, as seen in the past, even before a collapse in property values had even come into sight, certain homes could not be sold at any price.

When I first published my views on the residential property market in the early nineteen eighties, I was attacked, derided and mocked. As one critic put it, "Beckman is once again the lone voice of doom in a land of plenty." In reality, it was less a case of "plenty" than "too much." Too much credit and too many would-be lenders putting on the pressure to get someone - virtually anyone - to take out a mortgage.

As might be expected, considering the host of vested interests involved at every stage of the home ownership game, a major effort was made to discredit the research I had done; rubbishing the forecasts I made as a result. Many claimed that I had been predicting a collapse in property values as far back as the early 1970s. They sneered that it had taken no less than 20 years for my forecasts to be fulfilled.

It was a perfect example of one of the most effective weapons in a polemicist's armoury - the half-truth! It was a fact that I had predicted a collapse in property values at the time alleged. But that, I made quite clear, was primarily in commercial property. I certainly assumed that residential property values would also take a dive. But not to anything like the same extent. In the event, that is exactly what happened, when the collapse of the commercial property market in the 1970s triggered the second-line banking crisis. This, you may recall, had the entire UK banking system on its knees. It would probably have collapsed completely, had it not been for the Bank of England's taking its courage in both hands and launching the so-called "lifeboat."

In the forecasts I made in the mid-1980s I stated quite clearly that this time residential, rather than commercial property would bear the brunt of the decline in the market. The sequence I outlined initially involved a decline in values in "real" terms. That is to say taking inflation into account. It would then be followed by a fall in the general price level in absolute terms. I was careful to point out that the crash in residential property values would be "a crash that wouldn't look like a crash." That is precisely what it has been: a steep, slow decline lasting several years already. It was as though the firm rock on which the market stood was being corroded - rather than blasted away.

In my treatment of property values I was also careful to point out that during the continuing deflationary environment, commercial property values would fall in the wake of residential values. But they would do so to a lesser extent. In point of fact commercial property has never returned to the euphoria seen during the months preceding that earlier crisis. During the crazy eighties, "bubble" status was reserved for the residential property market.

In 1986 - the year of the City's Big Bang - I started writing *Into the Upwave*, the follow-up to *The Downwave*. I judged that the dangers threatening the UK residential property market were becoming acute. I therefore up-dated my views in my new book. Once again, given the power and depth of vested interests, it was only to be expected that attempts would be made to discredit my even more outspoken warnings. I have to confess that the acclaim which greeted me when I visited Ireland to promote the book was something of a surprise. A welcome surprise, I may say.

Eventually, even the blinkers provided by vested interests had to come off. The truth could no longer be avoided. Nor could the implications of what was happening be glossed over any longer. Too many people had been hurt on the way. Too many more were already set up to join the next wave of victims. The truth could not be concealed. All that could be done was to close the eyes and act as though the worst was over. That in fact is what happened; and to some extent is still happening. For how many years now has each month (let alone each quarter) brought forth one of its two familiar cries: "The market is showing signs of picking up at last" or "The expected recovery failed to take place?" Talk about England Expects! The full measure of what was happening has continued to be most effectively camouflaged making it possible for wave after wave of innocents to fall into the trap which they had been helped to set for themselves.

I am not a Conspiracy Theorist; and I find it impossible to believe that lenders and property interests have deliberately gone out of their way to cover up the seriousness of the property market collapse. So they must have been unable to see what was happening before their eyes. Many people, finding themselves on the boat deck of the Titanic would probably tip-toe towards the life-boats, saying - if challenged - that they were being quiet so as to avoid frightening the other passengers.

For many people the rule seems to be, try not to rock the boat; and never be the first to blow the whistle.

Look what happens when some stockmarket or banking scam is uncovered. No one knows anything. Yet somewhere along the line someone must have noticed something. The miscreant - who may have made a foolish but comparatively innocent mistake in the first place - cannot face the music. So he, or she goes off on a fantasy jag. In a flash they have cooked up a story which they are the first - but never the last - to believe. Tackle them afterwards and they will tell you they were playing for time, because they were convinced that sooner or later their luck must return. When it did, all they'd lost so far would be paid back.

Case after case down the ages has shown that the gamblers have forgotten that there will always be a point of no return. But that gambler's streak which they may not have known they had takes over.

THE DECLINE CONTINUES

YOU MIGHT have thought, when the FT carried that story of the collapsing bubble in December '89, reasonable people would have seen it for what it was - last rites for the Thatcherite home-ownership cult. But not a bit of it! Now, seven years later, the situation is far worse. For to the traditional threat of repossession for default has been added the current scourge of negative equity. Yet, read the advertisements, the feature articles, listen to the property marketeers and you would think that at any moment now the tide would be turning. As for repossessions, they have become almost routine. That is unless you happen to be a victim.

Returning to that story in the FT in December '89, we find there had been a modest rise of 1.8 per cent in the average price over the previous three months. This, it should be noted, had been achieved after builders had offered discounts and mortgage subsidies to attract still hesitant buyers. Outstanding had been the eagerness of the first-time buyers in '89. They had seen prices rise by 9.7 per cent over the year. Although that was double the rate of inflation for the UK housing market as a whole.

Some four months later, in March 1990, I gave readers of *Investors Bulletin* a further warning in a special feature on *The Continuing House Price Malaise.* This time I began by relaying the cautionary note in the *American Express Banking Review.*

Part of the problem, according to Amex, was that the boom in house prices in the North of England made many households feel richer than they thought they would ever be. It was simply an illusion. Nevertheless it encouraged refinancing and a concurrent consumer spending spree on the strength of funds borrowed by increasing the size of existing mortgages. In some cases new, unskilled dabblers in the market were encouraged to take out a bigger mortgage than was strictly necessary in order to buy that new Volvo or BMW, or going round the world or visiting Uncle George at Alice Springs.

One of the standard arguments used to persuade them - if they needed persuading - is that they would be helping the UK economy to recover. It would provide a healthy boost to the UK motor industry. Wasn't that what we all wanted?

(Buying a BMW or a Volvo would help the UK motor industry?)

It would help the retail end of the motor trade: and that's where the recession bites really hard! Besides it would be infinitely better to borrow a little extra to buy that beautiful, new vehicle...rather than leave it to rust away on the docks. Besides - there is our Import/Export trade to consider. Every time someone in the UK buys say...a BMW, there is a good chance that the money transferred to Germany will be turned around almost at once to buy something the UK is exporting.

Besides (the tempter would add) the borrower would not really be increasing his or her commitment. Indeed, taking a bigger mortgage than was absolutely necessary meant that the borrower would merely be syphoning off some of the "spare" equity in his or her own property. And that must be a good thing, mustn't it?

Certainly, it wouldn't be a bad thing! As for the extra cost: well, once the market woke up, house and car prices would both begin rising again. Delay would mean losing out price-wise. Why not do the deed while you can? As for that little bit extra on the mortgage...the money saved would mean someone else was financing at least part of the deal. Why pay more for the property by procrastinating? And why turn down the cheapest credit available? No motor trade finance company would let you get away with it as cheaply as the building society will.

If the would-be borrower was still hanging back, the final ploy would be to point out that however much you put on the mortgage - within reason - it would only be for a short time...in fact until property prices - and car prices - returned to normal.

The Salvation Army used to have a saying about not letting "the Devil have the best tunes." Maybe they should coin a new saying to apply to those whose business is to persuade Mr and Mrs Average Citizen to take on a long-term debt for the sake of cash in the hand. One drawback, which many failed to grasp, was that whatever words they used to describe what they were doing, they were irrevocably increasing a load of debt which was already proving to be somewhat onerous. It certainly meant paying more each month to service that larger debt. It also meant they really needed prices to start rising once more; and fast. Even those who boasted that they had to work out the simplest economic problem with a handful of matchsticks, should have been able to grasp what was happening. Despite the would-be lender's honeyed words, what their manoeuvres had done for the market in the 1980s should have been plain as a pikestaff. But it obviously wasn't.

THE PRICE OF DEBT

EASY credit earlier in the 1980s pushed up the demand for housing and reduced the available supply. That helped to send prices soaring. That in turn meant that borrowers were piling up the debt. Their inability to unload the property and lighten the burden of servicing the debt hardened their resistance to selling at what by the end of the 1980s would be a more realistic price. Many cautious first-time buyers hesitated. Their failure to enter the market, free from any selling/buying "chain", put the brakes on for the established owners. Recession, redundancies and cutting of staff did nothing to encourage first-timers to take their chance.

A sense of unreality still prevailed. Government, academics and other well-meaning bodies praised the courage of the small business man: seedcorn of Britain's future success. Somehow it got overlooked that in very many cases those start-up businesses had already been financed with loans raised by taking out second mortgages. They were in danger of losing home and livelihood at one blow. Middle class parents took out mortgages on the family home to enable the children to acquire a home of their own. Elderly folk went in for one of the home finance schemes, which enabled them to cash in on the equity in their property while still alive. It meant, in effect, disposing of all or part of the beneficial interest in their home in exchange for a home for life. This provided them with an annuity, purchased with the proceeds of the deal. It rescued them from the plight of so many of their age, who found themselves 'property rich but income poor'. However, under many schemes it left them extremely vulnerable to a fall in the market.

As the boom of the '80s continued, more and more ways of syphoning off some - if not all - the equity in a property were introduced to an eager public. Tags like "high income" and "with profits" were attached to all sorts of schemes. They proved highly attractive. There was generally a small-print note to the effect that anything offering a profit can end up with a loss. It might be a reduction in income or a loss of capital. Sadly, people did not take the warning seriously. Why should they? The Pyramids of 1980s were built not on hopes and promises, but on a solid foundation of bricks and mortar.

One of the most disastrous schemes, which sucked people into a morass of debt, was the sale of council houses at what appeared to the existing tenants to be generous discounts. In many cases the discounts evaporated when the value of the house fell to less than the former tenants paid after the discount. (Negative equity raising its ugly head.) Captured by the fantasies of saloon bar chatter and popular illusions about home ownership, thousands of council tenants all over the country found that they would have to balance their elevation in status as owner-occupiers against the fact that they were relinquishing extremely attractive, subsidised, controlled rentals which they would never again be able to acquire.

Nor were all the properties disposed of by councils in such good condition. The "bargains" of the eighties are now reappearing - by courtesy of the media - as the shock-horror stories of the tabloids. Frequently former tenants have been unable to cope with the responsibilities and financial demands of ownership. They require above all that they should keep their jobs: no easy task when there is a sharp decline in many unskilled and semi-skilled occupations. Falling behind with their mortgage payments, faced with repossession. Which would mean being homeless, with very little prospect of getting back into a council property. Bitterly they realised it had come about because they had accepted the Thatcherite and Neo-Thatcherite governments' invitation to "better themselves." The price tag on "their" property had made them feel "well off," if not "rich." It made the reality all the more bitter.

HARD FACTS MAKE HARD CASES

AWARE that a sense of unreality was still clouding many minds, I recalled for my *Investors Bulletin* readers the case of a couple who bought their council house at the knock-down price of £21,000. True to the creed of "People's Capitalism," the husband joined the burgeoning ranks of the self-employed. Unfortunately he failed to notice that 80% of all new businesses were failing at the time. The building industry, in which Mr W worked, was producing the greatest number of casualties.

"The Government," said Mr W, "sold us a dream. They told us we would be better citizens, a better class of person. I believed them."

In 1988 a surge in interest rates knocked Mr W sideways. Up went the cost of servicing his mortgage; and also the cost of servicing his overdraft, which he hadn't taken into account. He was also hit from another angle. The rise in interest rates caused a slump in the property market. That brought to an end the temporary improvement in the home improvement industry. You've guessed it! That was precisely Mr W's line of business.

Unfortunately, though property prices were weakening and business conditions deteriorating, would-be lenders were on the prowl. Trustful as ever, Mr W believed what he read in the newspapers. They said that interest rates would soon be coming down again, and property prices and the building trade would pick up before long. Mr W went for broke. He decided to capitalise on the increased value of his house, pay off his debts and inject much-needed capital into the business. He therefore remortgaged the property for £50,000; more than double the sum he had originally borrowed. This, he believed, would tide him over what he genuinely believed was no more than a bad patch.

The loan was granted in September 1988. By November everything had started to go wrong. Mortgage interest had risen to £800 a month. Mr W fell behind in paying for his building materials. By the end of the year he was in debt to the tune of £13,000. Of this £3,500 was in mortgage arrears. Finally, in November 1989, the crunch came. The local branch of the Oh-so-Friendly building society gave Mr W and his family 28 days to vacate their home.

"When I bought the house", said Mr W, "I never imagined I could fall into debt...it was so cheap."

COUNTING THE COST

IT WOULD be painful, if salutary, to discover just how many first-time buyers like Mr W still face repossession as you read this chapter. Many of those under threat as I write will have been dispossessed already. Others will have taken their place. It would be even more revealing - perhaps disturbing - to discover the proportion of first-time buyers who are still only potential victims. Generally they come to the surface only when the crunch comes. Meanwhile they carry around a psychologically crippling and demoralising burden of debt. Nor is it because they borrowed too much. It can be merely that the market value of their property had fallen below the total owed in mortgage and other loans. You might also say it is partly because that long overdue and over-rated recovery is still a long way off.

It is tempting - especially if you are not affected - to exclaim, "What fools some people are." But it would be wrong to imagine that it is only the feckless and less well-off who have been caught out. In his book, *Short History of Financial Euphoria*, Professor J.K. Galbraith dismisses the notion that only the reckless or the foolish suffer at times like these.

"I told of my hope that business executives, the inhabitants of the financial world and citizens of speculative mood, tendency or temptation that not only fools, but a lot of other people, are recurrently separated from their money in the moment of speculative euphoria."

In essence we, rather than "other fools," are responsible for our plight. However, Galbraith confessed that he was not too certain of the value of that warning for the individual or for society at large.

"Recurrent speculative insanity and the associated financial deprivation and larger devastation are, I am persuaded, inherent in the system. Perhaps it is better that this be recognised and accepted."

The message is clear enough. Face reality and make sure you understand the demands it places upon you. Remember that property-related enterprises across the UK are also at the mercy of the tidal forces operating within the property market; and from the uncontrolled growth of property values up to the day the market began to sink under the weight of accumulated debt.

Involved in the malign process of generating debt have been banks, building societies and other lenders. They have been the main contributors to an almost unprecedented outbreak of property speculation. Not that many of the lending institutions would admit to have played the role of speculator! However, the fact remains that the present mountain of debt could never have been created had not a wide range of lenders obliged with bank loans, merger financing, and first, second and third mortgages. Even that list fails to cover all their forays into creative financing. Perhaps their greatest achievement has been to persuade the public to keep their blindfolds in place on the strength of little more than honeyed words and a reassuring, professional manner.

The greatest illusion, which has to be seen to be believed, is the way in which a highly professional estate agent manages to make the would-be buyer feel at their first encounter that the agent is "really" on the buyer's side.

TIME TAKES ITS TOLL

FOR SOME seven years, we have been reading in the press, and been told by the media, that prices are about to take off again; and that the slump in residential property is now over. Only the brave - they tell us - will be able to score. Because they alone will have clambered aboard before the gravy train sets off again. But have you noticed one thing: how little there has been of any reference to debt. It is almost as though the relationship between debt and property was some up-market economic theory like supply-side economics or the Kondratieff wave. Then, it might be argued, there could be scope for a variety of interpretations. But that is not the case with property and debt. Here Professor Galbraith stands firm.

"The recession that began in the summer of 1990 and continued so obdurately in the face of the weekly predictions of recovery was almost certainly deepened and prolonged by speculative collapse...had there been no speculative excess and collapse with their larger economic effect, the political history of 1992 would have been far different."

I believe things have gone too far for a recovery in residential values alone to be a major political objective. The earlier "feel good/feel rich" sensation has been replaced by a chill reminder that from now on we must face reality. One aspect of this is the fact that the leading institutions are changing and changing fast. There are mergers and acquisitions on a scale not seen before. These are not taking place to make the property market more efficient. They are taking place because the institutions concerned have their own reasons.

That is why I believe it is putting the cart before the horse to claim that a healthy property market is an essential ingredient in a healthy economy. That used to be said about the Midlands' motor industry. A moment's thought suggests that it is the other way around. For the property market to be strong and steady, the economy as a whole must flourish. It must provide steady jobs and incomes, opportunities and incentives. The working man needs this even more than his white collar colleague. Nor does it matter whether he or she is an owner or a renter. The citizen must be able to meet his or her regular commitments, regardless of age, sex or class. The population must be kept healthy and educated to a certain level. Perhaps most important of all are their security and safety from war and crime.

You may say that these are tasks for government. True, governments can present manifestos, utter policy statements, make laws and inspire the people. They may even frighten off enemy and trade rivals alike. But they need to translate aims and obligations into action by performing everyday tasks. For this the right tools must be provided. It is the working economy which provides these tools.

Given a health economy, the property world can move ahead. But it will not be in the same way as before. Markets - like history - only appear to repeat themselves. Certain problems, certain aspects re-appear. But their relative strength, significance and methods change and develop with time.

It is not easy to monitor progress in this area. Trends in house prices are less visible than prices in other markets. There is no daily price monitor or index to watch; and houses change hands extremely slowly. We know from our own experience that negotiations over a particular sale will usually take weeks. They can take months. So comparatively few transactions take place and prices move slowly and ponderously over a relatively long period before a slow slide (or a hesitant rise) can be registered. Even then we are left to compare the price of one individual property with that of a quite artificial average.

It may be we would be wiser to keep an eye on the big battalions to see what they are up to. Particularly since the whole market place is in such an unstable condition. The "feel good" factor is something politicians are constantly on about, as though the act of so doing achieved something. Are bankers and brokers, building society chairmen and insurance tycoons similarly deluded? It would seem so. Otherwise they would not keep on about recovery being just around the corner. **That leaves us with only one practical approach - to discover where the big battalions are putting their money.**

Mind you, it doesn't mean they're always right. But let's see.

Last year Hambro Countrywide put money into buying Nationwide's estate agency chain. Unfortunately the market failed to perform as predicted. The under-performing branches dragged the group into the red. But Nationwide's other subsidiaries pulled it out of the fire.

Then there was Lloyds Bank's acquisition of the Cheltenham and Gloucester Building Society, which became effective in August '95. It was said there would be no closures among C and G's 230-plus branches. Nor was it planned to sack any of its 3,500 staff. Since then the enlarged Lloyds Bank group succeeded - at the end of a five-year courtship - in getting the Trustee Savings Bank (TSB) to agree to merge. Will this lead to substantial savings? The answer seems to be that both banks had already been slimming down staff throughout their long "engagement." TSB will bring with it a handsome dowry - its merchant banking arm, Hill Samuel.

Another August wedding was celebrated when the Halifax and the Leeds - the first and fifth largest building societies in Britain - agreed to merge. That, however was only the first step. The enlarged Halifax will cease to be a building society when floated as Britain's largest bank some time in 1997. The 4,000 jobs lost out of the combined workforce of 27,000 will be left to natural wastage. When the Halifax becomes a bank, however, it is hoped that more staff will be taken on. This was said at a time when high street banks have been showing every sign of closing down many of their counter positions and substituting cash dispensers for bank clerks. That means that another steady source of employment (and owner occupiers) will be coming under pressure.

But it goes still further. Analysts say that some 50% of the top building societies are likely to become banks in the next few years; and further mergers are expected among the smaller societies. At an earlier stage one might have asked, "How far is this trend likely to go?" Today the question must be how much further can it possibly go? In the 1920s there were 12,336 building societies in Britain. The disappearance of the Leeds Building Society and the transformation of C and G into a bank, left the Building Societies Association with no more than 79 members.

Are these newly forged unions going to make the housing lenders more efficient? More profitable? Simon Barrow, chairman of the consultancy, People in Business told the *Evening Standard* (18/9/95) that there was a "real financial cost to mergers and acquisitions, but a very large proportion of them do not show a profit in the long term". Why then, one is bound to ask, should mergers and take-overs have become so fashionable? Especially in view of the heavy losses sustained by banks and others when it was equally fashionable to acquire estate agency chains? In Simon Barrow's view, take-overs and mergers "...are done mainly to satisfy egos." Mr Barrow, who is also a Member of the City Disputes Panel, was unable to provide much comfort:

"The greatest number of mergers and acquisitions took place in 1988, when the greatest number of dreadful mistakes were made...but now the pace is hotting up again."

In 1994 UK-generated mergers and acquisitions rose by 32% to reach some £49 billion worth. How high will it climb? And what will be the consequences for the residential property market?

◆◆◆

CHAPTER THREE

WELCOME TO THE MADHOUSE

"Take the most intelligent and astute businessman and thrust him in a shrieking screaming crowd and he will immediately become a blockhead."

From: *The Crowd* by **Gustav Lebon**

IN THE early 1980s, wisdom was still nowhere in sight. Nor did the great majority of people remember what "wisdom" had once signified. Excess counted as energy, mania passed for dedication. The truth was that the inmates of the property madhouse were displaying all the symptoms of media manipulation. By that I mean they had nor merely surrendered to the press and TV the task of forming their opinions for them. They had delegated to the so-called news media the right to decide what was and was not a fact.

Had you sought proof you needed only to catch the sleeve of one of these razor-sharp citizens and ask what had been happening since breakfast yesterday. Providing you caught them before they had taken their morning dose of info-tincture, they'd have replied that they were sorry, but, "I didn't catch the headlines."

Had you gone one stage further and asked about one of the week's really big stories, there would have been no point in waiting for an answer. Unhappily, the kind of information we really need will not often appear in the headlines: not unless your milkman is a serial killer, or your brother is a top athlete, caught creeping into the room of an under-age groupie. The sad fact is that the things you genuinely need to know have little or no day-to-day "news value."

That is why we cling to every week-end supplement, as though the truth might be found here. Most citizens, for most of their lives, really do believe that the truth -

with a Capital T - is mysteriously revealed to Sunday journalists. This is especially true if property happens to be your main interest.

Let me introduce a caveat at this point. Be careful when an everyday event or routine activity that you know about DOES find its way into the headlines. It usually means serious trouble for one of the main players in the market of love. He, or she, has possibly been caught with one hand in the cookie jar; or is being accused of blasphemy or date-rape.

Go one stage further. Let a couple of feature writers with familiar by-lines begin pontificating about the prospects for the rental market or the pros and cons of an endowment mortgage. The odds are that no one is going to talk horse sense about the subject again. Not, that is, until it ceases to be "in the news"; or until the vested interests find another hare to chase.

That was what happened about domestic property - your home and mine - in the 1980s. By then the subject of home-ownership became a really hot issue. From 1982 on, it became a cult. The public were preparing to echo Mrs Thatcher's chant: "There is no prouder word in our history than freeholder." It was clear what she meant. But when you got down to brass tacks it was as romantic a notion as her call for a return to high-minded, sober, Victorian values.

It was happening anyway. All Mrs Thatcher was doing was giving voice to certain aspects of the radically changing culture. For all their terrors and disasters from the Cuban missile crisis to the total involvement of the US in Vietnam, the 1960s will remain the stuff of popular legend: remembered most for Love Not War, the Flower People and the New Freedom.

(Sure, the Cuban missile crisis brought the Western World within a few hours of mutual incineration, but it didn't last long enough to stop the fun.)

The 1970s, on the other hand, become the decade of bitter memory. The plan, which all political parties supported after 1945, had been economic growth, full employment and the implementation of the embrionic welfare state. By the 1970s the three-point plan was coming under attack. Disillusion followed in the wake of the three-day week, the winter of discontent and round one of the battle with the coal miners. Some observers described the atmosphere as "divisive". More thinking members of the public tended to regard the whole sorry mess as a return to normality. Towards the end of the decade, in 1978/9, pickets in some hospitals sought to bar the way to patients entering hospital.

Little wonder at the warm reception Margaret Thatcher received when she moved into No 10 in the summer of '79. She promised a return to domestic peace, confidence and enterprise. At the 1987 Conservative Conference, even luke-warm party members felt she could justly claim that Britain once again was:

"... confident, strong, trusted. Strong because our economy is enterprising, competitive and expanding. And trusted, because we are known to be powerful and a faithful friend."

It is no matter whether Mrs Thatcher was right or wrong. The main thing was that a very large number of ordinary people felt that way. In politics, as in the market-place, feelings frequently count more than facts.

Columnist Joe Rogaly wrote in the FT at the end of the 1980s that the mood of despair which had characterised the 1970s had been replaced by a sense of hope, at least among the successful classes. They were multiplying fast as were the entrepreneurs feted at No 10. Although they were not growing so fast as the worse off.

Looking back in 1988, Mrs Thatcher told the party faithful that the great political reform of the last century had been to enable more and more people to have a vote. "Now the great Tory reform of this century", she declared, "is to enable more and more people to own property."

As has already been said, the ethos of the 1980s was not entirely the creation of either the Conservative Government or the Prime Minister. The culture was already changing as the "Youth" of the 1960s began to age. Their Gospel of Youth - Never Trust Anyone Over 30 - was being transformed as successive waves of young men and women passed through the crucial age barrier. Many of them took on the harsher, materialistic tone of Edward Heath and his more dedicated followers. So fundamental were the changes that took place that it was no longer "strange", or a betrayal of their ideals, for the Youth of the early 1980s to declare quite openly that their aim was to become millionaires by the age of 30.

For the more capable graduates of the '80s, the property market became their tilting yard. Prepared to take a risk, and with lenders eager to oblige, funds were readily available. Property prices rose, profits were taken and the proceeds used to back an even larger loan next time. The smart operators flourished. At the same time, a mountain of debt was building up. The scale of the debt worried no one; even though they vaguely knew that some day it would have to be repaid.

Put in plain, everyday language, the equity in the ordinary person's property was rising. So was the level of debt. **But so long as inflation could be relied on, the debt caused no one the slightest anxiety. Every additional nought made everyone feel just that little bit richer.** It was so simple to make money - once you acquired the knack. You merely had to take advantage of the hot-house atmosphere of the 1980s. Lenders at this time were kept busy thinking up further ways to attract the borrowers, including 100% plus mortgages.

Even the less adventurous citizen began putting a timid toe into the water. It was as though the market had coined a new slogan:

"When inflation takes care of the noughts, only the biggest fool on earth will hesitate to add a few more if it guarantees their staying in the game."

So long as you didn't think too much about it, it was far too good a game to keep out of. What could go wrong so long as lenders continued to pile on the noughts; and there was a buyer, just as keen as you had been, to take the property off your hands? Each time that happened - perhaps as often as every 18 months - you would be collecting more than just a few noughts when the time came to sell.

THE GREAT GAME

ONE OF the more dangerous aspects of the game was that too few of the players could grasp the fact that it was a game. Many of them kept counting the noughts and telling themselves they really were "rich". To the seasoned onlooker, there was only one way the game could end - with one almighty upheaval.

It had happened so many times before. From Tulipmania in Holland in the 17th century, through John Law's banking extravaganza in Paris and the South Sea Bubble in the 18th, to the seismic shock which destabilised property in the United States in the last century.

For my own part, I warned of the danger of the whole home-ownership cult at the beginning of the 1980s. I was snubbed and derided for my pains. I had even given chapter and verse in my book *The Downwave*, to show that it doesn't matter what form the gambling takes. It must always end the same way, with someone getting hurt. A typical case was quoted by Jeremy Seabrook in an *Observer* special report in May 1989:

"One man, self-employed, who had three years loss of earnings through sickness, saw a £10,000 mortgage turn into debts of £70,000."

Jeremy Seabrook viewed the whole affair as: "...one of the great contradictions of this decade (being) that the appeal to prudent house-keeping has gone hand in hand with the irredeemable slide into indebtedness......Finance companies have been swift to exploit the sudden access to credit which owner-occupation confers: loans have been recklessly made, not only on the ability of people to pay them, but on the equity represented by house acquisition."

One is bound to ask how far its success among the population at large sealed the fate of the movement, in that it brought into the game many thousands of players who could scarcely afford the cloakroom ticket.

This, after all, is a situation which has arisen time after time on the stockmarkets of the world; and one which has served as a warning to wary professionals. This was a point I covered in some detail in my book *The Downwave*. But it is too important a factor, and one often overlooked, that it is worth repeating.

In my early career as a New York stockbroker, I shared a desk with one of

Wall Street's old-timers, Charlie Meyer. Charlie had known booms. He'd known busts; and had survived both. He was smart, but not greedy. Experienced, but never over-confident. He was an instinctive stockmarket operator. He could gauge the investment climate by the tempo of speculative activity.

Without balance sheets, charts or any other popular investment aids, Charlie managed to acquire several million dollars just by watching the prices as they travelled across the ticker tape on the old New York Stock Exchange. That ticker tape, I may say, was state of the art in that long-forgotten, pre-computer age!

As I recall, he would also monitor the expressions of greed and fear on the faces of his fellow investors: something you could have done, had you thought of taking the temperature of the domestic property market in the '80s. In that way you would have put aside what the media, building societies, banks and estate agents were keen to tell you. You might not have been a great expert, but you would at least have been using your own judgement. You would certainly have realised whose side you were on!

Anyway, one day back on Wall Street, Charlie spun round in his chair, slapped me on the back and said:"Beckman! Too many dummies are getting rich. I'm getting the hell out."

He was right. When the taxi-driver and the garage mechanic are boasting how they bought soya beans two days ago for half of what they are selling at today, it is a clear warning that the reservoir of buyers for soya beans has reached a low ebb. When the office cleaners start swapping "hot tips" with the elevator operator, it's time to head for the ground floor exit... fast!

Charlie did just that, figuratively speaking. He grabbed the 'phone, called the firm's floor broker on the New York Exchange, and yelled, "Sell!". He'd sold every investment he held within the hour. That was two days before shares peaked and began tumbling.

Where did you stand viz-a-viz the homes market? Are the dummies you know still trying to persuade you to "buy now...while property is dirt cheap...and avoid the rush?" What would be your response if they called you this very evening?

If, at the end of the '80s you had given them a firm "No", you would have been among the first of the few. Were you to have told them Charlie Meyer's story, a broad smile - compounded of pity and contempt - would have appeared on their faces. "Don't you realise," they'd have said, "that Charlie Meyer was dealing in stocks and shares: not property. Everyone knows property is different!"

How often have you heard friends or colleagues saying just that? Although you will notice that few of them will ever go on to tell you what makes the property market immune to disaster. You know it isn't, and I know it isn't. But did you know it THEN?

Even if you did, so many of the others didn't. So it's well worth taking a close-up view of some of the examples of post-boom collapse of which the United States has plenty to offer.

DEPRESSION, PANIC, DISASTER, DISTRESS

THAT was the sequence of events during the depression of 1819-1822, after a long cycle of wars in North America and Europe. These wars, ending in 1815, had encouraged every type of industry to reach boom proportions seven years earlier. Domestic demand supplied the stimulus: an unstable and over-developed credit structure, the means. There in place were the basic ingredients of every major financial panic.

The post-war depression of 1819 affected some three million people, or one third of the nation. News from Cincinnati told of "distress as beyond conception". Property values collapsed across the nation. Marshals and sheriffs everywhere were busy repossessing thousands of homes day by day as the banks foreclosed.

The housing market had been caught up in a wider storm. As Samuel Hopkins told the annual meeting of the Tennessee Agricultural Society, in October 1820: "Last year we talked of the difficulties of paying for our lands: this year, the question is how to exist... from this time onwards we shall have to contend for clothing and a few other necessities, without which we must become a miserable, and I fear, a barbarous people..."

Pauperism was now serious. Soup kitchens were out on the streets in Baltimore, Philadelphia and New York. The good people of Cincinnati left for the backwoods to raise food. One respect of the depression was to be repeated whenever property values declined for whatever reason.

If we see property as a superior instrument for investment, we would expect the propertied classes to have remained well above the general level of distress on account of their holdings.

But this was not so. The propertied classes were decimated. The burden of debt secured against property was such that it was liquidated the only way it could be, by sheriffs' sales at auction. The prices reached at these forced sales served to depress property prices still further.

The value of real and personal property in New York State alone fell from $315 million in 1818 to $256 million in 1820. In Pennsylvania, land swept up in the boom to around $159 an acre in 1815, fell to $35 an acre in 1819. Rentals in Baltimore plunged by approximately 50 per cent. The collapse in property prices was nationwide. In Virginia, many of the lavish homes of the plantation owners would not sell at any price. They were, literally, valueless. Poverty was so widespread that it was well-nigh impossible to find anyone prepared, and able, to assume the cost of maintaining the more imposing residences.

It was a state of affairs to be repeated in Germany shortly before the Second World War, when the magnificent estate of Edmund Goldberger failed to find a buyer, however hard he tried. No one, it was said, could possibly afford to keep it up. Goldberger had to walk away, leaving his empty home.

It is clear that far from protecting the owner, land and property have helped to bring about their downfall. Yet so often the pressure on the owner to borrow is matched only by the eagerness of the banker to lend. It's as though no bank could hope for greater security than a vault stuffed full with title deeds. That is until it happens, and the banks realise that they too are vulnerable.

There is one thing, it would seem, that bankers have difficulty in remembering: the fact that whatever triggers the collapse, the main charge capable of blowing any economy apart is in every case the over-extension of credit. No financial structure, however well-founded, can withstand the force of a credit based explosion.

There is no better illustration of this than the collapse of the Chicago land and property boom on Friday 17th March 1837.

THE CHICAGO BOOM BUSTER

SURPRISINGLY, perhaps, the Chicago house and land collapse did not arise as a result of depression; nor was it a speculative "bubble" like the South Sea Company's criminal misadventure in England a century before. Chicago was a boom town in its own right; the boom originating in a sober assessment of Chicago's potential.

It was known that the proposed Illinois-Michigan Canal would put Chicago firmly on the map connecting the up-to-date facilities of the new Michigan harbour complex with the Illinois River. This in turn would enable vessels to reach the Mississippi at St. Louis. It would also link the Great Lakes and St. Lawrence River, opening up a broad swathe of territory all the way down South to "the land of cotton"; specifically to New Orleans and the Gulf of Mexico. The new Canal would put Chicago at the very centre of the greatest network of waterways in the world.

Even with the American railroads still in their infancy, Chicago was becoming the depot for the cattle of the prairies, the grain of the Mid-West, the lumber of the great pine forests of Michigan and Wisconsin, and the minerals of Illinois and Missouri.

In a few years Chicago would become the Gateway to the Middle West; at a time, moreover, when the entire nation was imbued with the spirit of enterprise.

Money-making was considered a virtue. Ambition, almost a duty. It was bred in the bone that every street-corner newsboy or shoe-black had it in him to succeed. He might not end up as President. But there was always a chance of becoming a wealthy cattle man or head of a bank.

In the 1830s, immigrants poured into the territory in their tens of thousands. They become labourers on building sites and on the quayside; they supplied factory owners and warehouse companies with plentiful, cheap labour. They felt they were putting their shoulder to the wheel of progress and prosperity. The general mood of enterprise was helped by the fact that the people sensed they had the backing of President Andrew "Stonewall" Jackson. They were sure he knew what business and the country needed most. And that was money.

The country needed money to build; money to invest, and money with which to make more money. So President Jackson allowed the state bank to run its printing presses at top speed, churning out bank notes in ever-increasing quantities.

Unfortunately, President Jackson had become involved in a running feud with Nicholas Biddle, boss of the Second Bank of the United States. In 1836 the feud between the Man in the White House and the most powerful banker in America came to a head. This helped trigger-off the crash which reached its climax eight months later. But that was still a good way off when the boom began; when Chicago became recognised as the real estate man's dream.

CHICAGO — METROPOLIS AND MAGNET

AS CHICAGO developed, it acted like a powerful magnet. Settlers, or homesteaders, as they were called, arrived in droves. So did the land and property speculators. Banks were lending on property as fast as the teller could push a bundle of notes across the counter.

In 1836, Harriet Martineau, a well-known journalist of the day, viewed the scene as the Chicago boom was nearing its peak. A friend had told her to forget attempting to stay in any of the inns. She would find them "intolerable" at the period of the great land sales, which brought a concourse of speculators to the place.

By now the boom, which had earlier been based on Chicago's potential prosperity, was by now a price boom: a craze that would rapidly be transformed into a speculative mania.

Once any crowd is caught up in a speculative craze, the object of that craze will command whatever price you may care to name. No matter what the price! The object of the craze — in this case land and property — will be seen by everyone as undervalued. The higher the price climbs, the greater the perceived under-valuation. Once a mania is in full flood, price ceases to be a consideration. What counts is being able to raise even more credit on the strength of the last sale; and knowing that there is another buyer ready and waiting to relieve us of our next acquisition, at — it goes without saying — a handsome profit.

In Chicago's crowded streets, the speculators hurried from one sale to another. Tradesmen accosted Miss Martineau's friends as they passed their shops: "...with offers of farms and all manner of land lots, advising them to speculate before the price of land rose higher."

No doubt it all sounds most familiar! By speculating himself, one of Miss Martineau's friends had realised, inside two years: "...ten times as much money as he had before fixed upon as a competence for life."

Chicago, in hindsight, had everything that any city needs to generate an uncontrollable boom; including a plethora of bankers and other wealthy individuals, prepared to lend to anyone who could come up with a proposition that sounded in the least workable. By now the mania had reached such a pitch that it was not only lawyers and land dealers who were making their fortune. One poor man, wrote Harriet Martineau: "...had some pre-emptions to some land, for which he paid in the morning one hundred and fifty dollars. In the afternoon, he sold it to a friend of mine for five thousand dollars."

What went on in Chicago was typical of the boom that carries within it the seed of its own destruction. What begins as an exciting, yet practical, proposition gets swept up into as speculative mania. Normal standards of prudence and good sense are suspended. Once that has happened, there's no call (and no time) to start asking questions. "During a gold rush," said one old-timer, "you don't stop in your tracks to quibble over the price of a postage stamp." Certainly not when huge fortunes are being made every hour of every day. In any case, so long as the banks weren't worrying...who was?

Even those with a strong gut feeling that nothing — let alone the Chicago boom — could go on for ever, fell into a trap of their own making. They persuaded themselves that they, if no one else, would recognise the warning signs. So, at the first hint of danger, they would move with the speed of lightening to sell up and get out...like Charlie Meyer did.

That feeling of superiority is one of the more dangerous forms that self-deception takes. The truth is that there never has been a crash without an explosion of credit: credit that is extended on the assumption that prices will continue their rise indefinitely. Once that assumption has taken hold in the marketplace, normal prudence, doubt and fear give way to an overpowering greed that transforms mere mania into sheer, unadulterated madness. It is as though credit, which had nourished and stimulated the early boom like a powerful medicine, had been so wildly over-prescribed that it was now acting like a deadly poison.

A POWERFUL DRUG

CREDIT is, indeed, a powerful drug, the very lifeblood of every boom. But it is also the genesis of every crash. In the beginning, it is credit which alone enables us to pull off deals or execute coups which would be out of the question were we forced to rely on our own resources. In other words, by borrowing we acquire "leverage". With leverage, we can move financial mountains. When we have taken our profit on one deal, we may begin looking around for the next. Having shown once that we were onto a "good thing", we should have less difficulty next time in raising an even larger loan.

By increasing leverage, we have also increased our debt. This must eventually be faced. But not yet! The day of reckoning is still a good way off. Besides (we will tell ourselves) this is no moment for worrying what might happen.

As I have said, the basic component of every single crash is the explosive character of credit; raised in the belief that prices will go on rising for ever. In truth, prices will never reach the levels expected of them. One must be blind not to see that. But, with fear and greed as the ruling emotions, we are all blind. So credit creation leads to unserviceable debt, which will grow and grow until it is beyond the capability of the borrower to discharge that debt.

That means the lender will stand the loss, and the sum advanced will go, as we say, to money heaven. The lender's chance of recovery may be slim. So far as the market as a whole is concerned, the accumulated weight of unserviceable debt will eventually bring it crashing down.

In the early stages, a newcomer's fear of not being able to cut it will briefly be replaced by greed. But fear will not be absent for long. It is far too basic an emotion. In any rising market, alongside the greed of the holder of any speculative vehicle is the fear of "missing out." It gnaws away at the heart of every bystander who has yet to summon up the courage to take the plunge. When fear grips the speculator trapped in a falling market, it is greed that dictates the actions of the bargain-hunter.

Remember how the boom rose like a phoenix from the ashes of a previous crash? In the same way, it is at the peak of the market - the split second when it is perceived that prices can go no higher - that the boom is over. The crash - as yet undetectable - has begun. At first glance it might strike you as an unacceptable paradox. But it is a manifestation of the great mystery of nature, which has been felt and understood by the more visionary of Western philosophers.

It was as true for Heraclitus in ancient Greece as for the atomic physicist, Niels Bohr. It was as central to the oldest philosophies as greed and fear. The pinnacle of hope is in reality the first stage of despair: while the slough of despond turns out to be the birthplace of hope.

BUILDING THE BOMB

THERE was a further and unusual dimension to the Chicago land and property boom. It was not merely that individual banks were coming up with cash from their vaults each time fresh loans were granted. President Andrew Jackson was playing his part, encouraging the printers to keep the presses pouring out vast quantities of fresh notes. It was as though all that money was being shovelled straight into the furnace to raise an even bigger head of steam.

Between 1829 and 1837 (the year of the crash), speculation was rife. The number of banks in the United States more than doubled from 329 to 788. The volume of bank loans expanded five-fold.

Notes in issue maintained a parallel buoyancy, with the printing presses forever in top gear. In the seven years leading up to the crash, the face value of bank notes in circulation jumped from 60 million dollars to almost 150 million dollars.

In 1836, easy credit and copious amounts of new bank notes, had pushed the value of land sales up to an unheard of $25 million. But, in line with speculative manias of the past, land or property was being purchased simply for sale to someone else. Buyers were not in the least concerned with getting "value for money", or acquiring land or buildings because of their development potential. The main thing was that the market should still keep climbing. Therefore property in Chicago ceased to have any investment value. Its factories, office buildings, farmland and homes became mere counters in a crazy, state-wide game of Monopoly.

At the peak of the boom, the presses of some 634 banks were spewing out notes as hard as they could go. All in all, they handed out in freshly printed money no less than 525 million dollars worth of new loans. On the eastern seaboard, gold and silver-backed currencies were fairly plentiful. West of the Alleghenies, they were not. But the banks still continued to print more notes regardless. Theoretically the dollar was specie-backed. But the gold backing to that huge volume of paper amounted to no more than 35 million dollars. What did a mere technicality like that matter? Did anyone stop to ask?

What did matter was that the demand for more dollars never slackened.

However, when the crash came, it began to matter a great deal whether the notes were gold-backed or not. It became clear that a dollar from somewhere out West was not necessarily going to be accepted as readily as a dollar, say, from a New York or Boston bank.

DETONATING THE CHARGE

THE CRUX came, and the tightly packed charge was about to go off, in 1836. It was then the battle between President Jackson and Nicholas Biddle, who directed the Second Bank of the United States, reached crisis point. The President, having the political advantage, resolved the issue once and for all. He refused point-blank to renew the Second Bank's charter. This resulted in a veritable bank note orgy, involving almost every bank in the nation. Hoards of unregulated banks were drawing upon the seemingly bottomless pit of bank credit.

The final crunch came on 4th July 1836, when a large display of earth moving equipment rolled onto the streets of Chicago to take part in the Independence Day parade. They were to celebrate the grand opening of the Illinois-Michigan Canal.

Then Andrew Jackson delivered the final blow. It was fatal for the land and property market, as well as for Biddle's bank. Mr President publicly condemned the rush for land and residential property, and forbade the deposit of any federal revenues in Biddle's bank. He delivered the coup-de-grace in the form of a circular requiring that all payment for land and property should be made in fully gold-backed notes.

With land and property prices falling, there was a rush by speculators to unload before the market collapsed completely. Many Americans in business turned to London for credit. But they were too late. London had already begun to call in loans made to their American clients. The explanation given was that the funds were needed to finance a number of major ventures in Britain. England also cut back its American cotton imports: a further heavy blow on top of President Jackson's draconian measures.

Tension remained high throughout the autumn and winter. Then, on March 17th, 1837, a number of New Orleans cotton mercantile houses closed down. Their failure was due to the combination of extended credit and cutbacks in their order books. Instantly, almost one fifth of New Orleans banks became insolvent, and the entire commerce of the city came to a halt. The city's indebtedness, which included the liabilities of cotton factories as well as land speculation, totalled approximately 200 million dollars. It was an almost unimaginable amount for any city in those days. New Orleans banks were forced to suspend payment; and chaos spread to the money markets. By now, the entire Southern States were close to bankruptcy.

That was the last straw for the Chicago property market, which finally collapsed. Many businesses, which at one time could have repaid their debts 20 times over, also came crashing down. Too much of their wealth was held in notes which lacked a gold backing. At the same time, no one was willing to grant them credit on the strength of their grotesquely over-valued real estate. Chicago bankers reacted the only way they could. They suspended payment. Riots threatened. The State Militia had to be called out. As Joe Balestier wrote:

"The year 1837...was the harvest of the notary and the lawyer - the year of wrath to the mercantile...The land resounded to the groans of ruined men, and the sobs of defrauded women, who had entrusted their all to the greedy speculators...It was a scene of woe and desolation."

IN THE WAKE OF THE COLLAPSE

THE EFFECTS which follow the collapse of a major market spread like a brush-fire. A wave of default rippled through the money markets across America. Wall Street sank into the worst bear market it had ever experienced. Over the next seven years the stockmarket index sank to less than a fifth of its level at the market peak. It fell, in fact, to the levels of the early 1800s. You could say — as some said then — that when Chicago's credit bomb went off, it blew away the land and property market, along with 30 years of economic and industrial progress and prosperity.

You can be certain that on countless occasions before disaster struck, the solid citizens of that vast heartland between the Mississippi and the Great Lakes must have got together in their clubs and chapels, hotel lobbies and bar-rooms, board-rooms and brothels, to toast their new-found success. The record showed that in 1830 the first parcels of land offered at auction had been sold in small, 80/100-foot lots. They fetched $100 a time. By 1834, each $100 lot was changing hands at $3,000. The year after that they were realising $15,000.

The worthies of Chicago must also have asked themselves the question that is invariably asked on such occasions: "How can anything possibly go wrong after this?" No doubt they reassured one another that there could be no end to the prosperity they saw around them. It was, indeed, the fulfilment of every real estate man's dream.

The crash which came in 1837 did more than merely shatter a familiar dream. For, over the next six years, American society was to pass through a deep hollow of doubt and distress. The poor suffered, but the propertied classes were among the hardest hit. They were the ones who had absorbed the largest lines of credit. They now carried the heaviest burden of debt.

By 1840, the loss due to the depression was estimated at around $6 billion.

There were further losses which could not be measured. But the outcome of the distress selling which followed was no secret. Inside four years, the price of prime sites came down from $11,000 an acre to $100 an acre. Although even at $100 there were virtually no buyers.

The Illinois banks were unable to carry the burden of debt dumped on them by customers who had borrowed during the boom but were now unable to repay more than a couple of cents in the dollar. Frequently the price obtained for the property was insufficient to pay the interest outstanding on the loan. Negative equity with a vengeance! Throughout the State of Illinois, the banks did what banks always do in the circumstances. They closed their doors.

Nor did it end there. The State defaulted on its obligations. Work on the Canal was terminated. In the city of Chicago, property values fell even further.

By 1841, Chicago's troubles were spreading all away across the nation. The general collapse impoverished many hundreds of communities. As the most basic of values were questioned, prices took a fall. The tide of bankruptcy rose, engulfing nearly everything and everyone. Between 1841 and 1842, eight states would go into default. It was a nightmare situation, one which would not go away.

When, as was inevitable, the stricken nation made a concentrated effort to trace the cause of the disaster, the answer came up as might have been expected: over-extension of credit when the pressure of an over-inflated economy proved too great.

Now they had the answer. Fingers would be pointed, blame allotted and wise pronouncements made. But the knowledge alone was not sufficient to save California from a similar sequence of speculation, over-extension of credit and the collapse of land and property prices.

LESSON STILL TO BE LEARNED

CALIFORNIA'S land boom in the 1880s, like that of Chicago fifty years before, was initially based on real assets and genuine potential. But when the Easterners moved in to exploit — in the best sense — that fruitful, fertile land, the inevitable happened. The soundly based financial structure they planned to build ended up as a casino. As Theodore Van Dyke, who had written the epitaph of Chicago's boom, put it:

"We never knew what the cussed land was worth until outsiders found it out, and now we are green enough to let them make all the money out of it."

The losses this time were on a similar scale. Land worth $200 an acre in 1885 had been bid up by the speculators to almost $10,000 by the following summer. Credit as yet, was not all that easy. Nevertheless it was possible to borrow 75% at cost price. Hard headed competition gave way to fantasy.

As in all price booms, more and more players managed to persuade themselves that land in California was still under-valued. Therefore, they argued, when prices rose, they were merely trying to catch up with rising values. Since land was so grossly undervalued (in their eyes), the price paid was unimportant.

The crash came in 1888, and lasted through the following year. By the end of 1889, values had fallen by 75%. Many thousands were ruined. The answers were all there. But it made no difference.

FLORIDA FOLLOWS SUIT

IT WAS 1921, when state-wide land speculation flared up again, this time in Florida. By now the lessons of Chicago and California had been forgotten. It had all happened such a long time before!

The meanest-ever collapse in property prices, they called it. In the mid-1920s, the semi-tropical climate and the sandy beaches had attracted many farmers and retired couples who brought themselves - and their money - to this undeveloped paradise. The dollars poured in. The State prospered and the real estate business boomed.

On the heels of the dollars came the speculators, who appeared to cast a spell on the normally straight-laced, grim-faced Florida bankers. Within a year the loans on their books had all but doubled. A high proportion of the buyers put down no more than 10 per cent of the purchase price. Not that their aim was to take out the necessary 90 per cent mortgage. Their intention was rather to sell at a profit before the contract ran out and the time came to pay. In other words, they were into the classic margin play, which is a risky ploy at any time.

At first huge fortunes were made - at least on paper. Miami City Records show that one land plot - sold in 1914 for 1,500 dollars - changed hands in 1926 at 1.5 million dollars. But it was not to last. In the autumn of that same year, two hurricanes did massive damage to property in Florida. They tore the heart out of Florida land prices. It took until the 1960s for Florida real estate to regain its 1925/26 price level.

The immediate reaction of property market victims is to complain loudly. "Hell...if bricks and mortar are no longer safe, what is?" The short answer is the brutal one: nothing is 100% safe. Or ever will be.

Yet it is surprising how many of us in the UK still find that hard to believe.

◆◆◆

CHAPTER FOUR

BY WHAT DIVINE RIGHT?

"In Britain today there is more space where nobody is than where anybody is. That is what makes Britain what it is."

Gertrude Stein

FOR THOSE in the UK, who at this moment are screaming loudly about their ill fortune, there is an equally brutal question to be answered: "Do you seriously believe that there is some Divine Right which entitles you to live virtually rent free for twenty years, and then walk away at the end with a sizeable tax-free profit?"

I am merely asking that question. I do not intend to hang around for the answer. Although there is an answer alright. But not to my question. For the truth is that the tax-free gain had gradually become one of the main attractions in buying rather than renting. Mind you, there's no harm in hoping! Or taking a gamble. But remember: a tough game of whist in the front parlour is one thing. A cosy hand of poker at the casino is quite another. Especially if you lose.

I am assuming, by the way, that you would have learned all you could about both games before the cards were dealt. It would be sheer madness to get stuck into a game you knew nothing about. So - question number two - why act so crazy when it comes to property?

I can answer that one. In the first place, most people just don't know a thing about property. Why should they? It's not their business. It is something that will confront them out of the blue. Very often they become involved because someone in the family has got married, been born or suddenly died. In other words, they come face to face with the snares and snags of the property market at a time when rationally and emotionally they may be off balance.

Psychiatrists, and those lay-persons who enjoy dabbling in such pastimes as table rapping or a little homespun psychology, frequently say that moving house is one of the top three causes of stress and emotional upheaval. Moving house comes third after bereavement and divorce.

A cliché, but like most clichés there is an element of truth in it.

When they come right up against it, it's probably as a first time buyer - or seller. That could be just a little late to start learning the raw ...sometimes very raw...facts about the residential property market and the main players. It helps to know the ways of estate agents and those whom they are paid to serve. It is as well to know that chartered surveyors can be extremely hesitant when it comes to the main purposes for which our innocents are likely to require them. That is to say pointing out the hidden faults, and giving the client a fair and realistic assessment of what the property could be worth.

Then come the insurers - what are they going to charge? For what precisely are they willing to provide cover? Who is prepared to lend how much? For how long - and at what price? To say nothing of the manifold problems that can so easily crop up with leases, covenants and rights of way. There are now building regulations and district surveyors to be satisfied: planning committees to be won over and - if it comes to it - an appeal to the minister. That means winning over his inspector.

As John Donne put it, no man is an island. How very true when it comes to buying, selling, or just living quietly in one's own home. There can be awkward tenants and neighbours to be handled; builders - no longer interested - who tend to disappear or require to be chivvied. Then there are the material hazards: leaks in the gas or water mains, failure of the electricity supply. Did you have the company check it over? There can well be dodgy wiring and unsafe circuits that you wish you'd never mentioned to the Man from the Electric.

Then there are the really big snags, which can cripple you: a dodgy roof for one. Unhappily it cannot be blamed entirely on the big storm. True, the near-hurricane ripped out the whole of the two front gables and deposited them in the street. A clear case of storm damage! To this the company may well reply, "It is only partly the reason. If those roof timbers had not been so old and rotten, the gale alone would not have done so much damage." And there's that goddamned house next door...untouched, save for a couple of ridge tiles: positively leering at you and your wreck.

If the roof is OK, there's always a good chance of dry rot down below stairs. "Better have a look while I'm here," says the insurance man. "Nothing very much, right now," he reports. You sigh with relief. You can always get the previous dry rot merchants to pay up. You hold their guarantee. "The only way one can tell is by stripping out the plaster...and opening up that wall" A sharp intake of breath. The insurance man hears you. He pretends not to notice. That too, he suggests, would be covered by the guarantee. You don't react. For one thing, you can tell that the insurance assessor is not going to budge over the roof. "Course, I could always put it to head office. Have a quiet word." That is the last thing anyone in their right mind would want. Having a quiet word could take weeks. Meanwhile massive interest charges on that equally massive loan would be ticking away like a taximeter.

Besides, you've just remembered about that guarantee!! You seem to have read somewhere that the dry rot specialists in question settled the matter once and for all before they went out of business last year!

Not so long ago, merely to utter the word subsidence - let alone landslip or heave - was like screaming plague or worse. It could leave you stranded without a friend. Potential purchasers, who know nothing about subsidence, were frequently frightened out of their minds by the shock-horror stories in the media. Sometimes their solicitors helped. Knowing even less about subsidence than the paper boy, they'd claim to have "read all about it last Sunday." This could put their clients - the potential purchasers - into a real puckertairy.

THE PRICE OF INNOCENCE

STRESS, uncertainty, fear and panic would not be too bad if they merely sent the uninitiated scurrying for cover. But that is not necessarily what happens. Sooner or later, the harassed of this earth become slightly ashamed. They realise they are dithering - chickening out. So pride, rather than sober common sense takes over. Our innocents close their eyes tightly and have one last stab at making a firm decision. In sheer desperation, and under pressure from "the other side", the newcomer to the game can end up taking on burdens and responsibilities which would turn the hardened professional white over night.

There is another important question to be asked and answered here. Where is the innocent buyer or seller to go for sound advice? To the estate agent? To the bank? To the building society? To the insurance agent? To the Citizens Advice Bureau? To the rabbi or the priest?

Before answering, let me ask another question. Where do you go for advice over your financial affairs? Have you tried going to an Independent Advisor? If so, did he (or she) prove as successful on your behalf because they were independent? Or as you thought they would be?

I was not joking when I suggested the rabbi or the priest as a possible source of guidance. If they are well established, they hear things and know things about their respective congregations which rarely get to the ears of an outsider.

The first step is to get to know as much as you can about the neighbourhood, about the benefits you can expect and the burdens you're assuming. Ask advice of anyone - but bear in mind where their obvious interests lie. Be discreet in the way you use the specialist services. Ask the bank, the building society, the estate agent the same question if you will. How much and what you believe is up to you; to your common sense. Try shopping in the area if you don't know it already. Go to the public library. Find out about local societies. Take the pulse of the area. You will be surprised how much you can learn in a couple of weeks, or half-a-dozen weekends.

In brief, do what you would be doing if you were thinking of setting up a small business in the area. Spouses can help by looking in on the areas that interest them. There can be a role too for the teenage children. Read the local papers. Talk to the collection box rattlers. They generally stand near the entrance to the tube, the bus terminal, the railway station. Visit the leading local stores. Talk to the staff as well as to other customers. You may get some funny looks, but you will get some first class information.

If, in the end, you decide you don't like the area, there's nothing lost. Besides - think what grief and woe you will have avoided.

How is this book designed to help you? Firstly by removing several layers of myth and propaganda and exposing the real face of the residential property market. Secondly, and all the time, by introducing you to the actual concerns and opportunities we share with the recent past. Lastly, and very importantly, it enable you to view the disappointments and disasters of the past in a new light. This in turn should make it easier for you to anticipate the approach of their present day counterpart.

Let's pick up where we ended the last chapter: having realised that we should not be surprised at anything. Except, perhaps, how little anyone ever told us about the recent past, which helped create the uncertain world today. So - hold tight. It could be a bumpy ride.

A BUMPY RIDE

THOSE quite sensational disasters in the United States which we've already considered are equivalent - in Housequake terms - to the BIG ONE. In between each BIG ONE, there's a number of lesser tremors. Not all that terrible maybe; but sufficient to demolish your House of Cards. There are (and there will continue to be) a whole lot of bewildered people who'll keep reciting their creed: "House prices always move upwards, reach a plateau and then - after a brief pause - move higher still." Ignore them.

The somewhat elusive trend in house prices would appear to have an eighteen-year rhythm; with major peaks occurring at intervals of fifty to sixty years.

Residential property prices shadow the long wave of economic life to a more precise degree than any other capital market. As I pointed out in my book, *Into The Upwave:*

"The subdominant eighteen-year rhythm in real estate activity is linked to corresponding rhythms in new building and the marriage rate which also succumbs to major peaks in activity about every fifty to sixty years....As far back as the 18th century, which is about as far as available statistics on the subject of residential land prices and building construction can be obtained, we can see traces of the recurrent rhythm in real estate activity at work."

Figures showing the number of bricks produced in England and Wales during the period 1785 through 1849 were published by H.A. Shannon. This was possible as bricks were taxed at the time and records were kept.

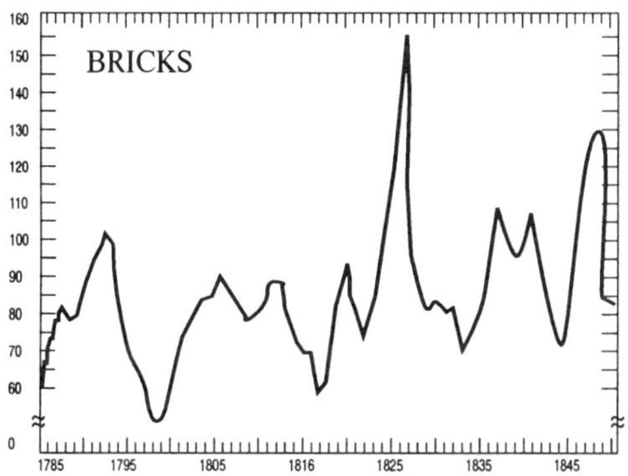

Figure 1: *Bricks produced per capita in England and Wales 1785-1849.*

Source: *The Price Series by G.F. Warren and F.A. Pearson.*

Reprinted by permission of Chapman and Hall, Ltd.

Warren and Pearson interpolated population data, adjusting brick production per capita during the same period. The result was further vindication of both the sixteen to nineteen-year rhythm of activity and the overriding fifty to sixty-year rhythm. The parallel between housing activity and long waves of economic behaviour was clearly revealed.

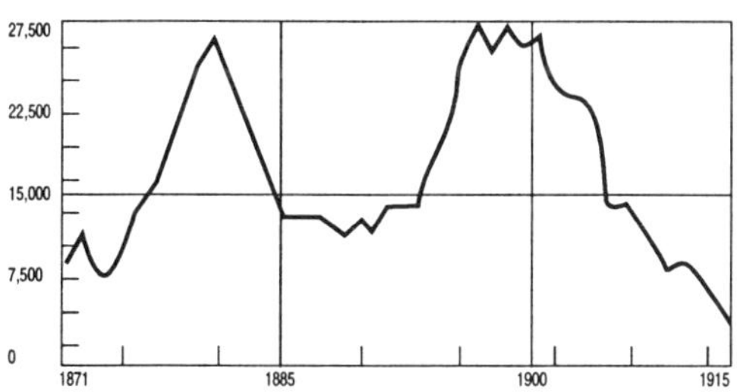

Figure 2: *New houses built in the Metropolitan Police District of London 1871-1916*

Source: *The Price Series by G.F. Warren and F.A. Pearson.*

Reprinted by permission of Chapman and Hall, Ltd.

It is likely that house prices edged marginally higher during the early part of the 20th century, embarking on a thrilling and explosive rise following World War 1. The prices peaked just about the time of the 1920-1922 recession. From 1920-1922, the combination of a sharp fall in land, construction and building material costs resulting from global deflation would certainly have affected the price of residential property. Nor were the effects felt in Britain alone. About the time that building costs fell by 50 per cent in Britain, France saw a drop of 28 per cent and Germany one of 37 per cent.

The periods 1891, 1895 and 1897-1899 saw sizeable falls in construction costs in the USA. The same holds true for 1901, 1903, 1904, 1911 and 1921. Between 1937 and 1939 costs fell there by 8.5 per cent. Between 1941 and 1944 they came down by 12 per cent. However the most severe drop in construction costs on record took place during the five years from 1929 through 1934. Then the cost of building a home in the United States plummeted by no less than 39 per cent.

Land prices in the United States have also fluctuated with the same degree of volatility. Between 1890 and 1920, the average cost of an acre of residential building land more than doubled from $747 to $1,507. But it didn't stay there for long. In 1920, residential building land began to slide. It continued to slide for 20 years, reaching a low point at $798 per acre in 1940. Then came an upward surge between 1940 and 1950 with the average price in constant dollars reaching $1,061. While consumer prices trebled between 1890 and 1950, and the population grew by two-and-a-half times, land prices increased only slightly.

A further variable in the house-price equation over the years has been the cost of land relative to the total cost of the home. Again, looking at the experience of the United States, the cost of land in 1890 accounted for almost 40 per cent of the total cost of a single home. By 1953, the land cost was down to a mere 17 per cent.

There is a distinct commonality in housing trends among industrialised nations. While the extent of expansion and contraction differs from one country to another, we have seen over the past 200 years that peaks and troughs in residential housing activity - directly related to price activity - have occurred in sequence without deviation among all the major countries.

A further interesting discovery is a tendency to major panics two to four years after peaks in building activity. For example, there was a peak of building activity in the United States in 1836. A major panic occurred the following year. In 1871, there was a peak in building activity in several countries simultaneously. There was a global panic two years later in 1873.

A most remarkable year was 1890 when a construction peak in Hamburg,

Germany, coincided with a record level of house building in London and brick production in Glasgow. At the same time the United States experienced a peak in real estate activity.

Exactly three years later, in 1893, there was a world-wide depression of immense proportions.

CHANGE AND DEVELOPMENT

FOR THE past century and more there have not merely been the wave-like movement in costs and prices which would appear to be the norm. There have also been significant structural changes in the residential property market overall. For the middle classes, the period has been one of evolution. For the working class, one of comparatively peaceful - but frequently bitter - revolution; with the rise and fall of public housing and the unparalleled advance of home ownership.

The changes, and the vast amount of government and private funds involved, have made property far more potent as a capital market than at any time during the past 200 years.

Strictly speaking, the surge in home ownership in the United States and elsewhere is largely a product of the past four decades. Although in the United Kingdom there has been a slow drift in that direction since late Victorian times. Several factors contributed to the gradual ascent of the residential ladder. One of the earliest was the desire of the better-off artisan to improve his status. Even if he and his wife never managed to rise above their working class origins, they might well enable their children to do so.

At the beginning of Queen Victoria's reign improving the condition of the urban poor was of intense interest to all classes. Primarily it was because the bad housing conditions bred disease, which in turn spread to all social classes. This coincided with a desire to move out from the centre of our cities, which were becoming grossly overcrowded. So many towns expanded into cities and the larger cities developed into sprawling conurbations. Until the third decade of the nineteenth century, house building had kept pace with the expanding population. After that, the rate of expansion was out of control and overcrowding became worse than ever before.

During the 1820s, the population in Birmingham, Bradford, Leeds, Liverpool, Manchester and Sheffield grew by 40% to 45% every ten years. Which still left them a long way behind London. Before Queen Victoria came to the throne in 1837, the capital city had no close rival. Glasgow and Liverpool had no more than 200,000 citizens and only five other towns had a population above 100,000. London, with its

1.75 million by 1831 towered head and shoulders above the rest. By the time the old Queen died in 1901, 33 towns and cities had a population of 100,000. Four had passed the half-million mark. But London still led with 4.5 million.

Queen Victoria's reign saw the expansion of the steam line railway network, enabling many thousands to move out to the suburbs. There was a vast improvement in heating, lighting and sanitation: and new homes were being built for the rapidly growing middle-classes on the outer fringes of the larger cities. They were the class which had been liberated by the expansion of the railways, since it was no longer necessary to keep one's own coach and horses in order to escape from the noise and smoke and over-crowding of the inner cities.

To this day one can see - and live in a flat - in the Victorian stucco villas built for men and families of substance. Young people, with their first child, still make their first family home in the red-brick terrace houses built for the less affluent. The cheaper, smaller and less well planned homes, built for the clerks and sales-people to rent, are still very much in evidence. Local history societies have them well documented. Local builders have modernised, improved and restored all three types of property, still in general use in the inner London boroughs, both north and south of the Thames. Much the same can be said for most inner-city areas, though on a smaller scale.

DESIGNED FOR THE MIDDLE CLASSES

J.H.WALSH'S *Manual of Domestic Economy* (1857) gives us an idea of costs. The sixteen-roomed house was deemed "sufficient for any ordinary (middle class) family." This house would provide good-sized dining and drawing rooms, with eight bedrooms plus two servants rooms in the roof. There would also be dressing rooms, and the kitchen would be underground. This, Walsh pointed out, was "universally the custom in London." The whole of the work could be executed for between £1,200 and £1,800. Price fluctuations might add another £100 to £150 to the cost. Such a dwelling would be "suited to families spending from £100 to £1,000 a year."

Walsh also quotes the price for two other models: the ten-roomed and the four to six-roomed house. The former was described as "the ordinary style of London houses in inferior streets." The rooms would be smaller than in the "large and roomy" 16-roomed house. It would probably be rented at an average of £55 a year: the rent rising and falling according to the situation. The cost of building such a house in London would run out at between £800 and £1,000. But, according to the Manual: "...in many cases where an inferior class of material is allowed to be used, £600 will have covered the cost. Here, however, the staircase must be of common description, narrow and dog-legged."

The four and six-roomed models were planned for people with an annual income of no more than £100 to £200. They would consist of: "...a basement, ground and first floor, in each of which there are two rooms, or sometimes...a basement consisting of a kitchen and scullery, while the other floors are entirely occupied by one or two rooms. They are seldom ornamented in any way externally, though...of late years, such an attempt has been made by means of stucco and cement, covering very inferior brickwork, and only resulting in premature decay.

BORROWED FROM FRANCE

ONE OUTSTANDING innovation in the 1860's was the "flat" system, described by T.H.S Escott, author of *England: Its People, Polity and Pursuits, as* "... borrowed from France."

Although flats were to be found in plenty in Scotland and on the Continent, they were a novelty south of Hadrian's Wall. In point of fact, the earliest family flats in England were "model dwellings" built for the working classes of Birkenhead as early as 1845. For once the middle classes followed the lead of the workers. 1854 saw the building of Ashley Place in London's Victoria. Queen Anne's Mansions in Queen Anne's Gate was the first "high-rise" building of fourteen storeys. In 1890, the height of London buildings was limited to 90 feet. Four years later, the height limit was reduced to 80 feet.

The demand for the original 116 foot high blocks was such that more and taller blocks were built. One attraction was the provision of a lift to reach the upper floors. Another was the panoramic views. They took in Hampstead, Highgate and Edgware to the north and the Crystal Palace and the Surrey hills to the south; to say nothing of the superb view of the Thames with its twin cities of London and Westminster.

A further inducement to the building of what today would be termed "luxury flats" for "persons of position", was the high rent which could be asked for a flat in these "Babel-like structures." Observed *The Builder* (2 June 1877):

"When a floor containing six rooms, without any grounds, commands £300 per annum, and two rooms £60 per annum, there is a strong encouragement to continue the erection of such a class of structure."

Bearing in mind the height of the buildings and the inevitable risk of fire, the journal's readers needed to be reassured that they were still safe more than 100 feet above ground. It was explained that the walls at the base were 4ft. 6in. thick: gradually reducing until they came down to 14 in. at the top floor. All floors, it was claimed, were strictly fireproof, with an iron girder framework filled in with concrete. As a further precaution against fire, there were water tanks at the top of every building, connected to each floor by means of hydrants, jets and hoses. The total capacity of the water tanks for each block was 40,000 gallons.

It was to take another 100 years before the giant towers of the City's Barbican challenged the feats of the Victorian developers.

T.H.S. Escott, writing in 1879, reported that "In the course of five years the rents have doubled....The sum paid annually for a suite of eight rooms on the ground floor (in Victoria) is not less than £250...and unless the tenant chooses to ascend to the lofty level of the garrets, no set of apartments can be procured in this quarter of town for less than £150."

Was there sufficient demand for such expensive accommodation? Apparently there was for few sets of rooms remain vacant for long. Even at a time when servants were cheap and plentiful, service flats possessed: "...what may well seem a great advantage to busy men or women who are anxious to purchase the seclusion of domestic life at the cost of as little inconvenience as possible. The tenant of a flat is able to compound for all the various petty charges incidental to the householder by payment of a lump sum."

There was a further advantage if the tenant intended to leave London. The flat could be sealed, threatened neither by the burglar "nor from the charwoman - the traditional custodian of the London house when the family are out of town." And, the writer concluded, "the strange relatives and unsavoury friends whom that person may invite into the drawing room during the period of her occupancy."

RISING RENTS

BY THE 1880s rents in the congested districts of London, declared the Royal Commission, were gradually moving higher, although wages were not rising at anything like the same rate. The contrast between the real standard of living of - say - the Victoria flat dwellers and their domestics was more pronounced than ever. High rents were due to competition at both ends of the market. It was competition which made slum properties as profitable for the landlord as top of the market property.

In south St Pancras, 4s. a week was paid for one small room, 10 feet by 7. Around the corner, 5 shillings was paid for a single room. Those seeking even cheaper accommodation might rent an underground kitchen which cost two-shillings-and-sixpence. In Spitalfields rents were higher: between 4s.6d. and 6s. a week for a single room. While the working class themselves were responsible for the overcrowding and the comparatively high rents, they had no choice; as the Royal Commission (1884-5) explained:

"Sometimes they hear of casual work to be had at a certain place provided they are there by 6 o'clock the next morning, so they must choose a central position from which no part of the town is inaccessible." In the provinces the rents of houses and tenements were considerably lower than in London. For example, a single cellar in Newcastle went for 3s. a week. That was higher than the usual price for a single room in the town, which averaged 2s.6d.

There is always a tendency when looking back to an earlier time to be too much influenced by what was happening in the capital city. In the case of London, it was by far the biggest city and growing fast. In 1881, London was twice as large as Birmingham, Glasgow, Liverpool and Manchester put together. It was also the centre from which both the authorities and the reformers were working, and which foreign visitors and writers tended to visit. It was the city around which the largest ring of suburbs spread. A leading article in the *Morning Herald* (20th September 1848) expressed astonishment over the rate at which virtually all the major cities were spilling over into the surrounding countryside:

"No one, who has recently travelled with eyes open....can have failed to observe that houses are springing up in all quarters, for the reception of the ever-increasing population of densely-populated London. In the vicinity of other large cities, especially if they boast the advantage of a railway the same observation will have been made....There is no lack of brick and mortar, east, west, north or south".

Money was scarce, continued the *Morning Herald*, and the whole nation was in difficulties: "But houses spring up everywhere in the outskirts of our great towns....You may get a new house, of almost every conceivable pattern, and at any conceivable price, down to £60 per annum...when we come to consider the number of pursy citizens that it will take to populate these snug suburbs, we are absolutely lost in wonder to determine where they can all come from".

The *Morning Herald* concluded with the thought that one would imagine there was an increase in population lower down than "the classes which rejoice in five hundred a year." It went on: "...when we contemplate the number of houses in the course of erection for the rich, where are the poor to be housed?" Where indeed?

COUNTING HEADS

UNTIL around the half-century, there was keen interest in improving the homes of the poor. Overcrowding was getting worse every year. With the overcrowding came disorder, squalor and filth, as workers and their families were packed together in the cast-off houses. They were houses the wealthy and the middle classes had vacated when they took off for the new quarters of the town or the increasing number of suburbs. It was not necessarily an enlightened philanthropy which gave the middle classes and the better paid artisans a desire to improve the conditions of the working classes. Social reform was more generally welcomed as a defence against the epidemics which started among the over-crowded, undernourished poor.

London, Liverpool or Glasgow might have been expected to provide examples of the worst housed among the poorer classes. But even in an area like Ipswich, there were horrifying examples of neglect and indifference. A bookseller and social reformer, John Glynde wrote a study of *The Moral and Religious Condition of Ipswich in the Middle of the Nineteenth Century.*

There were, he said, 106 courts in the town, containing 627 houses. The drainage from some of these was "very defective." : "In some instances all the refuse water has to be carried to a dead well, situated either in the middle or at the end of the yard....The demoralising practice of providing but one convenience for several houses is here seen in full force. No less than 67 courts, containing 358 houses, are in this position; giving an average of one to every five houses."

Yet the court dwellers were not all the dull, depraved creatures the better off - including some of the working class - held them to be.

"In the midst of all these disadvantages, the visitor of the poor meets with numerous instances of determined struggles for cleanliness and general purity of character....The clean bricks in front, the whitened doorstep, and the white muslin window blind....are indeed string proofs of a moral feeling which even the deteriorating circumstances around them have been unable to crush."

In Bristol, 35 years later, conditions were almost as bad. James Crosby, a journalist on the Bristol *Mercury* reported that within a stone's throw of the open space at the Haymarket and close to the "well kept carpet-like turf of the pleasure garden" lay "...a court of six or eight three-storey houses ... hemmed in...in what is known as a 'blind court' - narrow and without through ventilation. These are tenement houses - let room by room to families at 1s.6d. per week...(One) 'rookery' was a sample of the rest - from thirteen to sixteen or seventeen persons in a house, and in some instances husband, wife, and four children living and sleeping in one room."

The 1891 *Census - General Report* revealed that the six towns in which the percentage of "overcrowded persons" were the highest were:

Gateshead	40.78
Newcastle upon Tyne	35.08
Sunderland	32.85
Plymouth	26.27
Halifax	21.31
Bradford	20.61

NO REAL IMPROVEMENT

ONE OF the factors militating against the working class poor was the extent of demolition carried out for the railways, streets and public buildings, and what were called "improvement" schemes.

When Lord Shaftesbury and a future Prime Minister, Lord Derby had tried to halt the destruction of workers' homes, the comments of *The Times* newspaper showed a lack of either perceptiveness or humanity. Why should human beings be huddled together in filth and squalor?

"It cannot be for cheapness, for the returns show that the inhabitants of these rickety dens pay upon average a rent of £6 a year for a space of a thousand cubic feet, which, in proportion, is as much as a nobleman pays for his mansion in Belgrave Square...If lodging a poor man did not pay, there might be a danger that the labourer might be straightened for a lodging; but while he pays the builder a better percentage upon his money than can be got out of a Prince, there can be no fear that the labourer will be unable to find a roof..."

In *Good Words* (1872), Dr William Gilbert, author and champion of the poor, attacked the policy which led to the demolition of areas of bad housing without making any provision for the poor who inhabited them. This happened when Regent Street was projected:

"(One) great reason for its formation in the line it took was that it would destroy an immense number of poor dwellings...The inhabitants were ejected in crowds...In the western districts land was too valuable for them to find a home; and they migrated towards the Strand, to Westminster, and in many instances into Lambeth."

Gilbert compared the lack of any attempt to create new workers' homes in London when their old quarters were destroyed with the actions of the Germans when they entered Strasbourg. One of their first cares was to erect new dwellings in place of those demolished by their artillery.

The civic authorities, with their vast wealth, did eventually act over the so-called Farringdon Street Wastes - another vast acreage cleared of slum properties. An appeal was launched. The City fathers met and resolved that something like £20,000 should be set aside to build model lodging houses for "the better class" of the poor. The Corporation was warmly complimented on its action. Although "action" was scarcely the word.

Public imagination, reported Gilbert, either faded out, or the public interest diverted to other subjects: "(Some) twenty years elapsed without even the foundation of a house being commenced. The spot of ground was then sold (some say at a considerable profit) to the Metropolitan Railway Company..."

Among the vast quantity of evidence given to the Royal Commission of 1884-5 on the Housing of the Working Classes is the testimony of Andrew Young, surveyor and member of the London School Board. Some of the worst properties he had encountered were those purchased and demolished for the building of new schools:

Question – Did you give (the people) compensation for going?
Answer – Yes, some compensation was given

Question – How much would they get?
Answer – Those having one room might have from 5s. to £1

Question – Are they a class of people that would get into the Peabody building?
Answer – No, they are the class of people who are kept out...

Gradually the Government was obliged to take action. The Cross Acts (1875, 1879 and 1882) covered the clearing and rebuilding of large urban areas. The object was to guard against any excessive valuation of the property dealt with. The Torrens Acts (1868, 1879) covered single properties. The local authority was required to buy the land and carry out the demolition work. Rebuilding was left mainly to private enterprises. This created a problem for The Metropolitan Board of Works, forerunner of the London County Council (LCC).

They found they could sell only to charitable bodies. The Peabody Trust was one example. The land was bound to be sold at a loss since the authority had to pay the full market price, but the would-be developer would not pay more than the lower price fetched by land used for working class housing.

Joseph Chamberlain told the *Fortnightly Review* (December 1883) that the Metropolitan Board of Works had dealt in all with 42 acres of land, occupied by 20,335 people. A price of 17s. per square foot had been paid to the owners whose "criminal neglect" of the properties had led to their condemnation as unfit for human habitation. Even if sold for commercial purposes, after improvements had been made and streets laid out, it would still not have fetched more than 10s. a square foot. Designated for working class houses, and sold on that understanding, reduced the price to a mere 3s.4d. per square foot.

In the event, the net loss on the improvement ran out at £1,211,336 - approximately £60 per resident.

Despite improvements in the Housing Act of 1890, the law remained clumsy and expensive until the beginning of the new century.

◆◆◆

CHAPTER FIVE

TURN OF THE TIDE

"The man who goes up in a balloon does not feel as if he were ascending; he only sees the earth sinking deeper below him."

—Schopenhauer

"I CANNOT forbear to ask whether, before...we ride abroad redressing human wrongs in Turkey, Bulgaria, Afghanistan, and the ends of the earth generally, we had not better remember that charity begins at home..."

So said Dr G.W. Child, Medical Officer of Health for Oxfordshire, addressing the National Association for the Promotion of Social Science in 1878.

"...and before we spend £40,000.00 in two years for some Crimean war...reflect with advantage that the cost of two Crimean wars would...more than suffice to house the population of the country, even if all the money had to be found by the Exchequer..."

Dr Child was, in fact, an outspoken advocate of subsidising local authority housing. In this he was going far beyond the limit set by many genuine reformers like Joseph Chamberlain or Lord Shaftesbury. The latter set the boundaries quite clearly in the *Nineteenth Century* (December 1883 edition). He welcomed the current interest and concern of the public for the working classes and their living conditions. Though he found it strange that this feeling had:

"...lain so long dormant, for the disclosure of the evil was made more than 40 years ago, and ever since that date, the efforts of individuals, companies and associations have been...to devise remedies, and, in some instances, to apply them..."

His fear was that having done too little, there was now a chance that in some respects they might do too much.

There was such an outcry for the Government to "undertake this mighty question", that anyone setting himself up against that opinion was likely to incur much rebuke and condemnation: "Be it so. But if the State is to be summoned not only to provide houses for the labouring classes, but also to supply such dwellings at nominal rents, it will...utterly destroy their moral energies."

The *Westminster Review* (January 1884) rehearsed the economic and "practical" arguments: "We cannot pass an Act making it penal for landlords to receive the highest rents they can get...And it is difficult to see how the poor can combine to reduce the high rents they pay...Nor can we pass an Act compelling employers...to pay their men higher wages. That again would be disregarding every principle of political economy. And, moreover, it would be futile, for the price of everything would immediately rise in proportion: and the higher wages would...purchase no more."

There were many who still felt like the social reformer, Octavia Hill. A property owner herself, she was a good landlord and sought to improve the people themselves as well as their home conditions. She wrote a study of *Homes of the London Poor* (1875). Whatever was finally done in building for the people, she declared: "I most heartily hope...(it) may be done on a thoroughly sound commercial principle..(To) adopt any other principle...would be highly injurious to them."

Their homes were bad, she went on: "...partly because they are badly built and arranged; they are tenfold worse because the tenants' habits and lives are what they are. Transplant them tomorrow to healthy and commodious homes, and they would pollute and destroy them."

When she took possession of a property, each family had a chance to do better: "...those who would not pay, or who led clearly immoral lives, were ejected. The rooms they vacated were cleansed; the tenants who showed signs of improvement moved into them, and thus, in turn, an opportunity was obtained for having each room distempered and painted."

A thorny problem was solved for London when the London County Council (LCC) was established. This new body decided to retain all cleared land in public ownership, and put up housing for workmen. Some of the work would be done by the LCC's own Works Department; some by private contractors. The Council undertook 22 schemes between 1889 and 1900; and contributed to the cost of properties built under schemes run by the Vestries and District Boards. *Fabian Society Tract No 76* (1897) spelled out the LCC's achievements: "The Metropolis has done far more in the matter of housing than any other city - its total expenditure under the various Housing Acts amounts, indeed, to nearly three millions, or as much as that of all the rest of the United Kingdom put together - but it came into the field late. Not until 1876 did the Metropolitan Board of Works take action....clearing away slums at great expense without itself re-housing...."

The aim of the LCC, the Fabian Society tract explained: "...has been, not so much to reduce rents (which...would in the long run merely benefit the employer by reducing London rates of wages to the provincial standards) as to raise the standard of working class dwellings by supplying a better article for the same money...On the whole of the housing operations, taking one year with another, the rents received about balance the actual outgoings...."

Other cities followed suit: albeit haltingly. Glasgow began to re-build in 1889. By October 1900, the City had built 1,375 dwellings, ranging from one-apartment to three-apartment houses. Municipal enterprise built seven common lodging houses offering 2,414 beds at nightly charges of between 3d and 4½d. In 1899, a total of 867,338 overnight lodgers were housed, of whom 89,456 were women. Net profit, after an allowance for depreciation, was in the region of £4,400.

Liverpool built just over 550 tenements, let at between 2s 6d and 5s 6d per week. The dwellings paid about 3 per cent per annum. The Corporation decided that the very poor should be encouraged to build for themselves. This was done, with the building surveyor picking the foreman and his team. When completed, each room was let for 1s.

Obviously not all working class families lived in poverty and squalor. Some were even well off. Quite a few working men owned their own houses; or bought houses for letting. They were able to do this as a rule through either a friendly society or a building society. As early as 1871, the Royal Commission on Friendly and Benefit Building Societies received reports that 13,000 workers' houses in Birmingham were owner-occupied. Figures for worker home-ownership are scarce and not particularly reliable. But in York, Seebohm Rowntree was able to announce in 1899 that nearly 6 per cent of working class families lived in their own home.

PATERNALISM, IDEALISM AND SOUND BUSINESS

THERE were two other ways to approach home ownership - or leasing better class houses. One was through the estates which major industrialists had been building for a generation and more; the other was through the Garden City (and Garden Suburb) movement.

The village communities created by employers towards the turn of the century tended to copy some of the earlier philanthropic and idealistic schemes. Disraeli's fictional village in his book *Sybil* aroused a great deal of interest. It was possibly what inspired Titus Salt, a Bradford wool man, to plan Saltaire; the first independent community project on a green fields site.

The French economist, Leon Faucher, visited two early employers' villages. They were the 300–cottage Ashton project at Hyde, and Henry Ashworth's villages at Turton and Egerton. Faucher's report, written in 1844, goes into detail over the facilities provided for the tenants. Ashton's cottages, let for 3s or 3s 6d a week, came with free water, local rates paid and repairs carried out at no charge. With coal a mere eight or nine shillings a ton, the cottagers could afford to keep the fire burning away, which meant they could enjoy the luxury of constant hot water.

Ashworth's factory at Turton lay at the bottom of the valley. The summit of the wooded hills was the location, on one side of the valley, for Henry Ashworth's house. The workers' cottages were on the other. At Egerton, a second group of cottages built each side of the road seemed, wrote Faucher "...to welcome the approaching visitor."

Faucher was greatly impressed with: "...the order which prevails in these households...the polished furniture, and clean earthenware, with...the Bible, Memoirs of St Helena, weekly periodicals, and especially the Anti-Corn-Law Circular. The rent of each house is not more than £10 per annum; it costs £120 to build, and thus yields seven or eight per cent per annum."

The best known company schemes are the model village of Lever Brothers Ltd at Port Sunlight near Birkenhead, and Cadbury's Bournville near Birmingham. There was a dual motive in both cases: to give employees better conditions and thereby to encourage them to be better - and more loyal - workers.

When G.B. Shaw wrote *Widowers' Houses*, he tilted at the whole idea of boardroom philanthropy. But if the tenants felt critical or contemptuous of their landlords' motives, they could find consolation in the fact that their small houses had amenities many middle-class householders did not necessarily enjoy; like bathrooms and gardens and pleasant country air.

Lever Brothers' experiment was of great interest and importance to supporters of the Garden City Association, which proposed to take industry into the countryside and establish new towns for the operatives on model lines. One further point about the Lever Brothers' experiment was that it demonstrated that idealism in no way detracted from the benefits enjoyed by the tenants of newly created model villages. The houses were well planned and well built; and the workers lived reasonably close to the factory. The houses were of the Garden City type; each having its small garden in front of the house and a good yard behind. In addition to the gardens, there were allotments so the workers could grow their own produce; open spaces with trees and grass, and facilities for tennis, bowls, cricket and football. All in all the atmosphere was pleasing and cheerful.

As to the rents at Port Sunlight, they covered the cost of maintenance and repairs alone. There was no attempt whatsoever to seek a return on capital invested. The senior members of the firm would tell visitors that it was a "prosperity sharing" scheme. Lever Brothers believed that the firm enjoyed a fair return from the better health and increased efficiency of the workers.

At Bournville, the Quaker industrialist, George Cadbury - instigator of the scheme and founder of the Trust - let the houses to "suitable people" and proposed to use the profits to build more houses of a similar kind. He had a strong belief in the "civilising influence" of gardening. Therefore he arranged that each house should have one sixth of an acre of land. Mr Cadbury claimed that town dwellers who moved to Bournville "took to gardening as a duck takes to water."

The Bournville scheme took a step towards the Garden City model when it was decided that tenancies would not necessarily be reserved for Cadbury employees.

The Garden Cities themselves belonged to no single man or firm; nor was there any hidden benefit or agenda. Certainly there was no question of there being any tied cottages. James Silk Buckingham was an Owenite social reformer; and one of the pioneers of the Garden City idea; he prepared his own plan for "an entirely new Town, to be called 'Victoria'." Another pioneer of the movement was Sir Benjamin Richardson, a medical man and social reformer. He produced a plan for a model "city of health", providing such refinements as bath-rooms and hot and cold water in all the bedrooms. He wrote:

"...in this our model city there are no underground cellars, kitchens, or other caves, which, worse than those ancient British caves that Nottingham still can show the antiquarian as the once fastnesses of her savage children, are even now the residence of many millions of our domestic and industrial classes."

In the event, the first Garden City was founded at Letchworth in 1903, the year after Ebenezer Howard - its founder - had reprinted his book entitled *Garden Cities of Tomorrow.* In 1909 a survey carried out by the magazine *The Garden City* sought to establish how far former town dwellers took to living in the country. One of the local firms, Garden City Press, reported that, in its view:

"...slowly the working class population are beginning to get more contented with their surroundings here, as one hears less grumbling about the lack of town pleasures than say twelve months ago."

Similar reactions were reported from the so-called New Towns built after World War Two - Basildon, Stevenage, Harlow and the rest. It could have been a pioneering, socially minded architect, rather than Robert Louis Stevenson, who uttered those wise words: "To travel hopefully is a better thing than to arrive..."

The Garden City differed from the Garden Suburb in that the former believed that the work place should be part of the overall plan. The Garden Suburb, on the other hand, saw its mission as the creation of a purely residential, multi-class community. When Dame Henrietta Barnett and her friends founded the Hampstead Garden Suburb in 1906, their intention was to create a community of all classes. The tenants of the smaller cottage blocks, mainly East Enders would benefit in two ways: physically, by living in healthy surroundings in what was still "good country air"; and intellectually, because their minds and interests - and talents - would be broadened by the many opportunities offered them. They might enjoy the organised exercise classes; the stimulating walk across the edge of the Heath to the Hampstead tube; playing cricket, tennis or football on the wide expanse of the Heath Extension; or learning to practice the wide range of arts and crafts available at the Institute.

Although there was no comparison between the small workers' cottages and the grand houses, Dame Henrietta and her husband, Canon Barnett firmly believed that mixing the classes would tend to produce a more healthy and harmonious society.

Financially, the Hampstead Garden Suburb was comparatively well set-up. It had raised half the capital from the Public Works Loan Board. For the remainder, the Garden Suburb Trust and the Garden City Company looked to a new type of fund-raising agency - the co-partnership society, which sought to raise much of the capital from the tenants themselves. This approach had first been used by the Ealing project in 1901. Letchworth had followed suit.

None of these projects could really be considered mainstream. To begin with the "ordinary" worker was not the kind of worker to whom these slightly esoteric projects would appeal. Certainly the ordinary working man would not welcome the fact that there were no public houses on the suburb; any more than there were on Henry Ashworth's Egerton estate. Then the organisers themselves were not really looking for the "ordinary" worker. They wanted the studious young fellow with a Latin primer or a slender volume of verse in his pocket; the lonely walker, head in the clouds, determined to recreate something of the idealised English village. They wanted the sort of family that liked to bake its own bread, read aloud to the children around the grate, and - above all - were set on self-improvement; as the row of cheap reprints on their tiny bookshelf showed.

This was the Old World - the world before the First World War; when the bearded Edward V11 was the new king, and Elgar was composing the Cockaigne Overture. When Walter Sickert and Gauguin, Picasso and Degas were all the rage. When Orville and Wilbur Wright made the first flight in a heavier-than-air machine, when Liverpool and Manchester Universities were founded. When Mr C.S. Rolls was still only interested in the fine cars Mr H. Royce was building, and when Albert

Einstein was explaining Brownian molecular movement and beginning his work on relativity.

The first Motor Exhibition had opened at Islington, and Herbert Austin began manufacturing his cars, The Russians surrendered at Port Arthur, and the education authorities were to provide a meal for poor children. Hampstead Garden Suburb had just been founded.

The remarkable thing about the Garden City movement was the hold it would have on the imagination of planners and politicians alike. The town and cities were growing still, overcrowded once more. But there, in the outer suburbs - in the countryside - it was still possible to build in such a way that each cottager had his small garden, his ample back yard. Even the speculative builders tried to follow their example. A commendable effort - even if the longing for green fields did degenerate into ribbon development and three-bedroom mock-Tudor.

THE STATE MOVES IN

THE HOUSING (No2) Act was placed on the Statute Book on August 10th 1914 - less than a week after the declaration of war. It allowed the spending of £4 million on housing for the relief of unemployment over one year. The Act came to nothing in the end. But by mid-1915 the Government became involved when housing was needed for war workers. Lloyd George believed that the ultimate decision - victory or defeat - depended on the supply of munitions. This led to an expansion of the Woolwich labour force from just under 11,000 on the outbreak of hostilities to almost 74,500 by 1917. Much of the housing provided for Royal Arsenal and other workers was of Garden City standards. But time and the demands of war led to a fall in standards.

By the end of the war, some five million or so war workers, plus five million men from the armed forces would have to be returned to their normal civilian occupations. This posed a serious problem for the Government; not least because of the general mood of unrest. On the day after the Armistice, and in anticipation of this, Lloyd George promised a General Election and gave his word to create "habitations fit for the heroes who have won this war." Lloyd George was not alone in fearing that the United Kingdom could follow Russia and Germany and end up facing out-and-out revolution. The Home Office went so far as to express the fear that were serious disorder to occur, the rioters would be better trained than the soldiers.

TOWARDS HOME OWNERSHIP

THE FOUR years of the Great War saw the state driven to taking on responsibilities that no Government would ever have contemplated under normal conditions. The really important changes began to take place in 1915, when the allegedly scandalous shortage of shells on the western front saw H.H. Asquith swept from office by the coalition in which Lloyd George became Minister of Munitions. Here was the key man in a key post; and while the needs of the fighting forces were given the very highest priority, Lloyd George had also been the architect of important social reforms following the Liberal victory of 1906. By 1908 a pension of 5 shillings a week was provided for those past work and without means. Even then, it was insufficient to keep the unfortunate recipient from starving. Booth's and Rowntree's researches were to disclose that nearly one third of the population could not afford enough to eat. But it was an important, first step.

Labour exchanges were set up that year; followed by a National Insurance Act in 1911, calling for contributions from employers and workers. There was also an experimental unemployment insurance for a few trades. But it was not until 1920 that the majority of workers were allowed to subscribe. Even then, domestic and agricultural workers, civil servants and those employed by the still privately owned railways were excluded. They were judged to have sufficient security of tenure.

The building boom of the early 1900s had already begun to reduce overcrowding. But Chiozza Money, in his book *Riches and Poverty* pointed out that almost half of the national income ended up in the pockets of one ninth of the population. The Labour Representation Committee - from which the Labour Party would spring - had been established in 1900, the year before the old Queen died. From the Labour Party in due course would come a whole flood of Labour property legislation. In the meantime it was fighting for recognition.

The Fabians - political gradualists of the Left - with their icon, George Bernard Shaw worked away mocking, persuading and building up a following. For the moment, however, practical steps towards reform were taken mainly by the Liberals within the coalition. It meant that quite a few of the Ministers and their friends saw that the heavy, new responsibilities they bore for the conduct of the war gave them, as Christopher Addison, Under Secretary for labour affairs, saw it: "....a new kind of opportunity...Lloyd George and I agreed....(that) use ought to be made of the exceptional situation to secure a better and more humane standard of working conditions."

When it came to improving the war workers' housing conditions, it was only the powerful pressure exerted by the War Office which forced the Treasury to agree to a permanent housing scheme for the Woolwich munition workers. Later the

Treasury insisted that housing schemes should be supported only if they could be shown to be strictly necessary for the war effort. Moreover, the building of houses on generous Garden City lines could not continue.

Once under way with the various schemes which managed to wriggle through the Treasury's net, it became clear that building was only part of the problem. Roads, drains and mains services would obviously be required: and they were costly. Temporary buildings - which had been the first solution - were not necessarily an economic proposition; especially as the price of timber was rising fast. So far more of the wartime building ended up as part of the permanent housing stock than had at first been intended.

The Rent Strikes of 1915 and the gradual introduction of rent control changed the traditional relationship between the ordinary landlord and his or her working class, or lower middle class, tenants. Finally, there was the move by the local authorities into the provision of low-rent and subsidised housing. In the early years, a somewhat modified version of the Garden City model held sway. The plainer, less attractive dwellings were to come later; as were the blocks of flats. Massive tower blocks did not as a rule appear until after the Second World War.

Two local authorities were given the pioneering role in this new and significant task for local authorities: London and York. London served as a model for the large cities. But the municipal housing carried out in York was a more realistic model for the smaller towns. Apart from that the scale of the two operations was quite different. The first estate in York was located on the edge of the built-up area. It was no more than a mile from the centre. In London, by contrast, to find a suitable site, the LCC surveyor was forced to travel no less than 10 miles from County Hall. York enjoyed one further advantage. The investigations carried out by Seebohm Rowntree, and the example of the New Earswick Estate, which the Rowntrees had founded, meant that help and practical advice were both available and reliable.

GUNS INTO PLOUGHSHARES - WITH DIFFICULTY

THE SHORTAGE of skilled labour to carry out the Government's "homes for heroes" programme, and other essential work after the Armistice, had been solved initially by releasing "key" men from the services. Back at their bench, it was believed, these highly skilled craftsmen would help to get the peacetime factories and workshops going again, and create jobs for the less skilled. Without the creation of tens of thousands of new jobs, it would be impossible to avoid serious mass unemployment, once the expected post-war boom had burned itself out.

Unfortunately the "key" workers had not been called up with their contemporaries while the war was on. Instead, they had been left at their work bench as long as possible to maintain a skilled edge to the frequently diluted workforce. They had tended, therefore, to be among the last to be called to arms. Even then, many of them had never so much as heard a shot fired in anger - let alone fired one themselves. Not surprisingly their early release led to considerable resentment among the battle hardened troops many of whom were barely out of their teens. Understandably, they felt they had already "carried the tradesmen on their back" for long enough.

There were mutinies at Dover and Folkestone transit camps. On one occasion a mob had stormed Epsom police station. Winston Churchill, who became War Minister in January 1919 - a few weeks after the Armistice - hastened to introduce what seemed, when viewed objectively, a much fairer demobilisation scheme. Men were to be released from the Services according to their age and length of service. Those who had sustained war wounds on three or more occasions were to be released forthwith. Admirable as the plan was, it came too late to prevent a mutiny at Calais.

Trouble was to extend to the capital, and to the area behind Whitehall. On 8th February, Churchill was summoned to the War Office, to be told that three thousand men from the trenches, who were due to return to France after home leave, had assembled in the park, refusing to go back. They were determined to stand firm, regardless of the consequences. From his window at the War Office, Churchill watched the huge iron gates being closed by the Life Guards. The authorities were in no mood to tolerate any further indiscipline. Although Churchill had no direct view of what was going on, he learned that the Grenadiers had advanced slowly from one side - bayonets fixed - while the Household Cavalry advanced from the other.

Mercifully, the mere show of force did the trick. There was no need for bloodshed. Having come to their senses, the 3,000-strong leave party allowed themselves to be shepherded back across the park to Wellington Barracks. Then, after a good breakfast, they were escorted to the railway station, where they entrained without any further trouble for France. But it had been touch and go!

It is little wonder that, according to a memorandum by Christopher Addison, Lloyd George advised the Cabinet on 3rd March that: "In a short time we might have three-quarters of Europe converted to Bolshevism...So long as we could persuade the people that we were prepared to help them...he believed that the sane and steady leaders among the workers would have an easy victory over the Bolsheviks among them."

Following the example of the Russian Revolution, in November 1917, the German Communists attempted to seize control when the Kaiser fled the country and law and order broke down. In London this reawakened fears of a series of bitter strikes of the kind experienced immediately before the outbreak of war in 1914.

Only now it seemed possible that demobilised servicemen, war workers and the trades unions might band together and take to the streets. They might, it was feared, attempt to force the Government to carry out the reforms which many felt were merely being promised.

With hindsight - the only reliable kind of foresight - it seems that Lloyd George and the coalition had correctly judged the mood of the masses. They needed only to show the people that something was actually happening for them to send the hotheads and agitators packing.

The threat of anarchy, and the fear of revolution, may sound exaggerated today. But they were not all that different from the threats and fears which led to the introduction of the most draconian measures in the wake of the Napoleonic Wars. Then too the return of thousands of ex-soldiers, without money, jobs or somewhere to live had jolted the Government of the day into overdue reforms of the most basic kind. There was no future in attempting to meet force with force. Apart from anything else, the people were on the brink of some far-reaching social changes. Charles Furth refers to one of them in his book, *Life since 1900.*

"Between 1913 and 1937 the employed worker increased his outlay on clothes by about a half, but he spent two and a quarter times as much on his home. By 1939, most were in dwellings built after 1920, while working class families generally occupied 19th century buildings. By 1939...gross overcrowding was past, except in the East End of London, on Tyneside and in Scotland."

The uneven progress made by Government and local authorities alike in the development of public housing is a fascinating story. But not for telling now. Suffice it to say at this point that the Government's scheme for those "homes for heroes" was eventually launched. But it soon came unstuck with the collapse of the economy in 1920. A number of local authorities had been told to go ahead; some did - albeit slowly. Perhaps the most important decision was to rent out the state aided new properties at controlled rents, set at the 1914 level.

The Government was planning to give the local authorities a subsidy to cover any costs over and above a one-penny rate. Unhappily the 1920-22 recession, which ended the post-war boom, upset the housing market to such an extent that Addison was forced to pay far more to get a house built than would have been the case a couple of years earlier.

In March 1921, Addison left the Ministry of Health and became minister without portfolio. Shortly afterwards he left office for good.

However, in the steady move towards owner-occupation, it was the speculative builders who carried the torch through the brief 20-year period between the two wars.

BREAKING THE MOULD

VIEWING the property market at the beginning of the 1920s, it might not have appeared all that different from the traditional pattern. Taking London, we find the grand houses of Mayfair and Belgravia still accommodating the nobility, and those wealthy enough - whatever their origins - to join the upper echelons of a pleasure-seeking, post-war "society". The substantial four and five storey "villas" of Hampstead, Chelsea, Richmond, Kensington and the like were still in the hands of single families from the upper, middle and professional classes. Although the original leases, granted by the leading landowners and institutions like the churches, universities and Eton College, were beginning to run down.

Inside central London, and on the inner suburban fringe, were the familiar red-brick "mansion blocks", built in the 1880s, with their ornamental turrets and well-kept communal gardens. But even they were beginning to approach their fortieth birthday. However, one thing is certain: the vast majority of City men and judges, senior civil servants, MPs and peers, and the members of the learned, and well-paid, professions, were still more likely to be renting than buying their home.

The 1911 census showed that the population of Great Britain and all Ireland totalled just under 49 million. By 1981 the population of Great Britain and Northern Ireland had reached 56 million. 10.8 million householders were owner-occupiers. That is to say 56% of households. In 1914, one in 10 had been owner-occupied.

On the outskirts of our cities were small terraces of houses which some thrifty tradesman, builder or local bank official had purchased for the purpose of letting. That to the ordinary man was what "putting your money into bricks and mortar" really meant. One's savings seeking a sound investment should go into property rather than company shares or government stock. Few, it is safe to say, would have thought that saving meant sinking their entire capital - and then raising a massive loan on mortgage - to acquire "bricks and mortar" for their own use.

From the working man's point of view, his uncertain income was a barrier to house purchase. When he's working, he might be well paid. But when he wasn't working, he would earn nothing. The clerk or storeman, who might well earn less than the craftsman, had a regular wage coming in. Being able to pay the rent every week was what counted. The office worker might well be in a position to pay a reasonable rent; but he would probably never save enough to go on for "property".

NO LAND FOR HEROES

THE WORLD re-created in the 1920s was in a sense no land for heroes. It became the land of the superior artisan and the better-off fee or income earning members of the middle classes. Top society had its problems. Great and ancient families were frequently forced to sell the family seat. The cost of maintaining the property was beyond their means. But for their accountants and agents, bank clerks and master plumbers, the 1920s and '30s were ideal decades: for anyone, in fact, who had one foot firmly planted on the socio-financial ladder.

Apart from that, the citizen of the 1920s was not greatly bothered about being a hero. Young men - like their older male relations - had had their fill of "heroism" in the trenches. They had had more than enough of being used as cannon fodder and given orders as though they were some kind of slow witted sub-human. They had had quite enough of bosses and landlords.

It was not merely a case of "Jack's as good as his Master." To the ex-service man who had survived, Jack had no master. In the rural areas, the squire was no longer the arbiter of the humble cottager's fate. The upper classes, as everyone know, were "on their last legs". The great thing now was for the ordinary man - the ordinary family - to make up for the years, and lives, they had been forced to leave behind in no-man's-land. A feeling of independence could be yours, provided you could tear round the shires in your bright red sports car; or dance the hours away in the night-club of the moment.

The post-war equivalent of "the man on the Clapham omnibus", might still find freedom; if he could get one of those little houses strung out like beans along the newly built arterial roads.

It would be a typical three-up, two-down "semi", with its tidy little garden; and the pretentious shingle hanging in the porch, proclaiming that this was no numbered box. It was, in fact, "The Warren"..."Ventnor Villa"...or (if the couple happened to be named Sally and Raymond)...."Raysal House."

H.G.Wells had delighted in poking fun at the suburbs - and their inhabitants - in his novel, *Kipps (1905).* In *The New Machiavelli* (1911), he wrote of the fate which had befallen Bromley, where he had been born in 1866. Ruskin was even more scathing about the "pestilence" of houses and the "unseemly plague of builders' work" which had fallen on "the suburbs of loathsome London." The "man in the Clapham omnibus" was now "the man with the season ticket", travelling up and down each working day, with his neatly furled umbrella and his attaché case - containing an apple and a Bovril sandwich. There wasn't enough left over, when you'd paid all the outgoings: certainly not enough for a pub lunch every day of the week!

◆◆◆

CHAPTER SIX

THE PRICE OF ARCADIA

"I now have 275 marbles. Counted my stamps ... 305."

J. Paul Getty, aged 11

Two major town planning pioneers of the early 1900s had been Sir Raymond Unwin and Sir Ebenezer Howard. Thanks to their influence, the greater expenditure on the home and home surroundings coincided with an improved level of planning on the better speculative builders' estates. Arthur Marwick sounded a more gentle note than the literary lions. In his book, *The Explosion of British Society*, he wrote:

"Such houses as were built (in the 1930s) were reasonably well designed and situated in fairly well planned estates, laid out, however, according to a rigid class segregation. Ribbon development along the main highways was open to criticism on even broader grounds, and the many mannerisms of the domestic builder were to find an effective satirist in Osbert Lancaster: this was the age of Stockbrokers' Tudor and 'By-pass Variegated'."

The more expensive homes sold freehold in the new suburbs cost on average between £600 and £2,000. A worker who earned £5 a week had an above-average income. £3 was closer to what most employees were getting. Lodgings with full board would cost around £1.10s. or £2 a week at the outside. True, it was necessary in most cases to put down no more than £125. Nevertheless buying a £600 house could put a considerable strain on the average family budget. At that time it was not common for wives to have a full time job, with an appropriate salary. So the man-of-the-house was regarded as the breadwinner. His salary was what counted.

There were always extras; and with a small salary, the extras counted. There would be the man's fares - or season ticket; repairs and decorations to the house;

and "road charges" - payable when the local council got around to "adopting" the street.

It was not surprising, therefore, how long it took for home ownership to spread: from the 10% level in 1914 to no more than 20% in 1931. That was when the National Government took the UK "off the gold standard" after the European banking collapse. One third of houses built in 1931 cost less than £600. By 1939, that was true of 50% of new houses. Second-hand properties sold for between £400 and £500.

By now low interest rates and official encouragement brought the building societies into their own. During the late 1930s, the building rate had risen to between 300,000 and 350,000 houses a year. That was double the rate in the 1920s. As a consequence, woods and farmland on the edge of the already built-up areas of our cities were greedily gobbled up. Large old mansions with ample grounds and outhouses were demolished. The grounds were sold off as building plots. H. G. Wells was not alone in deploring the way the countryside was vanishing under a skin of asphalt and concrete. But the movement was too strong to be resisted. The middle class home owner was not going to be denied his chance to ape the wealthy and acquire his "place" in the conveniently adjacent countryside.

Property has always been one of the most potent status symbols; ever ready to be attached to the man or woman with the necessary bank balance. It was so in the Middle Ages, after the Black Death. It is today.

As the years passed, the lower end of the housing market became even easier than before. In return for a guarantee from the builder, building societies were prepared to raise their mortgage limit from 75% to 95% of the purchase price. So a £25 deposit would "secure" a £500 home. That meant that a clerk or a better paid blue-collar worker could hope to buy a place of their own on a wage of £4 a week. At one stage a particular model was reduced from £500 to £480. That meant it could be bought for £40 down and 13s.6d. a week over 20 years.

This did not alter the fact that in the mid 1930s some two thirds of all families still lived in rented property.

The wish - or longing - for a place of one's own grew stronger year by year. As yet a flat dweller was in a less favourable position. Except in Scotland, it was almost impossible to raise the necessary funds to buy a long lease. That would have to wait for the end of another world war.

But wait! I can hear some of you wondering whatever happened to the Depression. Or didn't the UK have a Depression?

There was, as we have seen, a fall in UK house prices during the 1930s. But there was no panic. Some people lost their homes through being unable to keep up with their mortgage payments. But there was no general collapse. Property prices had reached heights they could not possibly sustain. The fall that took place was that of a normal cyclical decline.

Right, then! Next question. If the UK housing market could survive the Depression of the 1930s, why couldn't it have survived unharmed the seismic shock of the 1980s: How ... and why ... did things reach the level of a full scale Housequake?

TWO DIFFERENT WORLDS

THE SHORT answer is that in comparing what happened in the 1930s and what happened in the 1980s is to attempt to compare, in a meaningful manner, two completely different worlds. The most important difference is that in the 1920s and 1930s the speculative builders were at risk. In the 1970s and 1980s, it was the ordinary home buyer who risked every penny — as well as his property. Today many thousands of ordinary citizens are in jeopardy, because the debt, which went with the house, was more than they could carry.

It would be impossible to stress too often that the inter-war years were but a brief pause in what has been called "the ten-year German war". Nor should we overlook the fact that the major changes in the boundaries and, indeed, the whole concept of social class did not take place until after the Second World War. In the inter-war years, class was a significant and stabilising factor in the housing market. Class divisions — and hostilities — were much as they had been in late Victorian and Edwardian times. It was after the emergence of the apparently classless society — which began to develop during the Second World War — that the majority of the population of the UK saw the fulfilment of the wartime promise of a New World. It means the old shibboleths were abolished. A man or a woman could achieve whatever they wanted to achieve: provided only that they could hack it.

In the 1920s and 1930s, however, the old ways and inhibitions still remained. Many believed that every man and woman had their place. The trouble was that too many had elected to overlook the fact. A generation later, in the second post-war era, the idea that a man or woman had their "place" was too ridiculous for most people to contemplate.

So far as the property market went in the 1920s and 1930s, there were four recognisable classes over and above the broad mass of the working class and the deprived, when viewed from a housing point of view.

These classes were by no means static. But there was just too little time for any fundamental change. There was, after all, no more than two decades between the Armistice in November 1918 and the fitting of the civilian population with their gas masks at the time of the Munich crisis of 1938. During that brief period, two years were taken up with the post-war boom and two more by the crash that followed. Another 18 months or so were overshadowed by the events leading up to the General Strike of 1926; and it took a long while for the effects of what came very close to open revolution to be shaken off.

In 1931, the UK was forced to come off the Gold Standard after the financial crash in Europe. The Depression, which followed, adversely affected the Welsh mining areas, the industrial North and much of Scotland; and was generally characterised by mass unemployment. There was one area which was mainly untouched: the south-east. Here were the new industries, in their new, clean factories. Powered by electricity, they brought a wave of prosperity to those lucky enough to be employed. They included many enterprising, skilled workers who had come down to the metropolis from the depressed areas.

House building in the prosperous areas continued apace. Despite the Depression, more and more land was swallowed up. More public transport was made available. New rail and tube lines were opened up, providing swift, comparatively cheap access to vast areas in the home counties. The Piccadilly Line and the Northern Line both played their part. The Metropolitan Railway's "Metro-land", reaching out from Baker Street towards Aylesbury and Amersham and the fringe of Buckinghamshire, was probably the best known example. This was due in no small measure to the sheer professionalism of the management. The "jerrybuilders", who had plagued the Victorian property market with their poor workmanship and shoddy materials, inevitably gained a foothold in the cheaper areas, but good, sound workmanship could be found provided one was prepared to pay a reasonable price. This was largely down to the strict standards demanded by the major building societies and certain local authorities.

By 1936, the international situation had worsened to the extent that the Government began building its shadow factories and preparing for a conflict which anyone willing to keep their eyes and ears open could not fail to see coming. The UK was slowly being put on a war-footing. Two years later, Mr Chamberlain returned from Munich, after his second meeting with Hitler, waving that famous scrap of paper. It was supposed to contain the promise of "peace in our time". That was the year that UK families tried on their gas-masks.

In short, those 20 inter-war years had been eaten up, leaving little time - or inclination - for radical social reform. There had been time to do no more than stagger, badly shaken, from the wreckage of the Old Europe of kings and emperors, and prepare reluctantly for the launching of the even greater disaster of the second world war.

There had neither been the time - nor the inclination - to introduce a pattern of social and political reforms which might have allowed the United Kingdom at least to recover its pre-war standing; avoiding (or at least postponing) what seemed like the inevitable conflict.

Comparatively modest middle-class families still managed to employ one live-in servant; and the advent of the "labour-saving age" was greatly welcomed. Dirt and heavy humping of coal and coke to the upper floors were replaced by electricity for lighting and heating, with easy-to-clean "boilers" in better planned kitchens to provide hot water wherever it was required. The refrigerator replaced the ice box and the brick-lined larder; and the gas-lit "copper", the outhouse with its coal-burning copper in which clothes were boiled on "wash-day". The replacement of the kitchen range by a gas or electric stove - with oven, hot plates and grill - added to the facilities which claimed to make house-work a "joy" for the wife and mother. Meanwhile the Super-Cinema, with its news reels and documentaries - to say nothing of the "wireless" - had opened up a whole new world to the masses. From 1936, those who were "really with it" were able to explore the new magic of television until Alexandra Palace was closed down on the outbreak of war.

The bright new homes, with their bright new "toys", for which the post-war generation would be struggling, were in many instances crude and undeveloped. But they already existed, and were in place, by the late 1930s. They also showed the way fashion and popular taste would be going once the "lights" came on again all over the United Kingdom in 1945. Much of the world would have to wait for at least another generation before it caught up with the living standards of the UK suburbs.

The outstanding development in the property market was the success of the speculative builder, who could offer the reasonably prosperous members of the working classes a home of their own on the "never-never". But the remaining classes of property were largely unchanged by the time Germany marched into Poland in 1939.

THE FOUR CLASSES OF PROPERTY

THE FIRST class of property still provided a home for the high society and the wealthy. They continued to cling to their vested interest, and a vanishing past. Immediately after the Great War, which robbed so many of the leading families of their heirs, the "old money" was fast draining away. Estate expenses were crippling, farm revenues fell and land and family possessions had to be sold merely to keep the estate and the family intact. The volume of "new money" was growing, but there was insufficient to maintain the lavish standards of that "long, blissful Edwardian summer" - as the saying went. Nor, to their chagrin, were the "new rich" immediately accepted by society.

Then there were the well-established upper-middle and professional classes, who sent their sons and daughters to the top schools. Their money and connections helped "the boys" to find a place at their father's university. (Or the university he would have gone to had it not been for that blasted war.) Many among the successful migrants from Scotland or the North would have scorned sending "the lad" to Manchester University or the like, although St. Andrews would have been acceptable. There were the group who would later be referred to, quite inaccurately, as "entrepreneurs". In truth, they resembled nothing more than a late model of the Victorian "little master", who began with a bag of tools and a couple of labourers and ended up with a large factory and a board of directors.

They occupied the prime areas - and prime properties - in every town and city. This, in London, tended to be Westminster or Kensington, Hampstead or Richmond, or the more accessible parts of the Home Counties. Many were the so-called "city and suburban squires", who regarded the weekend country cottage as their spiritual home, where they could act the squire.

In Victorian times, the "little master" who had just made the grade would often move from the dissenters' meeting house to the Methodist chapel. Then, if he managed to build the factory, complete with a couple of tall chimneys, he and his lady-wife would seriously consider deserting the Non-Conformists for the Established Church. A similar transition would often be made from a mere "home" to a "good address", ending up with "a rather fine place in the country".

Below the top boardroom level were the growing band of professional middle-management, executive grade civil servants and company promoters. They would claim they had sent their sons to a minor public school merely because Eton, Harrow and Winchester had become something of an anachronism. The wives tended to view their social climbing activities in a slightly shame-faced manner.

Whereas the wives of the top boardroom members might hanker after a knighthood for their husbands, the wives of the managerials would feel their husbands had done quite well if they "made" a CBE before retirement.

Fourthly came the Suburbanites: the better paid employees, accountants and oil company executives, the owners of small retail establishments, the buyers with one of the departmental stores, insurance company employees, statisticians, school teachers and retired folk - content with their lot and moderately contented with society and their place in it. They had bought their three or four-bedroomed home before the introduction of the Green Belt. It was too big for them now; so were the gardens. But you could always get a gardener in the 1930s.

There were in fact two kinds of Suburbanite: the first embracing the inner suburban ribbon-development dwellers. The superior kind were those who still claimed that their suburb was actually a village. "The Village", they called it. And why not? They still walked to Church; bought their stamps and postal orders at the store-cum-post office, and could boast of having a genuine village school. (Although, of course, it was suitable only for local children, or children from that row of council cottages beside the railway marshalling yard.

Looking back, it might seem that the people who "counted" were rather too class conscious. But in the 1920s and '30s class, in a sense, was a guarantee that everyone would know their "place". The newcomers who bought the Old Manor House and tried to force their company on the "county" were as much to be deplored as the proverbial council tenant who kept coal in the bath.

In point of fact, many of the far-out suburbs were still virtually a village. They would not be in-filled out of existence until after the Second World War. Not, that is, unless the War Department set up a firing range or concealed a military workshop in the Big Wood. Writers and intellectuals might mock; they might - with some justification - complain that Old England was being ruined. But until the late 1930s, you could walk out through the small gate at the end of the kitchen garden, and inside a couple of minutes you could be strolling through the woods to the edge of the Downs.

The sheer ignorance of one class about the ways of another would today seem unbelievable. Then it was the way things were. Leaving aside the Six Counties of Northern Ireland, Great Britain was far from being one nation. It would take that second world war to forge that alliance, although it would not last all that long once peace returned. Instead of the "old ways", promised the 1914/18 veterans, the 1940s would bring immense changes and - for just a few years - a new, unheard of prosperity.

THE CLASSLESS OF '45

AT THIS point, we must brace ourselves and recognise that the summer of 1945, when the nation went wild over the ending of hostilities, was half-a-century ago. Germany surrendered on May 8th; and - after the dropping of the Hiroshima and Nagasaki bombs on August 6th and 9th - Japan surrendered unconditionally. Now, said the ordinary man and woman, we can "get back to normal!"

It was pure illusion. There can never be any question of "going back". What may seem like "going back" is merely history catching up on us. History hates to be ignored. It has its own mean, nasty ways of reminding us of that.

However, the important thing was that 1945 marked more than the end of a cruel battle that had raged on and off for six years. For the people of Britain - who now felt they understood each other a little better - it was the dawn of a New Age. (Another time-hallowed and perilous conceit.) This, many people believed, would be an age in which prophecy and promises would be fulfilled. For the first time ever, service men and women, at home or on the far side of the world, had been recognised for what they truly were - the People. Once the guns in the West fell silent, every one of them was invited to cast his or her vote at the 1945 General Election.

The result was a shock to many. The People's choice was for the abrupt dismissal of the old war leader, Winston Churchill and his Caretaker Government; and their replacement by a Labour Government headed by Clement Attlee. True, he was a member of the pre-war Upper Middle Class. So were many members of his government, who would probably have stood as Liberals had that party not all but vanished.

It was also a Government which had a full quota of trade unionists and men of the Left. It had a full programme too for the nationalisation of "the commanding heights". Moreover, it had a majority in the Commons solid enough for the programme to be carried through.

The first on the list for nationalisation in 1946 were the Bank of England, the coal mines and civil aviation. The electricity industry, railways, canals and road transport were to follow a year later. The National Health Service was launched in 1948, followed by British Gas in 1949 and British Steel in 1950. In 1949, the House of Lords, which had done its best to thwart Labour's plans, had its powers reduced beyond the limits already set by the Parliament Act of 1911. Now the Labour Government looked ready to reduce the Lords to a mere cipher.

Some individuals murmured in dark corners about nationalising Land. Others hinted that a series of capital levies would reduce the bigger private fortunes sufficiently to control - if not emasculate - the property owning class.

Unhappily for Labour, they went to the people in 1950 and emerged from the polls with a greatly reduced majority. In 1951, the Conservatives took over. They were to remain in power until the 1960s.

Besides the nationalisation of the Bank of England and the utilities, there had been the long-promised social reforms based on the Report on Social Security and National Insurance (1942). Most people called it *The Beveridge Report.*

This was welcomed by virtually everyone. It was widely believed that the Welfare State would end once and for all the neglect and isolation of the poor, the hungry and the sick. From now on, each citizen would be entitled to the full benefits of this new and wonderful scheme, which guaranteed them protection "from the cradle to the grave". It was seen as guaranteeing them a decent home, regardless of class or income.

Housing would obviously be as important to the returning service men and women as it had been after the 1918 Armistice. In 1945 their expectations were higher than they had ever been. This time, the authorities were better prepared.

While the war was being waged - not all that successfully - serving men and women were told the basis on which they would be released once the war ended. When the war ended, the authorities released comparatively few service men and women right away. When they were released, gradually over the next couple of years, they returned to "civvie street" with a certain amount of paid leave. Jobs were taken care of as much as possible by the introduction of a Control of Engagements Order, which served to send the newly available labour wherever it could be best employed. There were arrangements for younger people to complete, or supplement their education at technical colleges and universities. Those who had been in employment when they were called for service enjoyed their right of re-instatement, always assuming that the firm was still there.

The ultimate goal for the majority of the ex-service working class was to become council tenants. It might be a purpose-built house or flat, or a requisitioned building. Fortunately local authorities had been running their municipal flats and housing estates for some years. They had gained considerable experience. But it all took time. Many applicants got no further than the housing list. Some younger people were able to return to the family home. Despite the many difficulties - not least lack of privacy - young-marrieds too were taken in by their family or their in-laws - just to tide them over.

After living out of a kitbag or sleeping in a hammock for several years, ex-service folk were less choosy than they would have been today. They hoped for a self-contained flat, but were prepared to make do with a privately owned flatlet. The main thing was to get a place of their own, where they would be independent of family and friends, even if it meant a rented room, sharing kitchen and bath.

It was by no means an easy passage for many. There was a nasty practice whereby the landlord charged for so-called "furniture and fittings", though they might be so old and dilapidated that no-one in their right mind would have given tuppence for the lot. In other cases the furniture and fittings existed solely in the imagination of the owner or his agent. Many landlords would simply demand "key" money - in greasy notes. No-one was very sure what to do about it, except pay up and have somewhere to live. For ten years or so it was still possible to find privately rented accommodation. Many landlords were ex-service men and women themselves, and tried to be fair. But costs were rising. Frequently the rent would in no way cover the cost, let alone give the landlord a penny piece. This had a knock-on effect. Some rents had been controlled ever since the First World War, and the small increases awarded by the rent tribunals, and the security of tenure which the tenants enjoyed, gave many private landlords the feeling that the authorities would always come down against them. By the 1960s, they were selling off their flats and houses the moment they fell vacant.

Such was the premium placed on vacant possession that the worst landlords terrorised their tenants, and left them without the essential services. Theoretically, they were protected by the Law. But comparatively few cared to face the wrath of an angry landlord or his strong-arm bullies with their dogs.

Understandably, the council dwelling appeared to offer the only hope for countless young people. Indeed, by now it was accepted as part of current folklore that when the children of council tenants became engaged or married, the young people would go straight to the town hall to get their name put down on the waiting list. This soon became regarded as one of the citizen's "inalienable rights".

With a declining stock of private lettings, the battle against overcrowding and homelessness was more and more left to the local authority. "Factory" systems of building - faster and cheaper - were employed. In the mid-1960s the tower block appeared to offer a solution. At first the tower blocks were extremely popular. Indeed, there was a race to get hold of one. They were constantly visited by delegations from other areas; just as the early LCC "estates" had attracted admiration and attention in the 1920s and '30s. In some areas, housing officers and local authority architects claimed that they were being "encouraged" to choose one of the "factory built" designs in preference to anything else. Some housing officers went so far as to allege that it was easier to get the necessary loan sanction if they fell into line.

Later, some of the tower blocks began to develop serious faults. One or two threatened to collapse. One block the writer knew quite well had steel joists inserted at strategic points to ensure its stability. The tenants disliked it. It made the inside of their flats unsightly. It was also a slow and costly process. Before long, some boroughs found it cheaper to demolish even comparatively new blocks and rebuild, rather than try to cure the faults.

By the end of the decade, and in the early 1970s, their unsuitability for young families was accepted without argument. Furthermore unruly elements, hooligans, yobs and delinquents of various kinds made established tenants on large flat complexes and estates feel insecure. The lifts - which tended to keep breaking down - frequently served as urinals. Or worse. That, obviously, happened only on the "bad" estates. On others, the tenants enjoyed a comparatively modest rent - although rents were rising, and special groups began to be catered for. The most important of these were the elderly and disabled for whom special "sheltered" accommodation was built. Another priority group in some boroughs was the single homeless.

In the 1960s some forward-looking councils had decided to try selling off their older flats and groups of houses on isolated estates. Applications came flooding in. But the number of sales concluded was comparatively small.

Nevertheless, the practice had been established, ready for the appearance of the Thatcher administration in 1979. Now the emphasis shifted once again to the private property sector. But before that was to come the commercial property crisis.

THE SURREALIST SEVENTIES

THERE was something surreal about the commercial property market in the late 1960s and early 1970s.

In the 1940s and 1950s, property developers had been quick to exploit the country's post-war/post-bombing housing needs. They took a calculated risk, and it paid off. Money was available at 5-6% in those days, and the return from a new development ranged between 8% and 20%. Soaring property values put icing on the cake. Yet, you may be surprised to learn, there was no rush from outsiders to climb aboard the development band-wagon.

But, as events showed, the ranks of the developers of the 1960s and 1970s were joined by newcomers from among the banks and financial institutions. The 1950s had seen the developers make quite sizeable fortunes, while the financial interests confined their activity to standing by on the sidelines, collecting the interest on their loans. That was their traditional role, rather than taking risks in order to chase after the big rewards. So far, the return the lenders received was adequate. Why not? They fixed the terms after all.

Gradually they began to ask themselves why they should lend to developers to enable them to accumulate a sizeable fortune. Why not us too? - anonymous voices began asking. Why not join the developers, and dip the odd institutional crust into that rich gravy?

From 1959 onwards, as John Plender explains in his book, *That's the Way Money Goes*, financial institutions, which had been mere spectators up until now, began to ignore the conventional boundaries and join the players.

The developers of the 1950s had known perfectly well that property values could fall as well as rise. They had fallen during the war, and a number of West End of London developers could remember losing serious money in the late 1930s. But, even though they began to take a keen interest in property, the institutions still did not really understand the game. Let alone the risks! Nevertheless, they started to insist on shares and options from the companies they were financing. By now, however, the current boom was near to its end. Moreover, most insurance companies paid over the odds for the equity they acquired in those entrepreneurial property companies. Towards the end of the 1960s, wrote Plender, it was banks rather than the institutions which were to power the second great post-war property boom. The lethal one!

Security, marketability and a potential for a rising income made property such an ideal asset. In the seventies it was virtually a substitute for index-linked Government Stock. By the end of the 1960s the newcomers began to pile in. The development game was a mechanism for making easy money. The market was now attracting the easy-money crowd, who are never far from the honey pot. Such characters may be wary about a calculated risk. But they are ever eager to go for a "good thing", especially if it looks like a "sure thing".

Unfortunately, says Plender, the danger was that:

" ... blind faith in the wisdom of the valuer will leave the British banking system vulnerable to collapse if property investment bubbles over into speculation. This is precisely what happened in the early 1970s."

The fundamental flaw was that surveyors put a value on a building by reference to comparable recent transactions in the open market, and by taking account of the position, scope for rental, terms of the lease and the state of the structure. Where there had been relatively few "comparable recent transactions", the chartered surveyor would still have to come up with some sort of answer for the client. So he did all he could do: hazard a guess.

But there was a more fundamental reason why entry of the easy-money crowd put the commercial property sector on the road to disaster. Once the entrepreneur turns speculator - be it in property, gold or whatever commodity you care to name - it changes the character of that corner of the market. It means that the first step has been taken along that relatively short path which leads from market to casino.

Here again the well documented experience of the American Railway Boom of the 1840s should have signalled danger to the main players. The 1830s had seen the start of a speculative rise in railway stocks. By 1842 the boom was halted by a sharp decline in prices. The *New York Herald Tribune* predicted that the approaching crisis would put paid to the current "fitful spasmodic system of american business". Did it?

Not on your life! It took another 19 years for the crash to come in 1873, when financial commentators pointed to the risk overhanging the market as a result of the perilous debt structure in the US banking system.

The New York Warehouse Company failed. Five days later Kenyon Cox and Company failed too. Rumours that other large companies were on the brink spread fast. On September 17th 1873 the US Stockmarket collapsed. Panic broke out on the New York Stock Exchange. By the end of the year more than 5,000 businesses had failed. Their liabilities totalled a staggering $228,500,000.

Yet, come to think of it, there was nothing fundamentally wrong with the railways themselves. The Iron Horse did more to open up the country than all of Custer's cavalry. Indeed, it's a fact of everyday life that natural disasters have led to fewer market crashes than the over-enthusiastic, moderate banker, fund-manager, or other "honest Joe" who thinks he holds an unbeatable hand.

A century later a runaway UK commercial property boom was to culminate in a threat to the entire commercial banking system, leading to the launch on 21st December 1973 of the Bank of England's so-called "Lifeboat". Today, alas, most "practical men and women" will tell you that what happened that long ago is "part of history". And history is something they wouldn't have the time for, even if they thought it relevant. But they don't. Which is why they are not asking - but positively begging the nasty side of history to repeat itself.

1973 - LAUNCHING THE LIFEBOAT

THE TROUBLE in the UK began over two years earlier, in September 1971, when the Heath Government published a White Paper, *Competition and Credit Control* (CCC). The plan was to abolish the existing ceilings on the size of loans to private borrowers, in force since the end of the world war. The idea was to stimulate competition between banks as they sought to finance Prime Minister Heath's "dash for growth". Theoretically there would be no free-for-all, since the price mechanism could be relied on to exercise a moderating influence. As the Governor Lord O'Brien put it in the *Bank of England Quarterly* in June 1971:

"What we have in mind is a system under which the allocation of credit is primarily determined by its cost."

Note, if you will, that the concept of "market forces" and "competition" acting as a safety-mechanism is similar to that on which Margaret Thatcher and Sir Keith Joseph were to base Conservative policy.

The CCC policy was implemented alongside a reduction in the liquidity ratio of the whole banking system from 28% to 12.5%. There were some spectacular results. Between December 1971 and December 1974, the total assets of British banks jumped from £36.9 billion to £85.2 billion. That was an increase of 131 per cent. Advances rose by a spectacular 160 per cent. As Douglas Jay wrote in his book on sterling:

"The banks' advances, their most profitable item, which had comprised 40 per cent of total assets in 1948-50, were nearly 80 per cent by the end of 1974... both advances and deposits had doubled in three years. More pounds sterling were created in these three years than in the whole twelve hundred years' history of the pound since King Offa."

It was not the Public Sector Borrowing Requirement that was the trouble, but the Private Sector Borrowing Requirement. The consequences of the credit boom of 1971-4 were damaging, writes Jay: "...because so much of the new bank credit was used ... to finance speculation in the true sense ... buying of assets - in this case property ... in the hope of capital profits through rising prices."

In the latter part of 1973, the inevitable occurred. People sensed that property prices could rise no further. Those who had bought for a rise sold. Those who sold at a loss could no longer repay what they had borrowed. Shades of negative equity! In July, the Bank of England's minimum lending rate was raised to the crisis level of 11.5 per cent, in an attempt to halt speculation. Property values came down. Borrowing became more difficult. The dash for growth was aborted, but the whole financial system had been shaken to such an extent that on 19th December 1973 the Governor of the Bank of England held a series of secret meetings which continued until 3am the following morning.

The fear was that if some of the weaker secondary banks collapsed, there could be a panic run on the High Street clearing banks themselves.

In a book entitled, *The City of Capital*, Jerry Coakley and Laurence Harris pointed to the contribution to the crisis of the so-called "secondary" or "wholesale" banks, which had more experience in hire-purchase, stockmarket dealing and straight money-lending than basic banking.

Some of the so-called "secondary" banks had been fully recognised for some time, and were referred to in official publications as "Other British Banks". They included associates and subsidiaries of both UK merchant banks and clearing banks. They were joined after the passage of the 1967 Companies Act by the so-called "Section 123 Companies". These houses relied for their newly-enhanced status on a judgement by Lord Denning in 1966, when he ruled that the court recognised the United Dominions Trust as a bank, not a money lender. When his judgement was incorporated in Section 123 it gave the green light to the secondary banks. By 1973, there were 133 such houses.

As a whole the secondary banks were financed by borrowing from the City. Some of the country's biggest banks and insurance companies owned almost 25% of the equity of a number of leading secondary banks. Once the property game got under way, they attracted some of the big names, like Slater Walker Securities, First National Finance Corporation, London and County Securities and the Crown Agents.

The secondary banks accepted deposits including the Euro-dollar deposits, which were rapidly expanding at that time. They used their funds to buy equity shares and real estate. In 1972 they went in particularly for the shares of property companies. At the same time real estate values rose steadily and steeply. Trouble came when property prices began falling in the summer and autumn of 1973. When the Bank Governor held the first of his secret meetings on December 19th, the problem was to prop up one of the less well known secondary banks, Cedar Holdings. It could not repay what it had borrowed because its depositors were withdrawing their funds as fast as they could. The thought that many other banks could find their depositors doing likewise concentrated minds wonderfully. A group of clearing banks and pension funds agreed to contribute £2 million to keep Cedar Holdings afloat. They also agreed to join in issuing what Jay calls "a tranquillising announcement" before the market opened later that morning.

Cedar Holdings had been saved for the moment, but secondary bank shares collapsed before the morning was out. Next day, Friday 21st, all the main City banks were called to a second crisis meeting. At risk now was a run on the High Street banks. But by that afternoon, the so-called "Lifeboat" had been launched, with facilities of some £1,000 million to be used to keep the weaker vessels afloat. The special bankers' committee set up to supervise the rescue operation was compelled to operate for several years.

It is spine chilling to consider what would have happened had there not been agreement that Friday, the last working day before the Christmas break.

In the event, some £1,300 million was loaned to keep threatened companies afloat. Loans were repaid by those which could do so by a gradual sale of assets over two or three years. By the end of 1976, there still remained unpaid debt of £783 million. The profits the major clearing banks had made during the boom period softened the blow somewhat when they contributed £50 million each. The Bank of England is reckoned to have put up something like £100 million. Since the Bank of England pays the Treasury any operating profits not put to reserves, the Treasury had to forego a certain amount of public revenue. That meant that a portion of the gamblers' debts were borne in the end by the taxpayer.

It should now be clear what went wrong. One thing was an over-anxiety to lend on property. Almost any property. It was said by cynics that you only had to appear before one of these street-market bankers, show them two pieces of wood and a bag of nails, and you were immediately accepted as a recognised "developer". Once you were in, you enjoyed unlimited access to easy credit terms against the security of some prestigious project which had not yet been built. In many cases, it had not even been conceived!

At the time, lending to property developers was thought to be as sound as lending to Third World countries. At that time, few could see the irony in that. Unfortunately the fringe banks went in with all the dash and bazzazz that the innocent - and the ignorant - display as they leap in out of their depth.

There was one further reason for their collapse; their willingness, at the outset, to receive a professional valuer's opinion as though it were Holy Writ. The money men tended not to grasp the insubstantial nature of a property valuation. As we have already seen, a "realistic" valuation depends on the sort of prices that similar properties have currently commanded. If no similar properties have exchanged hands, or it was a long time ago, then the valuer is driven to hazard a guess. Even so, if the figure quoted is not what the boardroom decision makers wanted to hear, it can soon be talked up - or down - until it fits in with their preconceived notion. Again, they may need to be in a position to quote the kind of figure that will persuade those not already committed to take the plunge. Thus the final discussion of a potentially money-making scheme may not be conducted in accordance with the traditions of the Banker's parlour, but horse-traded in the frenetic atmosphere of an ad-world brainstorming session.

Even more disarming - and more dangerous - is the strength of that gut feeling that has been with us at every stage of the game, namely that there must be a limit to the amount the market will be allowed to fall. Because, according to the consensus, far too many people would be ruined if it went on falling ... as it did in Florida. And that no United Kingdom government could possibly allow. The government - or someone - would have to launch another lifeboat.

The last time I was told that, I'd just closed my copy of the HMSO's *Housing and Construction Statistics 1982-92.* Over that 10 year period, repossessions had risen from just under 7,000 in 1982 to 75,540 in 1991. I dare say that when they fell to 68,540 the following year, some misguided soul began shouting: "Look. Possessions are going down. Recovery is on its way!"

I can just imagine the titter, harsh laugh that would have echoed across the almost deserted market place.

◆◆◆

CHAPTER SEVEN

RAW NERVES IN THE MARKET

"I felt like an undertaker in a plague."

Howard Ahmanson

IT IS difficult enough at any time to comment openly and realistically on the property market. To suggest that prices are going to run out of control evokes the kind of reaction that leaves you in no doubt. You have touched on a raw nerve. Do as I did, and suggest that property values will go into a sharp decline, and you are seen as wantonly and viciously drilling into that raw nerve.

At once the more exposed among the vested interests will accuse you of just about anything from sheer irresponsibility to something tantamount to sedition. At the very least they will write you off as a Jonah who delights in talking down the market on one pretext or another. You can almost sense the way the word goes out: "Rocking the boat is bad enough. But now that ******* is threatening to turn it over."

It is standard practice after that to accuse you of saying something you never said. That's smarter than attacking you for what you did say, since you might in that case put up a stout defence. Besides which, it is tantamount to an invitation to sit down and discuss the matter. The utterly false accusation lands you in the position of having to reply that you never said that! Very unconvincing at the best of times. However, this is the moment to put the matter straight.

I was accused of having said in the 1970s that the residential property market was going to collapse. It did. (Or weren't you around?) "But", they went on to say, "Beckman forgot to tell us we'd have to hang around for 20 years for it to happen."

Quite untrue. In the 1970s I did indeed warn of a collapse of the property market; but of the commercial property market. I made it quite clear that residential property would also fall, but not to the same extent. However, I must admit that I did not foresee the full depth of the secondary banking crisis. Or that it would almost bring down the whole of the UK banking system. Since then, incidentally, the commercial property market has never been able to return to the euphoric conditions enjoyed in the 1970s.

So - "Not Guilty" on the first count. It was, in fact, in the 1980s that I warned of the perilous instability of the residential property sector, adding that when the crash came the commercial sector would also be affected, albeit to a lesser degree. If only the specific weaknesses I pointed to had registered with a few of the leading operators, it might have saved some of the one and a half million householders who became trapped in houses they could not sell because their cash value was less than the burden of debt they were saddled with. The negative equity syndrome!

It is true that since the 1980s I have been the harbinger of bad tidings; and even less welcome predictions about home ownership. It is simply that I am (and hope I always shall be) unable to murmur a bland, "Caveat Emptor", and pass by on the other side. From the letters I still keep receiving, I find I have helped a considerable number of people to avoid the anguish and distress which the unthinking herd suffered. I only hope that the wise ones who listened have been able to perform a similar service for their friends.

The point to be made at this, and every stage of the game, is that once barter has been eliminated, it does not really matter whether you are buying or selling duplex apartments or nuclear submarines. Your needs and problems are very similar. You will still need to get your hands on big money in one form or another. If you can do that, no problem! You make your purchase and that is that. The problem starts when you don't have sufficient cash readily available; or just don't have enough cash! Either you must give up the idea or take some form of loan. Someone or other makes you a loan; or, more precisely, you persuade them to allow you to enter into their debt. From that moment on, you face a potential money problem. Let's say you take a 20-year mortgage.

If you're lucky as a mortgagor, you will be left alone to repay what you owe in the time originally agreed. If, however, the mortgagee - the bank or building society or whatever which makes the loan - suddenly needs the cash, the whole package may be sold to another party.

Again, you may be lucky. But if you are not, and the mortgagee demands early payment, you can be in deep trouble. From then on, you're flying by the seat of your pants. Maybe all the other houses in the neighbourhood did shoot up in price, and their owners did make a clear profit. That's not to say you will be so lucky.

Maybe no-one but your wife likes the location, or the outlook or the graveyard it overlooks! Maybe the house does have four bathrooms, a swimming pool and a triple garage. But maybe the rooms are dark and the place just doesn't appeal to the house-hunters blown by sheer chance in your direction. Maybe it is simply a question of price; or the fact that you must sell, regardless. So you are faced with a forced sale, which leaves you still deeply in debt.

There's always the possibility that the building society or bank you dealt with decides you're never going to be able to discharge your debt. So they decide to wash their hands of you, leaving it to a new mortgagee to seek re-possession. In this way, they not only avoid any hassle; they will also continue to maintain their bright and shining mortgagor-friendly image. That is something to which the sharks that infest the deep waters of the property world pay little regard.

You may well say you are not in the least surprised. In fact, you may know someone to whom the worst has happened. It could, of course, be hanging over your head at this very moment. So you are wise to what's been going on. But it will come as no surprise to find that in the 1960s and 1970s few such thoughts were entertained. They would have been dismissed as highly neurotic. There was nothing like the current level of awareness. Nor was there anything like the risk for the purchaser. So, when the cult of the owner-occupier began to spread, it was welcomed with open arms.

TOWARDS OWNER-OCCUPANCY

THE BASIC reason for the remarkable changes this would bring about was due - as so many social changes have been - to the demographic facts of life. Along with just about every major war there comes a baby-boom. By the 1960s the boom-babies of the Second World War were growing up. Whatever you may have thought - or think now - about the Swinging Sixties, it was not just sex that was having a field day. People - and especially young people - had money in their pockets. Not necessarily a lot of money, but enough to enable them to choose whether they would buckle down to work, or stick goose feathers in their hair and freak out. One of the first things the boom-baby wanted, as he or she grew tired of the family womb, was somewhere to live. A place of their own. This meant some sort of accommodation in a multi-occupation dwelling. It could be a bed-sitter or flatlet (shared bath and kitchen). It might be a share in an old fashioned, red-brick, turreted mansion flat. It could be in a newly built dwelling in the outer suburbs. After a comparatively short time, once the boom-babies had really made it, they would feel the urge to move. They would quit - let's say their Belsize Park pad - which they had always referred to as "Hampstead", or their crowded Fulham villa described as "just off the King's

Road". Or, if they were Australians, they might be seized with a desire to escape from Earls Court, by then best known as "Kangaroo Alley".

Whatever they were after, they would have to spend quite some time before they saw something which suited them, and which they could afford. What's more, it had to be vacant. One trouble was that too many people were seeking affordable, not too ghastly, rented accommodation. There was simply not enough. To make things more difficult, it became clear that landlords were selling off their rented accommodation, rather than buying or building more. The truth was that investment in property for letting was no longer the money-spinner it had been a decade earlier. Although it might not have seemed that way at the time, the owner-occupation bandwagon was beginning to roll. It was doing so well before the people began to discuss Thatcherism and the "property-owning democracy" in town halls, church halls and pubs.

I have been talking from the point of view of the metropolis; but a similar shift was taking place in most towns and cities. One is bound to ask, at what stage of the game does the public at large begin to scent the first hint of social or cultural change? Or, indeed, how many of them would recognise a fundamental change? Even if it walked up to them in the High Street and bit their ankle.

There was less get-up-and-go in the smaller towns and older industrial cities. Partly, for the obvious reason that a small town offers fewer opportunities for radical change, and partly because the more enterprising will in any case be off in search of opportunity among the Bright Lights.

Generally, the problem facing the would-be tenant as rented accommodation becomes scarce, is plain enough. But why, when the demand was there and growing, and rents were rising fast, should the multi-occupation landlords have sought to pull out of the game?

To come down to basics, most landlords prior to the mid-1960s tended to be investors who had chosen to buy property in order to secure a steady, safe return from renting out rooms or flats or whole houses. Many at the bottom of the pile were live-in landlords presiding over a "family" of tenants. They tended to be hardworking folk, content with a steady, safe income from the rents. In the early 1960s, for example, the going rate of return for multiple-dwelling units in a secondary market was 20%. Financing costs at the time were in the area of 4% - 6%. It was possible around that time for a high quality borrower to purchase a multi-dwelling unit at a financing cost as low as 4%. This yielded a positive return of 16% on the borrowed capital. The middle 1960s brought a change. Demand was rising, thanks partly to the boom-babies. Controlled rents soon hit their legal ceiling. Security of tenure enjoyed by controlled tenants further increased the immobility of a whole section of the rented property market. But there was no ceiling on costs.

Some smaller owners of rent-controlled properties could not afford to hold onto their properties. They began to offer to sell out to their tenants, merely to escape their liabilities.

In the case of uncontrolled dwellings, higher rents kept the landlords going. At the same time, as rents rose, the capital value of uncontrolled properties rose appropriately. At first this made comparatively little impact on the market. Traditionally, landlords were less concerned with capital values. What mattered was that they should receive a steady - and hopefully rising - income. True, it was comforting sitting on a small gold-mine. It made them feel "rich". That was not the way owners of controlled properties felt.

Given a sufficiently high rate of inflation which would not suddenly come down, there was no reason in the world why "good times" should not continue. Inflation could at least be relied upon to offset transaction costs associated with house purchase. That meant that smaller investment property "farmers" could afford to add to their "estate". Overall, it meant that one might expect to see more buoyancy and liquidity in the market through "trading up".

The thought that many rents would continue to be controlled, whether Labour or the Conservatives were in office, was not a pleasing one, although the more ruthless landlord could usually manage to make a bit on the side, even if it was only when there was a change of tenant. Then a charge could be made for "furniture and fittings". Some landlords would blatantly demand "key money". Tenants desperately searching for something they could afford were forced to pay up or give up.

In the 1960s it became clear that the capital value of multi-occupation units was rising faster than rental incomes. The more far-sighted saw that it might be well to sell off such properties, provided they could be sold with vacant possession. An alternative approach was to purchase - or clear - another property and "ask" your own tenants to accept "comparable accommodation". This rarely seems to have worked without a tussle. One of the snags was that tenants in uncontrolled properties tended to have comparatively watertight leases; moreover, tenants of the higher rental blocks tended to be of a class who would be prepared to fight the landlord. While they might not win their case, it could mean delay and unpleasant publicity. Far better, many owners felt, to put the pressure on the controlled tenants.

True, they enjoyed security of tenure; but a determined landlord would not find it too difficult to bluff or frighten the tenants into accepting a small sum as compensation for moving out. It was in this area that "Rachmanism" flourished.

Once vacant possession had been obtained, it would be easy enough for the owner to bring in a builder to convert the property from a rooming house to a dwelling of three or four flats. These could then be sold on a long (99 year) lease to lease-controlled "owner occupiers". Meanwhile, the shortage of rented accommodation continued to rise. From now on quite a few of the bigger private landlords began to consider selling off flats and houses to their tenants.

The longing of many thousands of households to escape from the landlord brought the dream of owner-occupation closer to achievement. After all, when capital values were rising, it was the owner-occupier who stood to gain. "It's our turn now ... not the landlord's," was the common cry. The Thatcherite creed of "blessed is the freeholder" caught on with the masses, although the vast majority of the new generation of property owners would not be freeholders at all, but merely long leaseholders weighed down with a sizeable mortgage. At the same time, the speculators continued to buy up the rental property market to cash in on what they deemed the guaranteed price increases. As I put it myself, in *Investors Bulletin:* "...the price of a piece of rental property began to float free of the actual income the property could ever be expected to produce."

The rise in the value of erstwhile rented property was further enhanced by the tax benefits offered the owner occupier. Whereas all earnings from letting an "investment" property were penalised by being treated as "unearned income".

As rented property was taken off the market in the early 1970s, and the supply declined, uncontrolled rents on the remainder soared to new heights. It began to be true for many families that it would be cheaper to become an owner-occupier than remain a tenant. The question was, could they raise the purchase money?

The rise in rents led to many hard cases among those for whom purchasing a property was out of the question. Very often they were elderly tenants and young families who could no longer afford the rent and service charges. The publicity such cases attracted persuaded still more families to look around for a place to buy. In the 1970s, the chatter at cocktail parties, and the inevitable pontification of wiseacres in the local pub, helped to spread the good news. **The message became more and more distorted with each telling. Eventually it was accepted without question that there was a fortune to be made in the residential property market.** The poor fools the fast thinkers professed to feel sorry for were those who had lost heavily on the sagging stockmarket. They were missing the boat.

There was virtually no risk in property was the message. Anyone could handle it - once they had solved the money problem and raised their first mortgage. In the 1950s, this had not been so simple if a pre-1918 property was involved. The mortgage would probably be limited to around 50% of the building society's valuation. But once that hurdle had been taken, you could feel you had taken your first crucial step up the property ladder.

The rules were quite simple. You raised your first mortgage. After that you allowed inflation to do its bit. Then, after eighteen months or two years, you sold your first property at a profit. Now you used the proceeds to pay off your first mortgage, making sure there was enough left over to put down as a deposit on a more expensive property. It would be little more than a paper transaction, since it only meant raising a bigger mortgage than last time. Each time you returned with your begging bowl, you were made even more welcome than before. From once having to chase after your first mortgage, the whole situation had changed so much that you were left with the feeling that your new mortgage had been chasing you!

Since it was gradually perceived as your "inalienable right" to make a tidy profit on each transaction, in the 1960s, residential property came to be regarded as "nature's hedge against inflation". At the same time, as one wag put it, you could sit there and watch inflation quietly melting down your debt like jelly on a hot spoon.

It became clear to property owners that the whole rationale of investing in income property had collapsed. Far better, it now appeared, to gain vacant possession and pay the tenants to leave if necessary. Then the landlord could give the property a good going-over, doing whatever repairs were necessary - or they thought they could get away with - and selling long (99 year) leases to this rapidly expanding class of tenant. From the leaseholders' point of view, there were two advantages. They would have real security of tenure, and would have a say (or so they imagined) in the management of "their" property. Disillusion was to follow. But not quite yet.

In effect, the small landlords were doing what the aristocratic land-owners had done back in the 18th century: handing the land over for a period years, along with responsibility for the upkeep of the land and the buildings erected on it, in return for a ground rent. When the lease expired, the property would be handed back to the landowner in good and habitable condition. In a sense, the land was being "put on ice" for a century. Naturally, the freeholder would be able to sell the land at any time, subject to the existing agreements with the leaseholders. There was one snag for the leaseholder, even a long lease was a wasting asset; and many of the properties being converted were on comparatively short leases. That was one of the things that often made a 1920s or 1930s house seem a better proposition - since many of the small houses had been sold freehold.

In the background inflation was roaring away. By 1976 it had reached the almost unbelievable level of 26%. It remained high for some time to come. Meanwhile great quantities of money continued to be poured into the market.

An important factor by now was that the boom-babies were ready to enter the single family home market. At Westminster and elsewhere, politicians made speeches extolling the virtues of home ownership. Their remarks by now were addressed to council tenants also. Legislation was making home ownership even more attractive. Building societies, which had taken a somewhat tough attitude to those seeking a mortgage, were encouraged to become more lenient in their lending policy.,

I summed up that phase of the residential property market in a special edition of *Investors Bulletin*, from the vantage point of March 1994:

"The diminution of the availability of rented accommodation was one of the major factors fuelling the rise in house prices with the tax advantages enjoyed by owner-occupiers providing an even greater incentive ... The problems that people have suffered as a result of the irresponsible attitude towards home purchasers is far greater than anything experienced when landlords were exploiting tenants prior to the introduction of legislation to curb rents and provide security of tenure."

THE ECONOMIC CONSEQUENCES OF '79

CONDITIONS were ripe for change when the Thatcher government took office in the summer of 1979. Almost at once the drive for universal home ownership was launched. As the stock of privately owned rental properties had been shrinking, many local authorities had pressed ahead with their plans for more and more council dwellings. Now the sale of council flats and houses became the order of the day.

The banking and commercial property crisis of the early 1970s had been rooted in the Government's economic policy. The same could be said of the residential property crisis of the 1980s. By now, I suspect, most of us have forgotten what actually happened ten years ago, or how few people were at all concerned. But what is past is past; and we shall gain little if anything by dwelling on a blow-by-blow account of that frightening episode. As for the consequences, they are still with us. They will not go away for many years to come.

The buying up of properties with vacant possession, and selling them on meant that large, unrealised profits found their way onto the balance sheets of major property companies. But neither developers nor the construction industry escaped unscathed.

It is difficult to know how best to convey the tone and dimensions of a great event. Whether it be a success story or the tale of utter disaster, the problem remains. Eyewitness accounts offer one way. So do surveys, opinion polls and statistics.

It so happens that on 15th October 1989, *The Sunday Times* published some figures provided by a leading London estate agent showing the extent to which the sale price of a particular terrace house had risen between 1918 and 1986.

In 1918, at the end of the First World War, the property sold for £500. By the mid-1930s, at the height of the new home building boom, this fading property fetched £1,500. That was the equivalent of two-and-a-half speculative builders' ribbon development homes.

In 1950, after the Second World War, the same house went for £4,500. That is to say, 9 times the 1918 price. Thirty four years later, in 1984 - when the Great British Property Boom was getting up steam - the price had climbed to £82,000. That was a staggering increase, you may say. But only two years later, the price had climbed to £120,000. In other words between 1984 and 1986 it had been climbing at a rate of £1,600 a month!

Incredible, of course! But it happened.

No need for surprise! We have had sufficient evidence to make it clear beyond doubt that it is not impossible for almost anything anyone can think of to happen, and to go on happening - to a degree. But there will be a point beyond which any further repetition will indeed be out of the question. Any belief to the contrary in the context of the market is a big, and dangerous, illusion.

THE BIG ILLUSION

AS WE have seen, the boom during the Great Depression of the 1930s was essentially a building boom, with tens of thousands of new houses being built. But there was never a price boom; not in the sense of an over-valuation calling for self-correction. On the way, house prices fell. But that didn't prevent the public from buying up the stock that was available. Remember, raw material prices and labour costs also fell. But in no case did the fall go on regardless.

One reason for the fall in the cost of materials was bulk buying and better site management. Some of the builders were operating on a sufficiently grand scale to enjoy appreciable economies of scale. What's more they could afford a good foreman and clerk-of-works to supervise the on-site operation. Planning controls and building regulations were easier at this time; far easier than today. More mobile equipment is employed on site today: cranes, bulldozers, dump trucks, trench diggers, pneumatic drills and the like. Many builders will erect a temporary roof of plastic sheets to avoid being held up by the weather. The muscle-power is reduced, but that does not necessarily mean a better, quicker or cheaper job.

Then you could say that virtually all power was muscle power. Labour was not difficult to find and far easier to get rid of. It was not difficult to stop building for a few weeks if the market suddenly sagged. Money could be borrowed more cheaply in the 1930s, whereas in the 1980s wage costs tended to race ahead of inflation. But, as we saw in the case of Florida, when you operate in Boom-town, it matters very little what things cost; not so long as inflation keeps running out in front. The great thing for any builder is to have buyers clamouring for every row of houses or blocks of flats completed.

The demand was certainly there in the residential property boom of the 1980s. So was a firm belief that the price of homes could only go up ... never down. As a reporter for the London *Times* put it, "House prices always move up, step by step, reaching a plateau, then moving higher."

A dangerous illusion; even if one is permitted to ignore history, sheer common sense must point to a price at which buyers pull out. It might be because they could not afford the price, or because the potential lender would not be prepared to take the risk. So the rate at which property prices were rocketing up in the late 1980s should have served as a warning. Still not convinced? Well, let's consider a simple example.

Suppose that the price of the average house in inner London suddenly started to grow at the rate of 15% per annum. This would mean one of two things - as I pointed out in my book *Into the Upwave:*

" ... either inflation would be rampant, and what you buy for £50,000 today would cost you £500,000, or that mortgages on a £500,000 house would be impossible to obtain, because the mortgage lenders would have crowded out of the market every single profit-making enterprise."

But given the rapidly escalating prices of the 1980s it is surprising that the rate of acceleration was insufficient to counsel caution - let alone sound a warning. Not even when everyone was not all that confident. In *Into the Upwave*, I quoted the words of one property man of vast experience, as he uneasily eyed the state of the market in the summer of 1986:

"It looks good. It feels good. And so long as everyone says, 'How nice! How durable!, as they stroll past ... on their way to raise another loan ... then fine. But try leaning too hard against the end wall ... or start getting worried about the level of borrowing ... and the odds are the whole impressive edifice of mortarless brick wall will come crashing down like the walls of Jericho."

It did look good - so long as you didn't think too much about it. Much had, indeed, been achieved in twenty years - provided you regarded the shift into owner-occupancy as an achievement. Provided too you were prepared to consider only the record up to that point. The record was impressive: between 1961 and 1981, the number of owner-occupied properties had jumped from 6.5 million to 10.8 million.

In 1981, the residential property boom was still at a comparatively early stage with no more than a quarter of all households owning their home outright - debt-free. Some 40% of the heads of those households were "retired" or otherwise "economically inactive". Among the number of households with mortgages, 62%

were headed by professional people, employers and managers. Among the semi-skilled manual, and personal service heads of household, 86% had a mortgage. But only 16% of unskilled manual heads of household had a mortgage.

Possibly more significant is that in 1961 some 5.5 million households still occupied privately rented property. In the following 20 years, the "flight of the private landlord", prompted by higher costs and a declining net return, almost halved to 2.5 million. Whatever you may think of the progress of home-ownership by the end of the 1980s, it is a fact that in 1914 no more than one-in-ten of all homes was owner occupied - and then by the "well-off".

Broad percentages, however, can tell us only part of the story. For example, in 1986 there was a significant gap between house prices in the various regions, as shown in the table below. It was published in *The Observer* of September 28th 1986, and based on figures from the Nationwide Building Society.

	Average prices (£)		
Area	Semi-detached	Detached	*All
Yorks & Humberside	26,870	45,260	27,080
Northern	29,150	NA	27,800
N. Ireland	24,820	37,370	27,930
Wales	29,140	35,260	28,950
North-West	29,180	50,530	29,140
E. Midlands	27,220	40,630	30,410
W. Midlands	28,950	46,080	30,650
Scotland	38,010	42,630	33,170
E. Anglia	36,190	55,600	39,710
South-West	38,980	56,020	39,710
Outer South-East	42,390	64,640	45,810
Greater London	67,470	89,770	56,210
Outer Metropolitan	56,950	85,320	56,280

*Includes flats, maisonettes and bungalows. Semi detached and detached prices relate to older properties.

Figure 3: House prices nationwide
Source: Nationwide Building Society 1986

So far as London prices went in the mid-1960s, a leading West End estate agent saw no reason to wonder at the surge in prices. In part, he said, it was due to the large number of foreigners who had been streaming into London and the South-east in time for the City's Big Bang. They had been prepared - and able - to pay high prices to secure a foothold both in the Square Mile and in one of the top residential areas. The erstwhile owners had then moved on. Frequently they went into the country - keeping a pied-à-terre in town. Usually they paid over the odds for the property they were after. But they could afford it. What's more, they were convinced that London after Big Bang would be another honey pot.

Tim Blenkin, director in York for Jackson Stopps and Staff, reminded the *Financial Times* in September 27th 1986 how quickly prices could rise in an over-heated market:

"Our vendor agreed terms for a sale at £58,000, where offers had been invited at over £56,000. After six weeks the buyer ... backed out. We re-offered the house at £60,000 and agreed terms at once, the difference being no more than representative of an improved market."

That "improved market" accounted for an increase of £2,000 in 42 days. What's more, that was the price actually agreed and paid! The market was really moving around that time. At the very top of the market, it took Knight Frank Rutley and Robert Bruce and Partners just under 12 days to sell Park House, one-time home of the late property and hotels magnate, Sir Maxwell Joseph. A wealthy European client of Beauchamp Estates had been looking for a house in the £1.5 million to £2 million range. Then, according to the FT, he saw this superb mansion, set in half-an-acre of grounds in SW7. The price agreed was £4.5 million, which made Park House one of the two most expensive London properties in 1986.

A property like Park House is virtually unique. It represents what an economist would call a "quasi-monopoly". That is something like a "pop" star or a best-selling author who has virtually no peer. Others might describe it as being rather like Georgian silver or virgin land. As the saying goes, "It's worth so much, 'cause they don't make it no more!" But that does not mean that the bottom cannot fall out of the market for either commodity from time to time.

Leaving such properties aside, what was creating the demand for residential property generally? Since it cannot all have been inspired by the cult of the "property-owning-democracy" the answer was that over-active lenders were playing their part. They were stuffing loans down the throats of borrowers who, a few years earlier, would have been considered bad news. In all probability they would have been turned down.

WELCOME TO LIBERTY HALL

TRADITIONALLY, building societies, banks and local authorities had been cautious when it came to granting a mortgage. They would want to know the personal details of a couple. Most important would be the husband's position and income. Usually, they would tend to dismiss the wife's earnings, limiting the loan to two and a half or three times the main earner's income. The exact figure varied from time to time, according to the individual valuer's assessment, and whether the society wished to take on the property and the client at that moment. But in any case the principle was to keep the loan well below what a forced sale of the property would fetch without too much difficulty. The building society valuation, in other words, would not establish the market value of the property, but merely determine its value to the lender concerned at a forced sale. Some societies used to discriminate quite openly against - say - certain occupations, rootless aliens and women.

When a woman sought to take out a mortgage on her own, she could encounter considerable opposition, if not a blank refusal. Whatever her income and standing, she would be regarded as nowhere so "sound" as her male equivalent. In the 1960s, a well known photographic model, who later became a fashion editor, was refused a mortgage for the flat in which she was already a sitting tenant. She succeeded in raising the loan only when her son (who had far less money than she) was accepted as a suitable (male) guarantor.

Even the general run of "suitable" applicants might have to be told that demand was such that mortgages were being "rationed". In a sense, it was understandable that when low interest rates were the order of the day, caution reigned, since a building society kept afloat mainly on the strength of the margin between what it earned from a borrower and what it paid to the depositor. By the 80s, that attitude had changed. So had the attitude of the British public. There had been two great discoveries. The first was how to make big money on the high street by making large loans on generous terms; and - from the individual's point of view - how to live with debt.

Both parties felt, rightly or wrongly, that the Government and the establishment in general were urging them to go ahead ... and not be shy! But it still took some time before both sides took the hint. For the average citizen, interest paid on loans was "dead" money. It was like having to pay rent, when you could own the property yourself. The fact that to acquire that property meant you would probably have to borrow was somehow put on one side. Illogical? Perhaps it was, but keeping out of debt was something one was taught at an early age. Incurring debt was treated as self-indulgence. Keeping out of debt was felt to be as wise as it was moral. You waited until you could afford whatever it was you'd set your heart on. But gradually debt had become "respectable". The use of "plastic money", instead of cash, was simply common sense. A charge account was "practical". A personal loan from the bank, or an overdraft, no longer made you a dodgy customer. On the contrary, it showed you were really "with it", and determined to be "enterprising".

Incidentally, you were helping the bank to make a comfortable profit. It was a great game, and one that neither party could lose.

A GREAT GAME

BANKS saw the building societies as their high street rivals. For the building societies, banks were the model they dearly longed to copy. By 1986, both banks and insurance companies stepped up their home loans business; and building societies prepared to join the banking community as soon as the Building Societies Act came into force. By the autumn of 1986, building societies had started borrowing on the Euromarket, and a number of foreign institutions entered the home loans business. Banks, building societies and insurance companies were dipping even deeper into the bran tub, buying up a number of estate agency chains. The theory was to soak up the commissions, and collect the profits from selling insurance. This so-called One Stop Shop move was one they would regret. Indeed in the mid-1990s they were still disentangling themselves from that unhappy venture.

As eager lenders of every kind poured into the market, competition became more and more intense. As mortgage rates rose, the rewards grew bigger than they had ever been. The gravy, as one operator put it, became that much richer. This was the Age of the Big Spend, and the Even Bigger Borrow! No reputable financial establishment would admit to having suggested to its clients that they should take out a mortgage for rather more than they needed. Then they could go on that special holiday or buy that brand new BMW. Anyway, that is what many of their clients did. In a short time it seemed to have become standard practice.

In the mid-1980s vast sums were owed to the Finance Houses Association. Government figures for August 1986 showed spending on credit to be rising at four times the rate of inflation. Infolink, a leading credit agency, reported in October '86 that applications for credit in August had been 6% higher than 12 months earlier. They were the highest August figures on record. Infolink's director-general attributed the rise to new car registrations, buoyant retail sales and increased activity in house purchase. The amount advanced by retailers, finance houses and card companies alone totalled to £2.68 billion.

The crucial fact that seemed to get lost in the overall euphoria was that when you buy a new car, take a foreign holiday or acquire a diamond watch, you are incurring a short- term debt. When you take out a mortgage, you are incurring a very much heavier and longer-term liability. Maybe you intend to pay it off in a couple of years when you sell the property and take your profit. But suppose you can't sell; or can only sell at a loss. What then?

Against that background, it is strange to think that people used to work themselves into the ground, and worry themselves to death, in case they lost their job or fell sick before they'd finished paying for the three-piece suite! "With the worries we have today," said my new neighbour, "it doesn't pay to have a memory.

Besides, if you owe enough to the bank, and they get too difficult, you can always hand over the keys and walk away. Then they can do the worrying."

Understandable as that attitude might have been at the time, I fear that my neighbour had a nasty shock coming the first time he bumped into the scourge of the UK residential property market today - I mean Negative Equity.

TOWARDS THE BRINK

THE LATE summer and autumn of 1986 seems to have been the time when harsh reality began to dawn. Nor was it too soon. By October that year, Blay's *Mortgage Guide* was listing no fewer than 25 banks, building societies and insurance companies willing to grant 100% mortgages. Among the most "generous" were Century, with a maximum of £60,000, followed closely by Walthamstow, with a top limit of £59,000. Dr. John Doling, of Birmingham University's Centre for Urban Regional Studies was dismayed at the practice. So was Barclays Bank's Chairman, who called for restraint. However on October 9th Barclays announced that they would be offering mortgages for second homes. Top limit for both first and second homes would be £200,000.

The Chairman of the Bank of England, Mr. Robin Leigh-Pemberton, had castigated the over-generous lenders. Sir Gordon Borrie, Director General of the Office of Fair Trading warned those institutions that were "falling over themselves in their eagerness to offer credit" that if they did not live up to their responsibilities to help solve the problem they had created, they could well "face the prospect of government regulation that would force them to do so." The Economic Secretary to the Treasury, Mr Ian Stewart, added his own warning at a meeting of building society officials at Eastbourne in October 1986:

"Although competition provides a healthy stimulus to business, it can also bring some extra risks ... It has never been a sound commercial principle that a lender has to do as much as possible of the available business regardless of price or risk."

The Economic Secretary also referred to their freedom, under the new Building Societies Act, to raise as much as 20% of their money from the wholesale market. He urged them not to abuse this new right, which should provide "a valuable degree of flexibility in the management of (their) funding and liquidity in volatile market conditions."

A construction analyst at stockbrokers Alexander Laing and Cruikshank (as they then were) seems with hindsight to have put his finger on the button when he said that if building societies had been quoted on the Stock Exchange in 1986:

"...their share price could well have been depressed due to concern over increased competition, and the amount by which lending is outstripping the inflow of funds."

But suppose the home buyers, who were successfully clamouring for a mortgage had been "quoted on the Stock Exchange"? What would the analysts have said about them?

I leave that one with you. Although in their *Quarterly Macro Economic Forecast* in October 1986, stockbrokers L. Messel Co. came up with its comment on the increase in mortgage lending:

"A projected 40% increase in mortgage lending in 1986 indicates the exceptional nature of the current boom in housing. While growth rates of this magnitude cannot be repeated, rises of 8% in 1987 and 4% in 1988 suggest continued buoyancy over the next 18 months at least ... (But) the long upswing in house building, which started in 1981, may end in 1988. Meanwhile, the rate of price increase, very high in 1986 and 1987, declines in 1988 as monetary growth falls to more acceptable levels."

I wonder how many interested parties read, or even saw that comment. And, if they did, how many of them worked out what they were being told, especially if they were floating on a 100% mortgage!

Besides, a 40% increase in lending this year and a 4% increase next! That sounded very much like the brakes going on, and the whole band-wagon screeching to a halt. One of the things it certainly must have meant was that if you were thinking of selling, it would be into a very thin market - unless all the potential buyers were men and women of substance who required no mortgage! That scarcely seemed likely. On the other hand, if you were hoping to slip your collar and get out from under that massive mortgage you had taken on, it looked as though the odds were stacked against you.

Of course, the market might be about to pick up. The downward slide might represent nothing more than a temporary correction. What did the big battalions have to say?

The Halifax, the biggest building society, had seen nothing very alarming on its way. I fancy you won't remember the message the Halifax conveyed to readers of *The Times* of September 30th 1986. So I'll remind you what it said:

"...we do not predict a collapse in house prices. If the Halifax had any such concern, we would feel it our duty to warn existing new borrowers."

Why, I have kept asking myself since that fateful summer and autumn...why did no-one see it coming? Or were they all afraid of frightening the horses?

◆◆◆

CHAPTER EIGHT

NEGATIVE EQUITY AND OTHER TEARFUL TUNES

"Property is illiquid. Most people know this; it's just that their actions indicate that they continually forget it."

Robert Ringer

CAN YOU point to one major economic power where property prices have not fallen disastrously at some time or another; or will never do again? The answer is you can't. Not, let me hasten to say, because there is something inherently unstable about property - especially residential property. Property itself is a "thing" like every other thing. By now, I hope (and, indeed, believe) that we have managed to clear out the many all-too-familiar myths about the property market; and have accepted - albeit reluctantly - what originally seemed a positively bizarre notion. To many members of the wrinkly-with-age set, it seems almost obscene to put property down fairly and squarely as one of the "everyday things" we need; things for which we may have to beg, borrow or steal. I am thinking of things like toothbrushes or - at the other end of the scale - a Ferrari.

Property is not a magic seed which, once planted, will grow and grow and grow until it makes a huge fortune for its owner. Nor, alternatively, is it a species of poison ivy that will end up harming its once proud possessor. No, indeed! The reason we have tended to regard property as lethal is that, for the vast majority of buyers and sellers, any property deal introduces a need to raise the largest sum of money they are ever going to handle in their lives. This cements the bond between themselves and those two supposedly friendly fixers - Master Credit and Mistress Debt.

Nor is money a consideration merely at the time that the sale or purchase is consummated. So long as an inevitably vast chunk of capital remains tied up in property, those funds cease to be available for any other purchase or investment by the new owner. Once the seller has got his or her hands on that money, a fresh round of transactions can begin. The man or woman who "has everything" can (and will) treat all that as a matter of course; a fact of life to be taken for granted. They will miss those few hundred thousand, but it won't change their lives. It's a debt - or investment - they can handle.

For many of those now in trouble over arrears or the fall in value of their home, the property they acquired and the debt they undertook was always way beyond their means and their power to control. The cost of having to surrender control over that immobilised capital - especially if they have had to borrow virtually all of it - will indeed be felt. They may say, nevertheless, "It's crippled us financially, but it was worth it." (Implying that something other than monetary value lay behind their decision.)

The non-monetary benefit will to some extent compensate for the other uses to which that capital might have been applied. Or, to be technical about it, they may see the non-monetary benefits as reducing the opportunity cost of that move into ownership. But they are still absolutely dependent on the property holding its value; just as they were dependent on lenders believing that inflation would send the value-as-security of that property even higher. Alas, that bubble had to burst.

Life is not all that accommodating. Most would-be buyers are forced to raise the biggest long-term loan they can to obtain a toehold on the property. That does not mean that the true cost is merely that on the price ticket. The way in which the funds are raised is crucial. However, mortgages and their characteristics are something we shall come to later. Suffice it to remind ourselves that the loan granted by the lender is given against the lender's assessment of the security inherent in the value of that property. Not, one must stress, the property itself. Does a building society or a bank want to end up with several thousand virtually unsaleable properties round their neck? What the lender has done is make the purchase possible. What he wants back is the capital sum he made available plus the price for allowing others the use of that money for a period of years. It is here that the concept of so-called Negative Equity comes in.

At its simplest, it can mean that the lender no longer feels the price he could obtain for the property - at a forced sale and with the minimum of fuss - would be sufficient to justify bearing the risk. This, to be realistic, will include loss of the profit envisaged at the start. That is one reason why the borrower's handing back the keys with a polite "thank you" is not good enough. The borrower still owes the same debt to the lender; so the key question is how keen the lender will be to get his hands on the property in order to sell it as soon as possible.

This has been a contentious issue in cases where the borrowers have claimed they could - or would have - sold for a much higher price than the lending institution. Hopes that any shortfall would be covered by the insurance which the lender may have been obliged to take out along with the mortgage is a very grey area. So far the lender has appeared to hold the whip hand. The weakness in the lender's position is that he must have ample grounds for asking the court for possession. If the borrower pays all his dues, and is not forced to attempt to sell the property for personal reasons - so forcing the issue - the lender may be virtually impotent. Considerable psychological pressure may be put upon the unfortunate borrower; pressure which he or she may find difficult to resist. But if the value of the property has fallen sufficiently below the mortgage figure, the lender faces the possibility that the borrower may opt for bankruptcy. Fortunately, this goes against the grain with most borrowers.

Some lenders have taken a longer view, and have allowed the Negative Equity victim to move to a cheaper property. The lender has agreed to provide the borrower with a mortgage to cover both the new property and a slice of the outstanding debt. This still leaves the decision in the hands of the lender, and depends to a considerable extent on both parties maintaining good relations throughout. It is safe to say that most major lenders will do their best to avoid an unnecessary confrontation. Some of the smaller lenders may find it difficult to make the necessary concessions. At the same time it has to be admitted that not all borrowers are angels, or prepared to seek an amicable compromise.

CHANGING CLIMATE

STRANGE how some words and phrases catch on, and how they serve to mark quite fundamental changes in public opinion. Such expressions as the "feel-good factor", "political correctness" and "negative equity" have certainly caught on. Their regular use, and general acceptance, enable people to discuss the state of business morale, to compromise on sexist and racial attitudes and to face up to the general collapse of property values, and to do so with hysteria or acrimony. To that extent, it also allows us to talk the problem through - and to do so again and again - until it virtually loses all meaning. People are then free to ignore the hard facts and decide - usually with some emotion - whether X or Y should be regarded as a "good thing" or as a "bad thing". Negative equity, the consensus would have us believe, is a "bad thing". That certainly is the way that politicians and the media usually approach it. That is due to their tendency to view the problem from the "human" angle. That is to say, from the standpoint of the unfortunate victim of the market collapse.

This is understandable, since the lender is almost bound to be seen in the same light as that traditionally dreaded figure, "the landlord". The question is not only whether this makes sense; it is also whether we can hope to see a more balanced view of the problem that is facing borrower and lender alike. This is not important from the point of view of the UK alone. It is not without its importance for other countries which have been moving along the same road towards owner occupancy. There were lessons enough to be learned from the American property scene in the last century. What about post-Thatcherite Britain? The tendency is for us to start asking, "How do we get there?", before we have decided where "there" is likely to be.

The first question, I believe, should be where we are going to end up if we go on as we are - doing nothing. In other words, do we leave it to chance, to the market, to nature or what you will? Is there anything to be learned from the way other countries are tackling their property market problems? It could even be that we have come to the end of the road so far as home ownership is concerned. Remember the great property boom began, went wild and came to grief in less than ten years. Now, as I write, some six years have passed since I warned my readers of my book, *Into the Upwave*, that the game was over. What has happened over those six years? To judge by the Prime Minister's remarks on June 1st 1995, very little seems to have been learned in that quarter.

John Major told Lincolnshire businessmen that he blamed the "crazy, almost unstoppable" house price spiral for the absence of that "feel-good factor". This at once brought howls of protest from Opposition MPs, charities and mortgage lenders. Their reactions were predictable. Building societies and City analysts, wrote *The Times'* political correspondent, "offered little comfort" to victims of negative equity. They reported that the market was still falling. The director of housing services for Shelter blamed the right-to-buy and the deregulation of the private rented sector, "which reduced social housing stock and increased private rents." For many people, concluded Louise Casey, "there was no viable alternative to home ownership."

Meanwhile more news, more figures came pouring out, some more imaginative than others: over a million people were said to be trapped in their homes by negative equity; many borrowers were sitting tight, saving what they could to pay extra off their mortgage: lender plans to help borrowers were dubbed "lifeline schemes"; some lenders were offering up to 125% of the value of the new home, plus a maximum £25,000 transferable from the old property. The straightforward, most logical, common sense remedy of allowing negative equity victims to pay off as much of their debt as they could, and then cease to be so-called "owners", does not appear to have found favour in any quarter. Moreover, I listened in vain for a firm voice calling for something to be done forthwith to revive and restore the rented property market.

At one time it seemed as though we might be thinking in terms of a partnership between landlord and tenant, lender and borrower, of the kind represented by the Housing Association movement. Then came the news that the Government wanted to give Housing Association residents that dreaded "right-to-buy". So we found ourselves once again, watching the trains go by ... and clutching one of those familiar Government issue platform tickets.

Meanwhile more and more repossessions have been taking place. It is not merely that the building societies and other lenders are mindful of the problems they would be creating for themselves if they took too "soft" a line. Building society members, like bank shareholders, demand that the rules be followed to the letter. Depositors with building societies and banks expect no less. Aside from which, this is a time when rumours of take-overs and mergers abound. A wise lender - like a wise soft-toy manufacturer - will want to tidy up his portfolio at a time like this.

Too many statistics, someone once said, are like too many monkeys. They demand attention and they aren't worth it. But this small handful, I believe, are worth repeating. What we have been considering in this chapter so far has been taking place against a rising tide of repossessions. In the first half of 1995, they rose for the first time since 1991. According to the Council for Mortgage Lenders, repossessions in the first half of 1995 were 25,200 against 24,196 in the last half of 1994. Neither of these figures covered those potentially at risk. That is to say those who have somehow managed to keep up with their mortgage payments, until they came face to face with redundancy and reduced government help. There were also those who had been fortunate enough not to have to move house, and face the full measure of the fall in the value of their property. This can be the crisis point. Facing an impending sale has driven lenders to get out their rule book.

So long as regular payments are made, a building society or a bank can use its discretion. But there must be a limit. On July 27th 1995, the *Daily Mail's* Consumer Affairs Correspondent reminded his readers that lenders would continue to help their borrowers. But in some cases the interests of those borrowers would not be well served by "allowing arrears to accrue for very substantial periods". Looking forward, it was felt in many quarters that any increase in mortgage arrears must be viewed with concern. In 1995 there had been a fall in arrears of 12 months plus. But there had been a rise in short-term arrears - those between 3 to 6 months. A spokesman for the Woolwich Building Society blamed this in part on the reduction in tax relief and tax incentives generally.

Strange how quickly we seem to have forgotten that in an ideal world - and market place - the degree of stability would be such that residential property deals would take place without too great a sense of loss on the part of either the buyer or the seller. Legal costs would obviously be incurred; and a whole army of professionals - from chartered surveyors to the local builder - would no doubt be beneficiaries. But no-one on either side would risk facing ruin.

It is because the major industrialised nations appear to be heading in the same direction as the United Kingdom, that an account of recent events has a relevance for just about every reader, regardless of domicile. Moreover the lesson offered buyers and sellers wherever they belong is so much better illustrated by the UK market, which has been like a gigantic arena, in which everything is still happening before our very eyes.

FEEL-GOOD FALLACY

WATCH those feelings! Remember, one of the more dangerous illusions in the '80s was that every £1,000 added to the value of a property made the owner that much better-off. Feeling better-off - and constantly being reminded they really were - soon meant that he or she felt a growing urge to lash out on that world cruise, send the boy to public school or buy that new car. Why not? There were all those kind, ever-so-friendly banks and other loan peddlers who were inviting you to do just that. You had the urge, they had the cash. Alas! Nothing like that in the offing today. Only quite an irrational feeling that if property were to recover, we'd all feel so much better. Once that happened, then the whole economy could get going again. Up would go turnover and the work force; down would go the losses and unemployment. The argument behind that assertion was simple enough, even if irrational. Housing was important. It was a shield against inflation and other monetary ills. It gave the individual dignity. It guaranteed a safe future, by keeping all landlords at bay. The only thing wrong was that the market was in the doldrums.

All that was required, folk told each other, was positive thinking, backed up by firm action. But there were two snags: the first was to persuade would-be buyers to take the first step, even though - the moment they signed on the dotted line - they might well find prices on the slide again. Nor would that matter, provided they merely required a home to live in. But for too many would-be buyers, there was a pressing, almost painful need to feel good and bask in the glory of what was inaccurately described as "ownership". The other snag was to establish precisely who ... or what ... would bring about the return of at least a "feel-a-little-better" factor. The answer to that was already on their lips. It was the Government's responsibility, of course. Unhappily Mr Major did not appear disposed to intervene. So the only focus of attention would be the November '95 Budget. It came, it went. Nothing changed. **The best the Government could do for the housing market was to keep inflation and interest rates low and stable.**

Many people and well-disposed bodies argued that it was only right to lay the burden on the Government, since the last thing they could recall was the Government's introducing new rules for helping (or not helping) those paying mortgage interest who fell ill or lost their job. The scheme, which did not cover repayment of capital, took care of the mortgage interest so long as the person remained eligible for benefit. But Government would no longer "send in the cavalry" to answer their call. From 1st October 1995, each individual would have to wait nine months before receiving help. Assume the mortgage on a three-bedroom house was costing something like £730 per month. Nine months worth of full payments would add up to £6,570 before any help came. This could be enough, critics felt, to tip the balance and send even more unfortunates down the chute.

Four months earlier, in July '95, there had been a Government Housing White Paper, *Our Future Homes*. It contained no promises to help close on one million people threatened by negative equity. Nor did it promise any tax breaks to stimulate the market as so many people had been urging. That task was taken up by the two financial giants, the Abbey National and the Halifax. Both launched completely new ranges of mortgage products to serve as a jab in the arm. Critics were again on their feet. Many Conservatives felt their Government was being too hard-nosed. On the other hand, it was undeniable that the building societies themselves had recognised the need for action; moreover they were doing something about it. Bearing in mind the extent to which their easy loans and honeyed words had contributed to the '80s boom, the Government would appear to have given the lenders a nudge in the right direction.

By now something else was happening, again with Government intervention. There was a steady build-up of activity in the rental market. This had taken place despite the fact that many interested parties were claiming that it was still cheaper — and, by inference, better — to buy rather than rent. Was there anything in that argument? Or had renting something to offer that buying no longer had?

RETURN TO RENTING

THE WELL organised House Builders' Federation were not surprisingly among the first to claim that renting was "a waste of money". So much so, they asserted, that home seekers were turning back to buying. It was certainly true that the increased mobility that renting could offer had proved attractive to young professional couples in particular. They, significantly, had earlier been regarded as "natural" first-time buyers. There were, however, other important demographic factors besides mobility. There was the growth in job insecurity for one thing. It was no longer a case of redundancies among a stable work force. More and more whole categories of operatives were no longer required. This applied as much to white collar workers, whether in banks, insurance companies or the civil service, again the backbone of owner-occupancy in earlier times. Cost was still important, and rents were rising fast. But cost was not the major consideration it had been. Apart from anything else, the more promising and determined among the lower age group were far-seeing enough to avoid hanging a 25-year mortgage around their necks.

There was a certain amount of displacement as the more attractive locations filled up, despite the rise in rents. As a consequence, less desirable properties in less choice locations became much sought after. In London, for example, soaring rents in Hampstead and Highgate drove many young people to see what Muswell Hill and Crouch End had to offer. These had been two areas to which young families in the past had tended to move, having decided to quit their more fashionable small flats in a more expensive locality when the first child came. This, thanks to the boom, they would usually manage to sell at a profit, as they began their journey up-market.

Now, by the mid-'90s, those young families were reluctant to buy a flat, a maisonette or an 80-year old house in an area in which they did not feel inclined to set up a permanent home. Hence the tendency to rent rather than buy. This led in turn to a property shortage in both Muswell Hill and Crouch End. Nevertheless, when the House Builders' Federation polled 6,000 houses, it emerged that nearly half of all home-seekers considered renting to be uneconomic.

On the other side of the fence, Cluttons London Residential Agency told *The Times* on October 28th that lettings in July, August and September had been 10 per cent up on the previous year. The spokesperson for another lettings agency, Robert Jordan Associates, believed that people were still wary of buying. They feared for their jobs and were worried about the future of the housing market.

It is not easy to gauge the true state of the housing market. Rents and mortgage costs can vary enormously. Indeed, to get anything like a true picture, we are driven to accepting the reports which major lenders offer us from time to time. According to September's rental figures, Winkworth's give the average rent for a two-bed flat in Islington, north London, as £250 a week. The average for a comparable flat in Battersea, south London, was no more than £150. At the same time, Cluttons pointed out that a three-bed cottage in Oxfordshire could be had for no more than £175 a week.

The net difference between renting and buying similar properties in the same area may come as a surprise. On October 25th 1995, for example, *The Times* published figures showing the difference in cost between renting and buying a three-bed house in Finchley, north London. Costs for the rented property included the rent, council tax, contents insurance and estate agent's fee. Together they added up to an annual cost of £10,197.77. Costs per annum for the property if purchased worked out higher at £11,922.97 per annum. The difference between renting and buying came to £1,725.20. The difference was due in part to the fact that the purchase cost package was somewhat different. The "purchase" package included monthly mortgage charges, buildings and contents insurance, Stamp Duty, valuation, council tax and water rates. The mortgage was for £120,000 at 7.99% over 25 years. (Gross £781.00. Net £751.04).

The main difference was that in any case the rent was bound to rise over the 25-year period, and would go on being raised thereafter. Whereas in 25 years the purchaser would take possession of the house - and all for an extra £1,725.20 per annum.

Now take the difference between renting in Finchley and renting in Manchester. The difference is considerably greater. The cost is £10,197.77 in Finchley, as against £6,694.53 in the North. That gives us a difference of £3,503.24. Finally take the comparative purchase figures for Finchley and Manchester: £11,922.97 and £11,829.17 respectively. That produces a difference of no more than £93.80. Can this be right, you might ask? I agree; it is not what one expects.

Despite the difference in cost between renting and buying, and despite the uneasy property market, it makes sense to contribute to your own mortgage, rather than help someone else to pay his. That is especially so with costs likely to go on rising. Nevertheless, a balance must be struck between cost and convenience. One has to be sure that if cost really counts, the ostensible saving is sufficient to be significant. It does not make sense to take a leap in the dark on the strength of a small saving either way. On the other hand, you will be forced in the end to take a calculated risk.

It might be making a sound, common-sense approach to the problem to be prepared to live modestly for a few years in rented accommodation which gives you a chance to save. In that way you could accumulate a sizeable nest-egg; in which case you could probably manage with a much smaller mortgage when the time came to buy.

Should you decide to rent, you are no longer left at the mercy of a bad or greedy landlord these days. In accordance with the Rent Act of 1977, you can always apply to have your rent assessed by a rent officer. Nor could the landlord prevent you making an application. The rent assessed by the rent officer then becomes the maximum payable, even if you had agreed to pay more. But be careful. If the rent officer thinks you are paying too low a rent, he can raise it.

CALCULATING THE RISK

HOW DIFFERENT life is at the top! Or is it?

Nature, they used to say, abhors a vacuum. Whether it does or not, the ordinary citizen certainly abhors risk, leaving it to the genuine entrepreneur to transform risk into opportunity. That does not mean they will sit there like martyrs, hoping (or even praying) that "it'll all come right in the end". Take, for example, Wimpey, the world's largest private homes builder, which made an asset swap with super-giant Tarmac, announced in November '95.

Specifically, Wimpey agreed to take over Tarmac's housing division at asset value, with Tarmac taking over Wimpey's mineral business and non-housing construction activities. The way the deal worked out placed equal value on Tarmac's housing division and Wimpey's mineral business; while Wimpey would be selling its construction business at nil value. This last would include its year-end cash balances. With the value of Tarmac's housing division and Wimpey's mineral business likely to be around £320 million each, it was a bold, strategic move. Moreover, both firms saw it as a winning move. A spokesman for Wimpey reckoned that quite a few boardrooms across the country would be discussing their joint announcement.

On Tarmac's side, its intention to sell its housebuilding capacity had been announced in August. So, clearly, both sides had moved fast. Wimpey expected to enjoy sales of some 14,000 houses a year, and shed the problem of funding its contracting and minerals activities. Tarmac would not merely be reinforcing its position in aggregates, but would also be controlling a world-class contracting capacity.

Around the same time, some of former Prime Minister Thatcher's "merchant princes" of the property world were shaping up to re-enter the post-collapse market again. In a number of cases, the end of the '80s had seen their companies tipping over one by one, like those proverbial dominoes.

Several of the big names, who had seen their massive fortunes crumble away, had already plunged in at the deep end again. For example, there were Godfrey Bradman and Stuart Lipton, who gave the City of London the world famous Broadgate office complex. Heading rival consortia, and backed by outside money, they were already competing for the jewel in Whitehall's crown - the £200 million redevelopment of the Treasury. At its peak, Lipton's stake in the Stanhope company had been worth in excess of £150 million. The crash wiped out his fortune. In 1995 he had watched British Land scoop up his company from receivership for no more than £3 million. Later he bought back the Stanhope name.

Other battle-stained armies had begun the long march back, headed by such familiar names as Ronnie Nathan of Waterglade, Trevor Osborne of Speyhawk, which crashed owing £350 million to 46 banks, and Gerald Ronson of Heron. The most spectacular return from the ranks of the presumed dead was that of Paul Reichmann's Olympia and York. Responsible in the first instance for Docklands' Canary Wharf - Olympia and York had managed to secure the backing of a powerful consortium and had begun buying back the complex once again.

A note of caution was sounded by Robert Maxted, who made a comeback in the autumn of '95. He was reported in the *Sunday Times* of November 12th 1995 as saying that it was a case of "familiar names in a very unfamiliar market". No-one knew where it was going, or what the rules were. Inflation was no longer a factor, and rental growth was not "something any half-intelligent surveyor talked about". The bottom line was that commercial tenant demand was virtually non-existent.

At the same time some choice property was gathered in by the bold and hopeful. Whether they would qualify to be dubbed "Major's merchant princes" remains to be seen. But one thing should be clear by now: the belief that a flourishing property market would be the salvation of the nation's economy was based on a myth. The reality could be seen in that pile of debt, disaster and broken promises, which still had to be cleaned up and cleared away.

That leaves the little people to find their own salvation.

RENTERS ALL

YES! We are all renters. We have a choice - provided we can afford to choose. We may rent a property and remain tenants; why should that be so bad? Or we can rent the money. If we take out a mortgage, we shall be allowed to call ourselves "owner occupiers", for want of a better name. But is that so much better? (Yes! Yes! - I can hear the cries.) My advice is think long and hard before you leap. Remember - until the last penny has been paid off, we are still only renters of one sort or another. Just as the really big names in PROPERTY - spelt large - are only players. They won't be allowed to get up from the table and cash in their chips until they have handed over a great deal of real money to their backers. Isn't that obvious? The difference between them and us is that they are professionals; we are only amateurs. But the game's the same; so are the risks.

Get this: Hollywood became the centre of the movie industry because that was where the pioneers in the new industry, the ex-rag trade pioneers took their chance. Many of the big names that once added glamour to the property market started out in another field of enterprise. Take Irving Sellar, one time chief executive at Ford Sellar Morris. He made his fortune in jeans when Carnaby Street became the No. 1 marketplace for the so-called swinging - and sexy - sixties. You had to be a real pro to make big money down the Street. Sellar was professional enough to build a property operation which, when it crashed four years ago, came down with debts of £150 million. It appears that he has little wish to dive in at the moment.

It could be that at the ordinary citizen level you might save, or sell your way out from under a load of negative equity. But you would be well advised to consider - at least for the time being - to becoming both tenant and landlord in a modest property, or properties, of your own.

You could become a full-time or part-time landlord. That means you'll be collecting rent as well as continuing to pay the overheads. You might decide to get out and let the whole house. Or you might decide to let the whole part of the property in which you are currently marooned and remain on the premises. Shock Horror is likely to be the reaction! "Nothing like that has been done in our family for ... fifty years". The response to that should be to ask how your parents or grandparents managed immediately after World War Two. Then renting meant getting hold of a furnished room or "flatlet". Unless you could pay "key money", you would be thrown back on your friends' or relatives' help. Or, maybe, you could somehow get onto the local council's housing list. No dignity of ownership - counterpart to the dignity of labour - then.

Get clear about one thing. You may feel the blow to your dignity if you find you're one of the "new poor"; if you are forced to do what the earlier generation had to do. So be it. If you are having negative equity problems, or decide to take evasive action so you won't, you could well find yourself moving swiftly into the ranks of the renters. Though by no means everyone will get the choice. It could be this month or this year, or some time in the not too distant future. It depends what happens to the economy. To your job. To the job your wife may decide to go back to.

TAKING A LONG, HARD LOOK

NEVER take a hasty decision about long-term responsibilities. If your building society, some helpful advice bureau or your wife's fat cousin comes up with a suggestion, do not immediately spring into action. Right ... we'll do that! It may be a great solution. On the other hand it may be a sudden rush of blood to the head. If you are well and truly worried you are likely to become a victim of the mirage syndrome. No, take the thought away! Take a good hard look at it. Do not rush off towards what only appears to be that longed-for oasis. If you feel you must move fast, do so only if you genuinely must. Even then, it must be for a real, good reason. Here I would say that not caring to think ugly thoughts is no reason at all for failing to look closely at your position right away, budgeting realistically, and working out your own Plan A. Think out a Plan B too, if you believe it might be necessary.

Despite what they say in the commercials, you don't need a computer to play the "what if" game.

Be discreet. Remember you give away much more by the shape of your questions than by any statement you make. No-one suggests you go around blabbing about it, and there is no call to hang out a bill-board saying, "We're the poor folks in this street". Remember too that potential lenders don't like dealing with losers; not if they have a choice. Believe me, they do have a choice! But ask yourself - frankly and without pulling punches - what you propose to do if the worst happens? What's more, once you have asked the question, stay in there until you have given yourself an answer. OK? And make sure it's an answer you can stick by. Having gone through all that, the idea of becoming a landlord as well as a tenant may not seem all that bad.

But here - as elsewhere - there are ground rules. Rule No 1 is "Get it right". You may have only one chance. So don't rule yourself out by failing to discover the rules before you place your stake on the table. Get the rules right, and adhere to them.

PLAY IT BY THE RULES

AS A landlord you take on several duties. Tough! But it's inescapable. Your first duty is to your tenant(s). Treat them right. Then, hopefully, they will respond. Some may not, but many will. Do not screw the last penny you can out of them. You want - you need - their goodwill. That is why you must keep your word. It is better to look sour and say, "I dunno about that!", rather than smile sweetly, say "Sure" and then do nothing about it. The hard fact is that a sullen, dissatisfied and vengeful tenant, who sees you as an ogre, a pest or a creep, can give you much grief and cost you even more money in the end. You want them to feel comfortable. If you become the "dreaded landlord" they are not going to take care of your property. Maybe there is a vine that needs watering; or pictures which call for gentle handling. Put the wrong polish on that bust, or stone vase or special hard-wood floor, and it can be ruined. Under the heading of careful handling, come the porter, the electrician and plumber, the odd-job man you always call upon and - above all - the cleaning lady.

And what about your immediate neighbours? Is your tenant going to get up their nose from Day One? The careless and noisy tenant can soon lose you the goodwill you so carefully built up. Need I say more? Take my list, lay it on one side and make one of your own. Then put the two together, and work on that.

Next comes your building society or bank, or whoever else might be the lender. You need to do more than merely play straight by them. You need to get them on your side. Lenders are as much under pressure as borrowers; different kinds of pressure, it is true, but pressure no less. Make it easy for them to make it easy for you. By that I mean, when they say, "Have a good day", make it easy for them to mean it. One way of doing that is to avoid presenting them with an accomplished fact. They do not like surprises. There is always someone at another level who is going to ask why they didn't foresee whatever it was you sprang on them.

To be specific, get the lender's permission if you intend to let. At one time that was difficult to get. One of the major societies, for example, will require their borrowers to complete a letting questionnaire. This is no mere formality. They will also ask for an administration fee. Some smaller societies still make difficulties. They have not necessarily woken up to the extent the property world has changed, and is still changing. Or, if they have, they have not yet taken on board the fact that they too will have to adjust - just like the rest of us. Knowing that there will be problems in getting permission, however, is no excuse for going ahead regardless. If more building societies follow the lead of their bigger brothers, and genuinely do their best to help you out of your difficulties, things will get easier. Here, let me repeat the warning - don't hide anything from them or spring anything on them.

The odds are you have never read your agreement. Try it. You will almost certainly find there are some small print obstacles to almost anything out of the ordinary. You really do need the lender to feel sufficiently confident that you will be given more latitude than is there in cold, hard print. Moreover, leave the cold print to them. Ask, yes! Suggest, yes! But do not write sassy and aggressive letters. Indeed, try not to write anything until you have spoken face-to-face with the key man you have to deal with. There is a good reason for this: your letter is going to go straight on file. Maybe, had you known a little more about the situation, you would have phrased it differently. But once that letter is on the file, that's that. The man - or woman - you have to deal with may understand what gave you that false impression. But the level to which your file is going to be shown will not. So, to vary the old saying by the Teddy Bear President, "Talk softly, cause the other guy carries the big stick". A final point. Remember that the man or woman behind the desk is probably worried about their job prospects as much as you are, or were until they were dragged out from under your feet.

There is another sound reason why you need the goodwill of the lender. That is because you may need to take out a second mortgage for the property you are buying to rent out. The need to keep away from the second mortgage sharks means you are going to have to bend the ear of your - hopefully - still friendly, first mortgage lender. Here you may find the going hard. That is why you need the reputation of being a "good borrower". That is to say, being pleasant, co-operative and paying promptly. If you are going to be entirely dependent on the rent from the letting, the lender may be very unhappy. If the lender feels you are becoming "professional", rather than merely trying to bail yourself out, the mortgage interest rate may be put up by as much as 3%. In a nutshell, the goodwill of the lender will be essential, because a lender who says, "No", means just that ... on pain of foreclosure.

You may be abroad when all this is happening, either because you are an expatriate Brit or a foreign national seeking property in the UK. The rules will be virtually the same. For the foreign purchaser, the first essential is to deal only with the most reputable agents or societies represented in his or her country. Face-to-face contact is most important. Ask for advice, but do not necessarily take it. Even if you do not, you will have scored on the PR front. People - especially professional people - like to be asked.

If the buyer abroad is an expatriate, it will still pay to go to a sound agent or society represented in the area. Apart from anything else, tax rules and trends are extremely important. Get it right now, is the rule. Then there need be no disaster in three or five years' time. Above all, that expat should not rely merely on "good old Charlie back home". "Good old Charlie", apart from anything else, is not so likely to relay the hard view of the uglier facts as a good professional. We all need to know the worst. But distance lends enchantment to the view; and enchantment in this context is only another, prettier word for distortion.

Most important are the relations which exist between your lender and the Inland Revenue. The lender must tell the Inland Revenue when the borrower lets a property. This generally means forfeiting the Miras tax-relief allowance. Take a mortgage of £60,000 and an interest rate of 7.9%, and the loss of relief could cost almost £33 a month. (Think of it as £396 a year off the rent.)

Naturally, Inland Revenue will be interested in your rental income. Mortgage interest, maintenance fund payments, agents' fees and insurance may be deducted. It could all add up to enough to reduce your tax on rental income to very little indeed. But it also means someone else, rather than you, will be collecting those expenses. It seems to be tempting enough already for some people to fudge their tax return. Self-assessment is obviously going to increase the temptation. We may expect the penalties to be increased as the drive on fraud continues to gain ground on all fronts.

Insurance can prove anything from a sensitive area to a minefield. The plain fact is that the insurance world does not care greatly for amateur landlordism. They can restrict the cover on both buildings and contents policies at one blow. Again, it is essential to tell all and tell it in time. Failure to disclose a material fact - however minor - can let the insurer off the hook. That is to say, no obligation to pay out! Insurers are generally quite clear about their attitude to letting; tenants are just not going to be so careful as owners. Therefore tenants mean a higher risk. If you have taken out your insurance through the lender, you may find yourself with a real problem. One of the major societies will at once restrict its cover for buildings, and withdraw its contents cover altogether.

Finally, the question of an agent. If you are willing to pay between 10% and 17%, the services of a good letting agent are at your disposal. Members of the Association of Residential Letting Agents reckon to handle some 40% of agent lettings in the private sector. Here the agents' services cover finding and checking on a tenant, making an inventory and ensuring that the telephone, electricity and so forth are in the tenant's name. Tenants can leave some huge bills unpaid. They will collect the rent, hold a deposit from the tenant and deal with maintenance problems. The main thing is that they are there and available while the landlord is going about his or her own affairs. Given a good agent, it is usually worth the money. Above all, they will ensure that the tenancy agreement is what you want, and they will warn you if what you want is not watertight enough - for your own sake.

Good letting agents are a front-line defence against some of the horrible mistakes that amateur landlords can make. Even the average-to-pretty-average ones are to be relied upon rather more than that know-all round at the pub.

Some would-be landlords find it difficult to handle the details, or the actual tenants. They are likely to end up dissatisfied and even out of pocket. Those who are a "natural" on the other hand are already beginning to sprout their entrepreneurial wings. One example which may encourage those with a natural bent is that of a young employee of a merchant bank who bought a one-bedroom, residential unit in London's Bloomsbury for £90,000. He bought it off-plan to secure a reasonably good price. From a tenant found by his agents, he received an income of £230 a week over a fixed 24-month period. The owner's outgoings are restricted to estate agency fees, ground rent and maintenance costs. The last, since it is a new building, should be minimal. Gross rental return: 13.3%.

The assured shorthold tenancy in this case gives the tenant security and removes the landlord's traditional fear of the renter becoming a sitting tenant in no time, and ending in a court case - which the landlord may not always win.

Beginners should not attempt to play the entrepreneurial game. But that does not mean they cannot take advantage of the fact that the everyday, low-level, practical entrepreneur is beginning at last to put a little life into the once torpid rental sector. In this way the steady erosion of accommodation to rent appears at least to have slowed down. There have also been signs to indicate that owner occupancy is no longer everyone's ideal. Indeed, as I write, there has been an interesting report by the Association of London Government - a body representing the 32 London boroughs and the Corporation of London. It revealed that the Government's Rent to Mortgage scheme launched in October 1993 had well and truly flopped. The scheme was launched by Sir George Young, the then Housing Minister, and was intended to persuade some 1.4 million better off council tenants to buy their homes. Two years later, his successor, David Curry, disclosed that no more than 13 properties had been purchased under the scheme.

Commenting on this quite extraordinary state of affairs in the *Hampstead and Highgate Express* November 24th 1995, the ALG's housing chairman, Councillor Pete Challis, saw this as proof that the Government's home ownership policies were not working. He believed the Government should rather be "promoting initiatives to boost the social rented sector ... so that people have a real choice between all forms of tenure."

A disturbing fact is that after eight years as "owner-occupiers", many former council tenants have found themselves under pressure to pay literally thousands of pounds as their share of improvements to the estate. The Government scheme for improving the worst council estates in the country was an ambitious one, and costed at £2,000 million. Those tenants who remained renters are charged nothing. But those who exercised their right-to-buy were charged in full. Some of the cases were reported in *The Sunday Times* of November 12th 1995 as being charged up to £42,000. This was not why council tenants - or any other tenants for that matter - bought the leasehold of their dwellings. Yet that is the predicament many thousands of leaseholders have found themselves in. In reality the leaseholder - whether the lease be for 99 or 999 years - has become the least favoured and protected tenant.

They bought their leases from a previous resident or from the landlord because it appeared to give them freedom from risk and that degree of "quiet enjoyment" which, they were persuaded, the ordinary short-term tenant could not generally enjoy. The behaviour of some private freeholders, who had been using excessive service charges and repair bills to get rid of leaseholders, had become a scandal by the mid-1990s. So much so, it seemed, that the Government would be taking steps to plug the hold in the leaseholders' defences.

Nevertheless, the market for renting has been taking off, thanks in some measure to the introduction of the assured shorthold tenancy, deemed to be the fairest form of agreement for landlord and tenant alike. Where a lender is involved, it is good to know that the landlord is not going to be lumbered with a bad or troublesome tenant, and that the tenant has an assurance that he or she can rely on the agreement being enforced if necessary.

The owner occupier who is also the freeholder is in the strongest position of all. But in the case of a converted house or mansion block, the freehold may be held by what is in effect a house committee. There the position of all can become difficult, should one of their number prove obstructive or refuse to pay his or her share of expenses. On the other side, a majority of the house may decide to spend heavily on repairs and improvements with the express aim of "winkling out" one or more of their number who, they know, will not be able to meet the bill.

The question no-one can answer at this time is when - or whether - we shall see a return to renting on a similar scale to that we saw before the early years of the 20th century, with home ownership restricted to a far narrower income and social range. In one respect, however, we are probably going to see more private individuals purchasing properties with the express purpose of becoming a landlord. It could be no more than a temporary arrangement. It could, if inflation is kept down and interest rates are lowered, signal the revival of an older pattern of investment, when bricks and mortar seriously competed with stocks and bonds.

◆◆◆

CHAPTER NINE

HOW TO... IF YOU MUST!

*"An estate agent is a man who holds a key in one hand and his dick in the other. In the end somebody always gets f****d!*

Michael Rhea - Architect

NOW THAT everyone has been rudely awakened to the fact that house prices do not always go up; and now that the gullible, arrogant exploiters of human need and uninformed, greedy property agents are back to driving taxis and waiting on tables, we can all settle down sufficiently to approach the subject of home ownership on a rational basis. This is important. It is particularly so if, like most folk, you need a place to live and would rather not join the ranks of the homeless.

A house or flat is merchandise. Its value is often a personal matter. Primarily the value of a home should be based on the use to which it is put. As merchandise, like a toothbrush, washing machine or automobile, you should attempt to buy what you need, when you need it, at the best possible price on the best possible terms. That is exposing yourself to the smallest possible loss if there is a re-sale consideration. Above all you must accept that a home as a possible plan for forced-saving, or as an investment, is not a viable proposition. It is unlikely to produce anything other than cost for the owner for quite some time to come. Accepting reality may be painful. But it is the reality of the housing market for the remainder of this decade and well into the millennium. The evidence to support this prognosis is overwhelming. Only a fool would argue with such convincing evidence.

From what I have outlined until now on the subject of home ownership, the prospect of owning your own home may begin to seem as welcome as a fart in a space suit. I can also assure you that no matter how dismal those prospects appear right now, they will get worse. But, for a variety of reasons, this may not apply to some people. They may be confronted with even more distasteful alternatives than merely the problems associated with owning a home.

Many may be in a position where they have little choice due to a lack of mobility and the scarcity of rented accommodation in the area where they must live. Maybe you're one of those who feel if you spend one more night under the same roof as your in-laws, you'll turn whacko and qualify as a candidate for the men with white suits and butterfly nets. Maybe the thought of paying rent in perpetuity seems like a fate worse than a lifetime of penury. After all, didn't mother tell you that paying rent was throwing money down the drain, leaving you with nothing at the end? Few would ignore the wisdom of their mother. Buying a house can also leave you with less than nothing. You can end up destitute and technically bankrupt — if you have managed to avoid legal bankruptcy. But, that's a chapter that's already been written.

Purchasing a home is not such a wham-bam, terrific idea in the current economic environment; nor in the one that is likely to prevail in the years ahead. Even though business conditions may improve quite considerably, the residential housing market is going to lag behind. In most instances home owners will have nothing but a depreciating asset for a long, long time to come. If I haven't made that point by now — and you still want to buy a house — that leaves you with two options: You can start re-reading this book from the beginning; or you can run the risk of committing financial suicide by embarking on an essay into home ownership for which you are unprepared.

On the other hand, if you are prepared to accept the potential risk and liabilities of home ownership because you need to buy a home, you can begin making preparations in a realistic manner. An acquaintanceship with the various ways of reducing your potential liabilities and limiting the risk, will prove beneficial. So I will now attempt to deal with these, because if you must buy a home, there is a practical way of going about it.

As a point of departure, it is vital that you acknowledge the most important caveat of all: Housing is essentially an illiquid market. For a time it was indeed a liquid market: a seller's market. Conditions of that kind happen only infrequently; maybe once or twice each century, lasting for only a few years. The rest of the time, housing is an illiquid buyers' market. Most people know this. It is just that to judge by their actions, they continually forget the fact. If you are planning to buy your own home, then you should do so only if you intend to stay on for quite a while. If there is any chance that you may not be able to stay put, forget the idea. If you have the slightest inkling at the back of your mind that you could reduce the cost of the need to move by making a profit on your house purchase, you might just as well take the deposit and lay it on the next ten long-shot flea-bags at Newmarket. In that case, you could at least cut your losses and move on when you'd had enough. But as millions of people all over the world have discovered to their dismay you may not be able to get rid of a house when you want to: not that easily!

On the assumption you've taken this caveat on board, it's time to take the first step towards home ownership.

More money has been made by more people in property than in any other market. There have been more property millionaires and billionaires than in any other field of endeavour. There is a reason for this; though the reason may not be what you would expect. So, has property been such a popular investment because it is intrinsically a more sound form of investment than any other? I don't think so. More millionaires and billionaires may have been created through property dealings than any other form of speculative activity. But there have been more bankruptcies, banking defalcations and economic disasters as a result of property dealings than any other activity. Can we forget the likes of Donald Trump, Olympia & York and the collapse of the property lending banks during the 1970s? The last disaster, as we have already seen, nearly brought the whole of the British banking system to its knees. We have ongoing, contemporary examples in the horrendous market dislocations in Hong Kong and Japan. Threatening the financial systems of both areas, they are attributable to property, borrowing and falling values.

No one knows the most beneficial area for wealth creation. Otherwise I for one would be far too rich to be writing; and you'd be far too rich to find time for reading. Therefore, all we can hope to do is study both the creation and destruction of wealth, and watch particularly for one to turn into the other as has happened in recent years in the residential and other property markets.

No sireeee! Property investment is certainly not based on any intrinsic quality which makes it superior — or less risky — than other forms of investment. Yet there is one element of property investment that distinguishes it from other forms of investment. It makes it unique and largely responsible for its popularity as an investment medium. Property — quite simply — has become so enormously popular because it seems so easy, simple and logical. That's why!

To make a business of property investment requires surprisingly little education, no knowledge, no special expertise and no training. You have to be neither numerate nor literate. To make a future in property, you don't even have to give up sucking your thumb or playing with your crayons and colouring books. You might imagine that successful property investment involves a willingness to assume risk. I do not accept that. Frankly, the level of intellectual ability demonstrated by the majority of property market operators that I have encountered is so low that on most — if not all — occasions these numskulls don't even realise they are taking a risk.

WHAT IT TAKES

A LAWYER friend of mine once said, "In order to make big money in property, you have to be blessed with a certain degree of stupidity." Individuals with little if any formal education, with no skills of any kind and who are essentially unemployable, have made fortunes in property. Yet there is no need to be surprised. Give me a migratory fruit-picker, a man who has made a career cleaning toilets, a check-out clerk at the local supermarket, a stripper in Soho, or the simple housewife and I will prove that each has all the ability required to make or lose a fortune in property and to do so at a level equivalent to, if not superior to, the average property magnate. Many innocent and unskilled people have tried. Whereas none of them would have remotely considered any area of speculation that required a bit of expertise like investing in a business or speculating on the stockmarket.

No other business has attracted so many — who say so much and know so little — as property. What I have said applies to commercial property to a far lesser extent than residential property. Dealing in commercial property — factories, shops and offices — requires a certain amount of knowledge and expertise. Basing one's livelihood on the exploitation of human need in the residential property market requires no knowledge or special expertise at all; merely greed, and an exceptionally low level of morality. Like the Rachmans of yesteryear and others. These are the true vermin of the property market.

The residential property market has got all screwed up because the market itself attracted a lot of individuals who were all screwed up. It is an area that has attracted the cerebrally deprived and in many cases the mentally deranged. Those who might have risen to their level of incompetency in semi-critical functions like punching holes in buttons, tending goldfish, delivering magazines and other useful activities, were seconded and seduced by the quick and easy riches of the property game. It is suffice to say that when you make your first acquaintance with the many who have become self-styled property "experts" you will not have been dealing with mental giants.

The good news is that this should place the average individual — who can add and subtract and may have read a book — at a tremendous advantage when it comes to negotiating the purchase of a house.

The first step when considering the purchase of a home will be to contact a local estate agent. In dealing with this hardy breed, it is helpful to realise that you are dealing with a group who are performing a task that could be executed with equal efficiency by a chimpanzee if that chimpanzee could drive a car.

If you are determined, there is a strong chance that you will be able to arrange the purchase of a home at the best possible price on the best possible terms in spite of the distractions most people encounter when dealing with an estate agent. You must be bold. You must be intimidating; and never allow yourself to be intimidated by an empty barrel making a lot of noise.

Have you ever considered how little it takes to launch an estate agency business? I can tell you now...not a lot! In fact, all that is required is a telephone and some headed note-paper. Given the basic equipment, the would-be estate agent can get busy telephoning around to recruit his staff, who will be the selling agents.

Likely candidates are not too difficult to find. The would-be agent may have a source of friends able to find "an opening". But, if that source fails; the local job centre can probably offer a suitable candidate; although anybody who has some spare time on his or her hands can be an agent and enter the lucrative field of selling property. In many cases, the would-be estate agent need not worry about paying any wages or similar staff overheads. Property agents will frequently work on a commission-only basis.

No one has to be a rocket scientist to drive a prospective purchaser to the property the vendor is relying on the agent to unload. While the budding home-owner looks around, the agent will answer his questions and make suitably encouraging noises. So the minimum that is required of a selling agent is a neat appearance, a natural fluency, a reasonable sense of direction in the locality and a vague acquaintance with what the future owner is likely to ask about the house. Property agents normally get paid what they're worth. That is why staff overheads are lower than in other fields of endeavour. When a property agent finds himself becoming instrumental in the execution of the purchase or sale of a property, he then gets paid a lot more than most clients think he's worth; which is another facet of what makes the residential property game such a bagatelle for everyone involved. True, I have been describing the lower end of the "profession". But that is the end with which most would-be home-owners are going to be dealing. So it is better to know the worst.

A TIME WASTING EXERCISE TO AVOID

EVEN at a higher level than I have described, anyone who wants to enter the fantasy world of property broking can do so quite quickly, arranging staff and the means of communication with surprisingly little capital outlay. Once the location of the telephone has been decided upon and the requisite number of staff enrolled, it becomes a matter of building inventory. In most businesses, inventory is paid for. In the business of property peddling no payment is required.

The inventory of the back-street estate agent is displayed on the little

"Property For Sale" signs that he puts in his window: if he has a window. If he doesn't have a window, he must go all out and make a financial commitment by placing an ad in the local paper giving details of the property along with his telephone number. The manner in which an estate agent goes about forming his business, doesn't concern the prospective house buyer too much. I've created this hypothetical figure merely to demonstrate the foundations upon which the practice of property broking is frequently built in order to discourage any false confidence that the industry might inspire. Although a do-it-yourself estate agency business is unlikely to be of paramount importance to anyone looking to buy a home, the manner in which your friendly local parasite goes about accumulating those little "Property For Sale" signs, should be.

Small and newly-formed estate agencies will rarely generate the confidence a prospective vendor requires when placing his property on the market for sale. The owner is going to want a quick sale, with an established agent who appears to have the facilities which would ensure a quick sale. Although a large estate agency is unlikely to be any more effective in executing that quick sale than a small one, the established practice will have one advantage. That is direct contact with the vendors of property. Small agencies are often forced to resort to co-broking. While the small agency will still be able to accumulate a number of little "Property For Sale" signs in this way, a prospective house buyer dealing through a co-broker is placed at a disadvantage.

An amateur salesman with little experience will often fail to differentiate between a saleable property and one that is unsaleable; a workable deal from one that is unworkable. Any professional salesman knows that the worst possible way to obtain a deal is to get it from another salesman. An estate agent usually decides to pass on a property to a co-broker because the property is difficult, if not impossible, to sell. It would not be unreasonable to assume that a selling agent would have to be pretty stupid to bang his head against the wall, trying to sell a property that no one else has been able to sell. But, as you can gather, being pretty stupid is a quality that is not in short supply among those involved in the world of property peddling.

If for one reason or another, a property has been on the market for some time and no one wants to buy it, you shouldn't buy it either. It could be that the property is overpriced, owned by a vendor who is not really a serious seller. There might be a serious structural defect that you're not going to find out about until you shell out a very expensive survey fee. The property might be of a design that has an extremely limited market. There could be strings attached to the purchase that you won't find out about until you're well into the negotiations. There are a wide range of reasons why a property might be difficult, if not impossible to sell. By becoming involved in a co-brokerage arrangement, you are inviting these problems. A marketable property in a good location that is structurally sound does not need a co-broker.

A large proportion of the inventory of co-brokers will be property that's been on the market for some time, which no one wants to buy. I have observed from my own experiences that co-broking is a way of life for many people in the estate agency business. Rather than spend the time, energy and money necessary to solicit listing directly from principals, many estate agents will take the easy way out and just work on deals passed on by others. Properties that are impossible to sell get dumped on inexperienced salesmen, who in turn offer them to equally inexperienced and unsuspecting home buyers.

An estate agent who operates in this way is rarely involved in the ultimate sale of a property. As I have already implied, the average home buyer who has acquired the education and skills necessary to earn an honest living, is far more prudent and discerning than the lower grade property salesman. It would be highly imprudent of you to consider purchasing a home unless you took an active part in the negotiations.

In any pursuit in life, you are only "co-broking" if you avoid the area — the place where it all happens — choosing instead to work with counterparts whose interests may conflict with yours. The odds against reaching a satisfactory conclusion — in any type of business transaction — are pretty high. The odds shorten when the two "principals" — buyer and seller — start talking together. To try to achieve a gratifying result in the purchase of a property with an agent and a third party between you and the vendor, the only one in a position to say "yes" or "no" to your offer, borders on the masochistic.

DO-IT-YOURSELF PROPERTY VALUATION

THIS may come as a surprise. But, when purchasing a property, it is highly unlikely that you will have any reliable guide to help you determine whether you might not be paying twice what the property is worth. Many people believe that if a bank or a building society are prepared to lend them the money, then the property is worth the purchase price. This may be the case if you take out a 100% mortgage. But if you only require 50% of the purchase price, you may be paying double what the property is worth. The bank or building society is concerned only whether the property will offer sufficient security for the loan they are making. As we've seen, banks and building societies are replete with bad debts because of their poor judgement; the value of the security they were lending on being insufficient to cover the loan.

Don't for one instant expect your local friendly agent to give you any real idea of what the property you are buying might be worth. As already spelled out you are not his client. He has been taken on by the present owner. So far as he is prepared to go, he will probably tell you anything he offers you will be a "snip" and underpriced. Now I'm not suggesting that your local friendly agent says to himself, "What kind of cock and bull story can I make up to sell this property". I am prepared to believe that his intentions and motives are far more innocent. He may even try to convince himself very badly that you are getting value for money. He may often succeed in doing just that...convincing himself very badly.

In short, property valuation is not so simple as may appear. There are no hard and fast rules. There are guidelines, such as the price at which similar properties were sold in the locality. But these guidelines are less than reliable. For one thing, no two properties are ever alike, even in the same road. For another, two or three people may come along with more money than sense, willing to pay far more than properties were worth. By and large the value of the recently sold property lies in the eye of the beholder. At best, valuations are arbitrary. At worst, they are unrealistic — especially in a falling market.

Despite the vagaries associated with any attempt to put an absolute valuation on a property, certain guidelines are likely to prove useful when considering the purchase of a property. A familiarity with the basic principles should give you a lead over the prospective vendor and his agent in negotiating the final price.

To pursue the purchase of a property diligently and prudently, with knowledge and foresight can save you many thousands of pounds. But, as a matter of urgency, there is one class of property that should be ruled out from the beginning. If you consider this type of property, you will be exposing yourself to the possibility of entering a financial black-hole from which there may be no return. The type of properties I refer to are the "Handyman specials".

THE "HANDYMAN SPECIAL"

IN RECENT years, a piece of advice frequently given to home buyers was to purchase the worst property in the chosen area; fix it up, and then sell it at a substantial profit. In this way, dilapidated homes which would have been unsaleable in earlier days were gobbled up by buyers who were anxious to have a home and get in on the property boom at the same time. These properties keep being offered for sale. Known in the trade as "handyman specials", they are properties where the owners have invested their own time and effort. They now have to charge the new home buyer for the time and energy spent on the property. The greedy, glitzy 1980s witnessed a surge in such properties. Some were intended to live in. Others were intended for resale only.

Certainly, "handyman specials" were quite profitable for certain investors during the 1980s. Many might not be such a bad buy now, if offered at a realistic price. But the type of investor who has done well out of "handyman specials" would be those with experience in carpentry, plumbing, and like skills. If the vendor of a property is a professional, the work will show it was done by a professional. If the vendor is simply a do-it-yourself, it will usually look like it. That could well undermine the value of the property rather than enhance it. It could cost you thousands — on top of the purchase price — to undo the work of the handyman.

On the other hand, you might be offered a property as a potential "handyman special" on the premise that you become the handyman. Remember, if you do it yourself, it will look like you did it. If you hire skilled craftsmen to make a property habitable, it is likely that it will be a very poor financial proposition. Even if you have the skill to turn an uninhabitable property into a habitable one (or to make good a schedule of dilapidations) you must be careful. All too often "handyman specials" are grotesquely overpriced, and incorporate an estimated cost for repairs that is quite unrealistic.

While I was researching this book I was offered a property priced at £65,000. I was told that the repairs could be carried out professionally for £30,000; and upon completion of those repairs, I would be left with a property worth in the region of £125,000. One of the consultants who had been assisting me in the compilation of this manuscript was a quantity surveyor. His advice was that the work that needed to be done could not be carried out for less than £45,000. This meant the all-in cost of the property would not be £95,000 but £110,000. I also made enquiries among several local agents who knew the property. I asked for an estimate of the likely value of the property if it were in a good state of repair. The estimates ranged from £90,000 - £100,000 at the time of my enquiries. Given the downtrend in the housing market, the time taken to complete the purchase, and to complete the repairs, it became more than likely that any purchaser would be left with a property worth even less than that estimated by the local agent.

It must also be understood that if you consider purchasing a "handyman special", you are going to need a significant cash reserve. You will need the cash to begin with to pay for the repairs and the materials. Unless you are buying the property for cash, it is likely you would have to put up a bigger deposit than usual. Clearly, it would be difficult to obtain a high mortgage on a property in a poor state of repair. You might be able to finance some materials and a few other items. But when you need a new roof, boiler, complete bathrooms, stairways and kitchens, that's going to set you back thousands of pounds. Moreover, the builder is going ask for a substantial deposit up front before he will start work.

Probably one of the most dangerous minefields of all is making certain that the work is carried out in a satisfactory fashion. Here beware "cowboy" builders. In the case of a "handyman special", the work will usually be too small for one of the larger firms. You will therefore have to use a smaller firm, which is where most of the "cowboys" are employed.

Many people resort to employing an architect. You may think the architectural profession is one upon which you can rely. Forget it! Once you employ an architect, your minefield really become a no-go area. If you employ a builder directly and his work is unsatisfactory, you can refuse to pay, or make a retention in the sum due, until such time as the work is carried out satisfactorily. If you employ an architect, the situation is quite different. You will sign a "Small Building Works" contract with the architect. This document gives the architect the right to issue certificates of approval for work which could have been unsatisfactorily carried out; or which may not have been carried out at all! It has been known. Once an architect issues these certificates, you are legally obliged to pay the builder. Whether the work is satisfactory or not.

Your only recourse for unsatisfactory work which an architect has approved is to sue him. In this area, your chances of success are very slim. The architect knows this and the builder working with an architect knows this. In the first instance, you would be exposing yourself to thousands of pounds in legal costs which could amount to more than the cost of the project. You may also find yourself waiting years for the final legal outcome. In the meantime, the value of the property could be steadily falling, adding even further to your liabilities.

On many occasions, a property dealer will buy a "handyman special", in order to "make a turn", without going to the expense of repairing the property himself. By offering the property on the basis that it is a "handyman special", the seller sometimes can make a bigger profit by leaving the property in a dilapidated condition than by fixing it and selling it at a higher price. Although the price may be lower, the "mark-up" for the seller with a knowledge of the market is far higher. During the 1980s "handyman specials" actually seemed to have a value of their own among certain dealers.

The best advice I have for anyone tempted to buy a "handyman special" is to sleep on it. If you wake up in the morning and still consider buying a "handyman special", sleep on it again! Repeat the process until the self-destructive urge disappears. "Handyman specials" should be left to professionals who have enough money to renovate a property correctly and sell it at a profit. They could even live in it if they so choose.

"Handyman specials" must be avoided by anyone who wishes to minimise the potential cost of buying a home. The property market is a very sophisticated one, dominated by greedy professionals. Don't expect a "free lunch". Don't expect a bargain. What looks like a bargain can, more often than not, turn into the most costly undertaking you could ever have imagined.

DO-IT-YOURSELF PRICING

A MAJOR consideration in evaluating the viability of a property purchase is the determination of its price as opposed to its value. It may come as a shock, but the two are not the same. The price of a home is the agreed-upon number of pounds exchanged between buyer and seller. We can call this the exchange price — for lack of a more suitable term. This exchange price may be different from the property's value on the open market. It will certainly be different if offered at auction as a "forced sale". Before we go any further, let's examine a standard definition of market value. The following is one that was published in a university textbook:

"Market value, also called fair market value, is the highest price in terms of money that a property will bring if, (1) the terms are all cash to the seller; (2) the property is exposed on the open market for a reasonable length of time; (3) the buyer and the seller are fully informed as to market conditions and the uses to which the property might be put; (4) neither is under abnormal pressure to conclude a transaction and (5) the seller is capable of conveying marketable title."

Bruce Harwood, Real Estate Principles, Reston Publishing Co., Inc. 1977

It is worth considering the implications of this definition. It can be seen how the final selling price of a property may not coincide with the "market value" of the property. For example: notice that the definition specifies that the market value is the "highest price". This stipulation assumes that the seller is aware of the highest price that other buyers are willing to pay. Of course, this is an unrealistic assumption. Just as most assumptions associated with the property market are unrealistic. The requisite knowledge of a buyer represents an ideal situation. Even though the property investing community may lay claim to making a considerable effort to achieve this ideal condition, it remains only an ideal, rarely — if ever — achieved.

A failure to fulfil any of the conditions specified in the standard definition on value as presented affect the price of a property, effectively widening the gap between the selling price and the true market value. But, the most important point should be clear: the price of a property and its value are not necessarily the same.

The difference between price and market value is important to you as a home buyer. Obviously, you do not want to purchase anything that is overvalued; you're probably anxious to find a property that is undervalued in order to reduce the cost of home ownership. To achieve this objective, you must yourself attempt to determine if the price of a property is in line with its value. You're certainly not going to get much help from your friendly local agent, or from the vendor, since their interests are contrary to your own. So, you have to do a bit of valuing yourself. While it is totally impossible to determine the true value of a single property, there are three methods commonly in use for approximating value. They are: the income approach, the replacement cost method, and (the most widely used) the market-oriented technique. Replacement costs and the market-oriented method are appropriate for all buyers. The income approach, however, can be used only when the rental value of a property can be ascertained. That can be done when a property, which had previously been rented, is now being sold: or when the buyer have been offered a choice between renting and buying.

INCOME VALUATION

THE INCOME method of valuation is based on the return on capital employed that the owner of a property receives. The computations involved in capitalising the value of a property based on the income received range from the very simple to extremely sophisticated mathematical models. There is no indication whatever that the extremely sophisticated mathematical methods have been any better in determining the possible value of a property than the very simple approach. I will therefore focus on the simple approach which most home buyers can use to good effect.

An initial assessment of the value of a property based on the income approach can be computed in the following steps:

1. Determine the total amount of gross rental for the property.
2. Estimate the expected annual expenses for maintaining the property: rates, insurance, utilities, repairs, etc. An additional amount should be deducted from the gross rental to allow for periodic vacancy.
3. Subtract the expenses from the gross rental. This will give you the net operating income.
4. Compute the capitalisation rate of the property by dividing the net operating income of the property by the price. If you wish to establish the value of the property, simply divide the net operating income by what would be considered a reasonable return and you have an estimated value.

Back in the early 1960s multiple dwelling units were priced at auction in the area that would produce a 20% return. During the late 1980s, the same properties that would have produced a return of 20% on capital invested in the 1960s were producing returns of 2% to 3%. Property owners assumed that "total return" — "the sum total of income and capital gain" — would actually exceed the 20% returns of the 1960s. Rental values can often be as arbitrary as values in general.

The capitalisation rate of a property will usually run between .05 (a 5% return and .10 (a 10% return). The higher the capitalisation the better, since that represents a high income-to-price ratio. If the capitalisation rate is below 5% you probably should avoid the property. If, on the other hand, the capitalisation rate is 9% or 10%, you should give the property your serious consideration, provided other factors have been considered and are consistent with good value.

The economic approach is far from an ideal method of valuing a property. There are many inherent faults. One aspect of the income approach projects current income into the future and makes numerous assumptions about what future rates of return are likely to be in other areas. Even the best economists often miss the mark when trying to predict future conditions. The income approach to assessing the value of a property is best used to compare a prospective property with others on the market. The income approach does not necessarily give you a precise measure of true market values. The information should be used with great caution and must be interpreted only as a ball park figure. However, you need to understand the approach and the computations involved so that you can be in the picture when others discuss it.

REPLACEMENT COST VALUATION

DURING a period of rampant inflation — or even modest inflation — the replacement cost method of valuing a property is usually a more reliable and quantifiable one than the income approach. The replacement cost method involves the computation of the cost to construct a new building equivalent to the one already standing in the property in which you may be interested. The cost of constructing the home is added to the likely value of the land on which the house stands in order to determine the total replacement value of the property. The land value is determined by the market value approach. The replacement cost of a home is determined in one of three ways:

1. A quantity survey may be taken to compute all of costs for all of the necessary materials and labour. For example, the number of bricks may come to 1,594. The number of bricks will then be multiplied by the cost of each brick, which is, 17 pence. 1,594 x 17 pence = £270.98, which is the cost of the bricks. The same

calculations are made for all of the other components of the building. This is the most accurate method of replacement cost valuation, but also the most costly and time-consuming.

2. Building components in place, such as fireplaces or an installed roof, may be priced individually and added to compute the total estimate. This is generally considered the second most accurate method of establishing replacement cost.

3. An estimate can also be made more simply be determining the size of the building (either in cubic feet or square feet) and then multiply the size by the standard cost per unit foot. The cost per unit foot of a house of standard architecture can usually be established by making a telephone call to any of the building advice centres. Assuming building costs of, say, £35 per square foot, the total replacement cost of a building comprising 4,000 square feet would be £140,000.00. While this third method of computing replacement cost is usually the least accurate, it is by far the most frequently used. This is because the differences among the three replacement cost methods are often not large enough to warrant the additional time and expense required to gather all of the necessary information and making the additional computations for the two alternatives. When comparing costs per-square-foot in an effort to determine value, be sure all comparisons involve identical constructions.

There are as many faults with the replacement cost method of determining a property's value as there are in the income approach. For one thing, there is the element of profit margin. A property that is sold on the open market will involve three factors which are (1) the cost of the building; (2) the cost of the land and (3) the expected profit margin of the developer. Obviously, no builder or property developer is going to consider selling homes at cost, if he can avoid it. Yet, sometimes, the developer cannot avoid selling at cost; or even at a loss if he wants to survive. The point to be made is that profit margins vary enormously but must be added — and sometimes subtracted — from replacement cost when attempting to establish the value of a property.

The vendor of a property will also attempt to use the cost of building the property as an aid to establishing its selling price. Few vendors are acquainted with today's economic realities and will assume that the price of a property today will always exceed the cost of building the property. It may be true in the case of properties which were built 10 or 15 years ago, or in the case of properties older than that. However, it is often not the case when it comes to homes built in the past 7 or 8 years.

It will probably come as no surprise to learn that land prices have fallen. What will surprise many is the fact that material costs and the costs of construction have also fallen. It is likely that the replacement cost of a home built seven years ago is now lower than the original cost. Many vendors will find this fact of economic life a little difficult to accept. Many will refuse to accept the fact, and will therefore not sell their home until they are forced to at a sacrificial price. One reason there are so many unsold homes is the number of vendors who are either unaware of today's economic realities or simply refuse to accept them.

I must caution you again that if you want to use the replacement cost method of valuing a property it should not be used for anything more than general comparison.

THE MARKET METHOD

THE MOST common method used for the purpose of attempting to arrive at a value for a property is the market method. This method compares properties in the area that are similar to the property in which you are interested and which have recently been sold. As an accurate measure of value, this too has its limitations, since few properties are anything like identical. As a consequence, it is therefore necessary to make adjustments for significant differences in their price. The condition of repairs, number of rooms, size of rooms, amount of land, location and so forth: all can make sizeable differences in both the value of properties and their price.

Most prospective house purchasers who have previous experience in this enterprise will look at a large number of homes, comparing various aspects of different properties before taking the decision to buy. The first-time buyer should do the same. The different kinds of comparison include properties in the neighbourhood, similar properties that have recently been sold, and similar properties currently for sale.

In a comparison of other properties in the neighbourhood, as a general rule, the astute home buyer will try to make sure he is not purchasing the nicest, most expensive home on the street because the people who could ordinarily afford to buy such a home would be attracted to a more exclusive locality. Consequently, such a home will have become difficult to sell or its price will have to be reduced so much that the vendor will be reluctant to accept a realistic price.

Comparisons of properties that have been sold recently give the prospective buyer a reasonable price range for the property in the area of his choice. By comparing properties currently for sale, the home buyer can consider other possibilities. It is important to remember that every item in a comparison should be reflected in the price of a property. For example, if the home buyer is comparing two detached houses and one is located on a busy street and another is located in a more secluded area, then the busy street is probably going to reduce the value of that property in comparison. Or at least it should do! The number and size of rooms, age, amenities, location, construction, design and other factors should all be considered to determine the relative prices of the properties compared.

Do not allow your taste to become an obstacle in executing a fair value purchase. Your taste may veer to a property that might be aesthetically magnificent but extremely difficult to sell. This should be reflected in the selling price. In general, standard designs with standard floor plans, which those with opulent lifestyles might find mundane, are far easier to sell than homes which are non-standard designs and floor plan. While an eccentric design may perfectly suit one individual, that same design may turn into a white elephant for another buyer, or for the majority of buyers. One example might be something that looks like a castle in the middle of an otherwise conservative middle-class residential area. Non-standard floor plans would include such things as having access to the living area of a home through the master bedroom; the front door opening directly into the kitchen, no provision for a dining area, or mirrors on the ceilings and walls of the bedrooms. The problem with non-standard designs are: (1) they cannot be changed, except at great expense; and (2) the property might be very difficult to sell. Although the prospective home buyer should only consider a house purchase as a long-term commitment, it should be appreciated that ease of resale is a major consideration in establishing price and value.

There is an old rule of thumb in the property business: "The three most important factors in evaluating a property are location, location, location."

While this may largely be true, it's a philosophy that is highly overstated. Desirable locations for properties can differ appreciably with different objectives like aggregate resources, investment attitudes and other considerations. What could be a totally unacceptable place for a home for one person, because of its location, may turn out to be another's dream home. Also, the desirable location may change over time. The trend of values in some larger inner city areas is a perfect example of this change. I would strongly advise against paying a high premium for any property because of its location, especially if that location is in a currently fashionable area of suburbia.

Those considering the purchase of a home should be acutely aware that condition is a major factor in establishing the value of a property. Consideration of the condition of a property goes much further than mere appearance. The income method of valuation and the replacement cost method of valuation, along with the traditional market method of valuation, all assume that the properties being compared are in NGN (Nearly as good as new) condition. If this is not the case, the probable cost to achieve an NGN status must be deducted from the selling price. It should not be considered in the offer price.

Cosmetic blemishes generally can be fixed at relatively low cost. Structural problems can be serious and far more costly. Most investors shy away from properties that have severe structural damage unless considerations overwhelmingly compensate for the cost of repairs.

Other elements affecting the value of a property may not have anything at all to do with physical condition. Items such as judgements, charges and local planning are conditions that will also greatly affect the desirability of a property. You certainly don't want to buy a property that may be subject to compulsory purchase at a lower price than that which you might now be willing to pay. You also would not want to purchase a property where the local planners are considering running a super-highway through your back garden. A thorough title and local planning search are perquisites for any house purchase. Here the good solicitor is well worth his fee, and the cut-price substitute can prove extremely costly in the end.

DO-IT-YOURSELF NEGOTIATING

IN NEGOTIATING the purchase of a home and the possibility of a fully, or partially owner financed component in the transaction, it is always wise to carry out these negotiations with the vendor on a one-to-one basis, not through any agent. Once you have decided that you would like to buy a certain property and are willing to make an offer, it is time to by-pass all third parties. This should be a prerequisite for any deal.

Remember, the seller is normally the agent's client — not yours! Nor is the agent normally concerned with serving the interests of both parties. If you decide to instruct an agent of your own, remember there are a few skilful property negotiators in existence, albeit few and far between.

Most property agents are out of their depths in the field of negotiations and are only interested in a quick turnover and rapid fire commissions. This is a counter-productive attitude. But, as I mentioned, when it comes to dealing with property agents, you're most unlikely to have access to another Donald Trump. Most agents — like their clients — have yet to learn that in a falling property market it is to their own advantage, as well as that of the seller, to press for a price level which is as close as possible to the "forced sale" price. Many agents continue to promise vendors they will get prices that could never possibly be achieved in these markets. This is one reason that the residential property market is in a state of stagnation and why a vast number of properties remain on the market month after month, year after year.

Contributing to the stock of unsold properties is what I have defined as the "fantasy market". In my investigations, I have noted two tiers in the residential property market, one of which is genuine, the other of which is totally unrealistic. This two-tier market, is principally the product of the greedy owners and the inefficiency of agents who waste a great deal of their own time and that of potential buyers.

There are some individuals who have neither the need to sell their properties, nor any intention to do so. But they would be willing to sell if an offer was made which would result in an acceptable profit, such a profit is usually based on some preconception which is factored into the selling price of a property resulting in a price that bears no resemblance to the value of the property. Home owners, encouraged by agents wishing to increase their costless inventory, will leave their property on the books of these agents, sometimes for years on end. The agent will keep these properties on their books at the price asked, hoping that a sucker will come along one day. Needless to say, the "fantasy-tier" of the residential property market is one to be avoided.

If you want to buy a home at a good price on fair terms, you'll be well advised to do quite a bit of homework yourself. You cannot possibly rely on the information a property agent will provide in terms of price and value. The agent will try to obtain the highest possible price for the seller, while appearing to achieve the lowest possible price for the buyer. Unless you have Siamese twins acting for you, what is implied is not possible: unless you instruct another agent to act on your behalf. Before instructing an agent to act for you — which means paying him commission — it's wise to make discreet enquiries among those living in the area you favour to determine the price levels at which properties have been changing hands in the vicinity. Those who are employed at local building societies and banks can be a reliable source of information and assistance. You will want to make comparisons between the current prices at which properties have been changing hands and the level at which similar properties changed hands six months and a year ago.

Journalists or local newspapers can also prove a useful source. Scour the "property for sale" advertisements for those owners who are offering their properties directly, and not through an agent. If possible, ascertain the prices that have been achieved through forced sales in the area. If you have the time, go to local auctions; go to one of the mass auctions that some large societies hold. When you have collected this information, begin making comparisons with the price levels of homes offered through local property agents. Do not be surprised if suddenly enormous disparities appear. A large number of disparities will be the product of the "fantasy-tier" of the property market where sellers are only sellers at an inflated price, having put their property on offer in the hope of meeting a sucker. It's the way the game is played. You may find you prefer to play it too, rather than instruct your own agent.

You can save a great deal of time by determining the reason for the sale and the length of time the property has been on the market along with the extent to which the price of the property has been reduced since it was put on the market. **If the reason for the sale appears somewhat vague and obscure, watch it! Some properties have been on the market for a year or more, not because the owner has decided they have become surplus to his needs but he is just waiting for a sucker to come along.** These are among the big-time wasters; especially if there has been no substantial reduction in the asking price since the property was first offered. Owners who have built their own properties, or renovated properties as speculative developments are also time-wasters. If the property is a second-home, or if the owner doesn't live there while the property has been on offer for a year or more, don't expect a good deal. It's likely that the owner hasn't yet faced up to the realities of the residential property market. You certainly don't want to subsidise his dreams. Dreams can be lengthy and persuasive if not counter-balanced by more realistic motives.

The year the property was purchased by the existing owner is also likely to influence the price at which a property is offered. Any property purchased after 1989 will fall into this category, especially if there is no pressing need for the owner to sell. Many owners cannot possibly accept that they might have to take a loss on their property. They may be anxious to sell, but do not have a pressing need to sell. Such owners will be adamant in refusing to accept a price below the price they paid. As it happens, anyone who purchased a home after 1989, or during the descent in prices that followed, will have to take a loss if he is to sell his property at a realistic market price. His only option is to hold out for a buyer who — for some reason of his own — is willing to pay above the odds. Otherwise, he will not be able to sell the property at all. As usual, the length of time the property has been on the market should serve as a warning.

At the other end of the spectrum, there are a few people who have yet come to terms with the state of the housing market and it often takes a bit of time for its present nature to sink in. The average seller may point to a house down the road that was sold for such and such an amount two years ago, adding on 15% for his perception of growth and the common delusion that his house is better. Another property offered at an unrealistic price! Compounding the unrealistic price fantasy could be the fact that the property was purchased after 1986. Although prices may have peaked after 1989, the break-even level in the mid-1990s is the 1986 price figure...for now!

An owner may have a genuine need to sell, but it may take a few months for him to realise that the price he is asking is highly unlikely to attract a buyer. If a property has been on the market for a few weeks, or a month or so, and the price is at variance with what you have discovered when doing your homework, it is likely the seller will have to spend a few months coming to terms with reality. This usually dawns after about three months, after which the mark-downs begin. So don't waste your time on properties that have been on the market for less than three months with no reduction in the original asking price; not even though offers may have been made. Before beginning negotiations, it is wise to determine what unsuccessful offers have been made. The fewer the offers, the stronger your negotiating position.

Don't expect a local property agent to educate these sellers who offer their properties at unrealistic prices. He may try. Time is of the essence for him too. But, many sellers will go from agent to agent until they find one who tells them what they want to hear. There are some agents who will promise anything, just to get a few properties on their books. Many small, local agents have yet to come to terms with the true state of the market. The better ones are aware of the uncomfortable position they're in. Recommending a cut in the asking price may lose them clients. Hanging about trying to get an unrealistic price out of a buyer can just as easily lose them both credibility and money. At least it has the advantage that the battle will be won or lost in a matter of minutes, rather than weeks or months.

I've now outlined the property situations in which you are likely to have difficulties in negotiating a reasonable price that represents fair market value. There are many more, but the general principles discussed should serve as a guide for most situations. Now let's consider the situation where you're in the driving seat, and heading for your destination.

If you're a cash buyer, your best deal will always be at a property auction. Unfortunately, the number of available properties to suit your tastes and requirements is almost certain to be limited. So is the number of people able to buy for cash. Those who can, will tend to be professionals, as well-heeled as they are experienced at the game. So, doing battle in the salesroom can be a tough number.

Which brings us to the next important topic....

◆◆◆

CHAPTER TEN

CREATIVE FINANCING AND OTHER MATHEMAGICAL FEATS

"Figures don't lie, but liars sure as hell can figure."

From: *How To Lie With Statistics* by **Arthur T. Denman**

A LARGE number of factors must be taken into consideration when approaching the final stages of buying and paying for a home. The price must be in accordance with your resources and the true value of the property. If the price is beyond your ability to pay, whether in cash, institutional finance, owner finance, or a combination of all three, the proposition is a non-starter. It shouldn't even be considered. If the property is overpriced...ditto! A person who purchases an overpriced property exposes himself to serious financial loss in the future. You may say the property is a lifetime commitment. That might apply to your life, but not the life of your loved ones who could well be forced to sell at a serious loss.

When evaluating the resources at your disposal, include your time, skills, negotiating ability, money and the availability of finance. All of these will help when committed to an effort to get the best possible value in your home ownership venture. Even if a property is offered at a very low price, should it need work and the investor doesn't have the resources to repair or maintain it, then he or she should look elsewhere. On the other hand, given the right combination of resources, some properties that it might have been unwise to consider may become highly desirable.

Although you may not have the necessary skills, never overlook the value of your contacts. Good plumbers, electricians, carpenters, roofers, wholesalers and bankers can be of great assistance to you when you decide to buy or change your home. It may be possible that you can exchange your skills for theirs. Say you are a lawyer. You might provide a builder — who needs legal work — with your skills if he provides his. If you are a retailer, a similar exchange could be negotiated. You might offer to supply goods at cost, if a plumber you know also supplies his efforts at cost.

Probably the most important resource of all for anyone buying a home is money; having access to money. It is ridiculous for anyone to purchase a property that he can't afford. Too many building society agents, property agents, housebuilders and insurance consultants have been trying to convince uninformed people to purchase property they cannot afford. They have been very successful; much to the subsequent chagrin and dismay of those whom they convinced. By misusing financing methods and acting on the basis of what these salesmen presented as an attractive proposition, first-time buyers and others have placed themselves in an extremely risky and precarious position, jeopardising their financial future for years to come. While it is possible to purchase a home with a comparatively small amount of money and easy initial repayment terms, the house buyer must be careful and coldly objective in the evaluation of properties and the resources available. When it comes to the presentation of financing terms for purchasing a home, the figures won't lie. But when a liar presents these terms, he sure as hell will be adept at figuring.

RENTING MONEY

FINANCING terms include the amount and timing of payments. The terms of financing comprise such things as interest, the deposit, the downpayment, mortgage payments, second mortgage payments, third mortgage payments, rent charges, owner-financed payments, balloon payments, deferred payments, escalating payments, front-end capital payments, back-end capital payments, interest-only payments, up-front interest payments, level capital and interest payments, fixed interest payments, variable interest payments and so forth.

The method of financing should always be factored into the price of a home. Financing can involve many hidden costs. These, in the final analysis, can increase the cost of the purchases quite considerably. On the other hand, by varying the terms of a purchase, a property that might otherwise be undesirable and far too costly, could be a practical proposition given your objectives and resources.

Unless you have 100% of the purchase price of a home in cash and are willing to absorb the "opportunity cost" of putting the cash into that home, you're going to have to rent something. Either you must rent a home, or you must rent the money to buy a home. Whichever is the case, a form of rental is involved; that is something most people don't seem to appreciate.

If by paying a weekly, monthly or quarterly rent for a home you appear to be throwing money down the drain, then it must be recognised that the rent paid for money in the form of interest is going down the same drain. Not convinced? When you borrow to finance the purchase of a home, you pay for the home plus the cost of the rent paid on the money to buy that home. That takes the form of interest. If you decide to purchase a home and rent money instead of renting accommodation, it is at the end of the day, the rental cost of the money that will have gone down the drain, but you will be left with a home that is fully paid for...provided nothing goes wrong.

On the other hand, you might decide to rent accommodation, investing the money that might otherwise be used for capital repayments if you were to purchase your home. If you go down that route, the rate of return on the money you invest will serve to offset the charge for rented accommodation. At the end of the day — I am referring to the same day as the individual who buys a home with a mortgage — you may not be left with a home that is fully paid for, but you could be left with a nice chunk of cash enabling you to buy a better home or one which is more consistent with your needs at the time. If the cost of renting accommodation proved lower than the cost of renting money, you will have come out well ahead of the game.

The big question is whether in 10, 15, 20, or 30 years you would have been better off living in rented accommodation (and harbouring a nice nest egg) as opposed to having a home that is fully paid for. The answer depends on quite a large number of variables. They are extremely difficult to predict, establish and quantify. Many of these variables can be of a personal nature, due to circumstances which you might never have anticipated and could never have predetermined.

The financial variables, although difficult to project, can be ascertained and established to a more meaningful degree than your personal circumstances. One of the financial variables is the prospect for mortgage interest rates. Another is the outlook for rental values. They will often be influenced by general interest rates, but they are also influenced by availability. The most important variable of all is the outlook for the residential property market in terms of capital gain or capital attrition. If mortgage interest rates rise and you have a variable rate mortgage, rental values fall due to an increase in the availability of rented accommodation and house prices continue to fall for the better part of the next ten years and just level off after that for another five to ten years, the scenario which would have been the most beneficial is without question. If you decided to rent accommodation, saving and investing the difference between what you pay in rent and what you would have to pay on a mortgage, you will come out tens of thousands of pounds ahead...if not more! Renting money can be a far more expensive proposition than renting living accommodation. Back to that key question: is it going to be better to rent money than accommodation?

Home ownership could place you in a position where more money would have gone down the drain in interest payments and asset depreciation than if you had rented accommodation during a period of rising interest rates and falling house prices. If, during the life of the mortgage, you were unable to keep up the payments, you could then find yourself in default and possibly in the "negative equity" trap. This could leave you bankrupt, precluding the chances of buying a property again until that bankruptcy was discharged. The variables which determine whether or not you are better off renting a house or buying a house, have always existed. At no time in history has the mathematical equation relating to these variables ever given absolute assurance that owning a home was the best financial strategy that an individual could employ. The answer is clear: if you have to rent something, you must begin by considering the likely cost of both scenarios.

As is the case with many financial matters and the approach to business, investment and finance generally, conventional wisdom seeks the lowest common denominator of acumen and intellectual achievement. The simplistic answer (which is the result) is often dangerous and misleading, much to the detriment of those who act on the basis of conventional wisdom undeflected by serious thought. The conceptual approach to the residential housing market has been wrong for decades. Assume the correct conceptual approach to a problem and there is no guarantee that you will be successful. But, you will certain avoid some of the worst pitfalls. If the conceptual approach to the residential property market is wrong, you may still achieve success, but it will be by accident. The fall in property values in recent years was no accident. It was a phenomenon that the "accident" — the residential property bubble — made inescapable.

MONEY MATHEMAGIC

IF YOU are going to approach the subject of home ownership in a reasonable and astute manner, an appreciation of the time value of money — especially the present value concept — should prove highly beneficial. The basic idea is that time is worth money. Given a choice, most people would rather receive whatever money might be due to them today, than in a year from now. Receive what is due you today, and you can invest it so that it can earn interest enabling you to have more money than you now have in a year's time. That is the reason why you must pay back more money than you receive when you borrow. The difference is the interest — the price you pay for the period over which you use the money until you return it.

This is an extremely simple explanation of the definition of interest payments, which can be strung out into extravagant complexities and usually is. As most people are aware, the price of money, or the interest rates you pay, can vary enormously from time to time, and also from one lending institution to another at any given time. Many factors influence the rate of interest you have to pay on a mortgage. Some have to do with market forces; others simply have to do with greed. But that's the subject of a different book.

Let's now consider how what was devised by the usurers at the temple has evolved. Suppose, for example, you borrow £1,000 on the January 1st, 1996. You promise to pay it back on December 31st, 1996, plus 12% interest. At the end of the year you will pay back £1,120; representing the £1,000 you borrowed plus £120 (.12 x 1000) interest. The same principle holds when you have a series of monthly payments. Suppose you must pay back the £1,000 loan in 12 monthly payments. Once again, let us assume the annual interest charge is 12%; 1% per month for each of the 12 monthly payments. Your monthly payments will come to £88.85, which will total £1,066.20 (£88.85 x 12 monthly payments for the full year). The difference between the total payments you make and the amount you borrow represents the interest charged by the lender for giving you the money. It is the amount you have paid for the use of the money during the course of the year.

Now, unless reading newspaper advertisements has blunted your ability to employ deductive logic, you will have noticed something quite interesting. In both of the above cases, you borrowed the sum of £1,000 to be repaid in a year. But the total amount you paid back was not the same in both cases. In fact, if you had decided to pay back the amount you borrowed in monthly instalments, the interest charge would be about half the amount you would have to pay if you didn't pay back the sum borrowed until the end of the year. Actually by paying back part of the money each month, you did not use that part you had paid back for a full year. Consequently, you were not charged as much interest. When you borrowed £1,000 and paid it all back at the end of the year, you paid £120 interest, and when you made monthly payments, you paid only £66.20 interest.

Unless you intend to live in a gopher hole on the Kensington fringe of Hyde Park, it is most unlikely that you're going to borrow £1,000 and pay it back in a year in order to purchase your dream home. Albeit, you might require monthly payments to leave you with a bit of spare cash to construct an entrance to the hole. If you're like most folks, particularly a first-time buyer, you'll require a mortgage over 25 or 30 years that you will repay in monthly instalments. I shouldn't have to describe how iniquitous the equation could become if you paid monthly instalments but were charged interest on the basis that the sum you borrowed was outstanding for the duration of the mortgage. Before demonstrating how investors were bludgeoned into penury by this equation, let's deal with the mathemagic involved in the purchase of a house over a realistic time frame with the amount of money that might be needed to buy the house.

Let's say you're a reasonable size player and find the home of your dreams in the £125,000 price range; and you manage to secure a 100% mortgage at 14% over 30 years. To repay the sum of £125,000 over 30 years attracting an interest rate of 14% would require equal monthly instalments of £1,481.09. After you made those 360 payments of £1,481.09 per months for 30 years, your dream house would have set you back a cool £533,192.40.

If I were your friendly, local estate agent, trying to sell you a house and told you that it was almost certain that its value would quadruple over a period of 30 years, that might sound like a reasonable deal. Actually it wouldn't be such a terrific deal at all. I would be promising you only the return of what you paid, but nothing more. An investment that gives you a nil return after holding it for 30 years, is not such a terrific investment.

Because we're dealing with such long periods, the mathemagic of housing finance gets worse. Back in the days of grocery store finance and rock-and-roll banking, when former Prime Minister Margaret Thatcher was telling everybody they should go out and buy a house, mortgages repayable with an endowment policy were all the rage.

These potential financial demons seemed simple on the surface. You took out a mortgage on which you only paid interest for the life of the mortgage. You paid a monthly insurance premium for an endowment policy which would mature in the amount of the mortgage. The way the tax structure was put together at that time - to encourage home ownership, of course - you would receive tax relief on a portion of the insurance premium that you paid. You would also receive tax relief on the interest you were paying. If you took out a "with profits" endowment policy, you had additional tax relief on the additional premium that a "with profits" endowment policy attracted. In theory, the after-tax cost of the home would be far, less than if the home buyer simply paid back equal instalments of principal and interest, plus the added bonus of being insured against a terminal experience which might inhibit mortgage repayments.

This seemed to be a government giveaway because it was perceived that taxation was such a pernicious evil; and that the dream of owning a home was the inverse nightmare of a man waking up without his penis. Anyway, more people were encouraged to buy homes via this new found mathemagical miracle. The insurance industry made a fortune out of endowment policies that had been previously difficult to sell, due to the high cost of life insurance and the derisory returns on premium investment. The insurance policy peddlers along with the mortgage brokers — the latter an unknown species in the 1960s — made a fortune in commissions on these policies. The position of the individual who took out an endowment mortgage was totally unquantifiable, contrary to the benefit promised, right from the beginning.

OPTIONS AND VARIABLE

AS I mentioned previously, whether you're going to be better off buying a house or renting a place to live, involves three variables. They are the level or mortgage interest rates, the prospects for the price level of residential housing and rental values. Those are pretty formidable variables for any one to cope with. Individuals who purchased their homes with an endowment mortgage exposed themselves to a whole new set of variables. But, before dealing with the additional variables, lets look at the size of the commitment undertaken when embracing this mathemagical fiend, the endowment mortgage.

Interest payments on a £125,000 30-year mortgage where there is no reduction in capital until the end of the 30-year period attracting an interest rate of 14%, will come to £1,458.33 per month. Over a period of 30 years, the total amount paid in interest will therefore come to £524,998.80 (360 x £1,458.33). This compares with the cumulative total of interest payments of £408,192.40 which would have been the interest charges if capital repayments had been made in equal monthly payments over the 30-year period. The difference between the interest you would have to pay if capital repayments were made in equal monthly instalments over 30 years, rather than a lump sum payment over the 30-year period, amounts to £116,806.40. That is about £9,000 less than the price of the property on which you got your 100% mortgage. If you were to repay your mortgage in equal monthly instalments of capital and interest over 30-years, you end up paying for the house about three times over in interest charges. If you take out an endowment mortgage, you pay nearly four times over in interest charges. For the individual who repays equal monthly instalments of principal and interest, the problem ends there. For those involved with an endowment mortgage, it doesn't.

In addition to the interest payments you must make under the endowment plan, you must also pay a monthly insurance premium; this will accumulate sufficient principal to repay the debt. I am told that the average insurance premium on a "with profits" endowment policy for a man aged 28, maturing in the sum of £125,000 in 30 years, comes to £357 per month. At this stage it should be noted that insurance premiums can vary enormously from one company to another. The individual could end up paying appreciably more than the premium quoted, but not significantly less.

Based on the average premiums for a "with profits" endowment policy in the amount of £125,000 maturing in 30 years and taken out at the age of 28, an additional £128,520 (£357 x 360) must be added to the £524,998.80. The total sum you would have paid into the plan for your £125,000 house on which you received a 100% mortgage would therefore come to £653,518.80. This compares with £408,192.40 you would have paid under a plan involving equal payments of principal and interest over the period. It is a difference of £254,326.40.

In order to come out ahead purchasing your house under the endowment plan, you'll have to be certain that you will be entitled to tax relief in excess of the £245,326.40 that represents the additional repayments above and beyond the mortgage involving only payments of principal and interest, plus the lump sum available to you in profits that the insurer may have declared. With an endowment policy, profits are never guaranteed. According to industry sources, profits are currently averaging 60% of the sum assured. That amounts to 2% per annum.

The "with profits" element of an endowment policy is another variable that has been added to the equation. Moreover it is a variable that does not act in your favour. The variables you expose yourself to under the endowment plan are quite considerable and difficult to quantify. Can you really predict what your income is going to be over the next 30 years? If your income falls, your entitlement to tax relief will also fall. Are you certain that you won't spend part of the next 30 years without a job and without income? If you have no income for a period your tax relief entitlement will also drop. If you're a single man without dependent children, who is planning to marry a single lady without dependent children, and want to keep your full tax relief under an endowment mortgage over the next 30 years, you had better put that thing away right now. Suppose your prospective bride decides to stop work after marriage and start a family. Then, as the number of your dependants increases, your tax bracket decreases along with your tax relief entitlement.

I have used a man, aged 28, for the purpose of this illustration. As you get older, your insurance risk gets higher, a fact which is reflected in the level of your insurance premium. As you get older, you get closer to retirement, which will also have a considerable impact on your tax status. If you're aged 45 and you take out a mortgage on the endowment plan, it is likely that you will reach retirement age during the life of the mortgage and become an old age pensioner. It would be ludicrous to project the tax relief forward for a 45-year-old man in the same manner as for a 28-year-old. In order to determine whether or not you are going to obtain sufficient tax relief to justify a mortgage on an endowment plan, you really have to be fairly certain what your income is likely to be during the entire life of the mortgage. I doubt if one man in a million can make such an assessment with any useful or meaningful degree of accuracy.

I have only outlined a few of the variables which are likely to have an impact on your future tax bracket and tax relief entitlements, according to your personal circumstances. You know your personal circumstances far better than I do; and I am sure you can think of an even greater number of variables than I have presented which, due to unforeseen circumstances, could make endowment plan mortgages a highly costly and onerous undertaking. The variables inherent in the future of each and every individual amplify the risks of home ownership. The variables do not end with the various twists and turns your future may take.

There are certainly some variables inherent in the insurance contracts themselves. For example, you may not be able to transfer your insurance endowment policy to be used as security when you purchase another property. Remember, under an endowment scheme, you do not repay any of the loan until the end of the contract. If you have a contract that runs for thirty years, you have still not paid off any of the loan. You have a house with a mortgage in the same amount that you started with, and an endowment policy with a surrender value which will presumably offset the lack of capital repayment. But it may not do so.

If you wish to change your home at the end of 5, 10, 15, or 20 years, and you are unable to use this endowment policy as security for another property, you must sell your existing property to repay the loan. The proceeds of sale, may or may not be sufficient to repay the loan. The equity you might have built over the period remains in the endowment policy which you would redeem. From the equity in the policy (that would ordinarily reflect capital payments if you had been repaying capital) must be deducted the cost of the life insurance for the period during which you had held the contract. Depending on the state of the housing market and the period you had been holding the contract, the equity in the policy may or may not be sufficient to repay the balance of the outstanding mortgage. The value of the home could have fallen below the level of the mortgage. In these circumstances, everything you had paid — endowment premiums and interest charges — would have evaporated. You might still be left with an outstanding debt that you will have to repay from your own resources. If you were foolish enough to consider purchasing another home on the endowment mortgage scheme you would face even higher insurance costs. Because you will be that much older!

This brings me to another variable in the structure of the insurance contract. It involves "guaranteed" surrender values year-over-year. These can have an enormous impact on your financial circumstances; depending on the nature of the contract. Those who design endowment contracts can get up to more devices than a ten-year-old with a Meccano set. What's more they usually do.

HIDDEN COSTS

THERE are two costs in an endowment policy contract that the individual must absorb, which are not a consideration when taking a mortgage repaying equal instalments of capital and interest. These costs are rarely referred to by mortgage brokers and insurance agents, although they involve the commission the insurers pay to agents, along with the charge for the life insurance element in the contract. Both are an element in determining the "guaranteed" surrender value of the endowment policy after any given period. An agent will normally receive a commission of £2,500 on the initial sale of a £125,000 endowment policy, in small annual increments for as long as ten years. The cost of the life insurance element in the contract varies enormously. More often than not it is based on the maximum amount the insurer can get away with through actuarial jiggery pokery in the terms of the contract, while remaining competitive.

The cost of agents' commission and the amount the insurance company charges for the life insurance element in an endowment policy contract reflect in the "guaranteed" surrender value of the contract. The commission charges are usually levied at the beginning of the contract. The sum total of commission charges and life insurance charges can mean that several years may elapse before the endowment policy acquires a "guaranteed" surrender value at all. Several more years may elapse before the "guaranteed" surrender value approaches the sum total of the premiums paid into the policy.

The variable which involves the "guaranteed" surrender value of a policy can have a tremendous impact on the poor house buyer, who for some reason or another is unable to use the policy as security for another property and must sell his house in the early years after purchase. It could well turn out that after making interest payments for a few years, the premiums paid into the endowment policy have gone for nought, since the policy has no "guaranteed" surrender value. This leaves the level of the mortgage where it was when first taken out.

Up until now, I have been discussing the traditional endowment policy. In recent years, new innovations have been introduced to help insurers market their products. The most pernicious of all is the equity-linked endowment policy. Under this scenario, the "guaranteed" surrender value of the policy, which will ultimately be used to redeem the mortgage, is linked to the performance of the stockmarket. If the stockmarket performs poorly during the life of the mortgage, it is possible that there will never be a sufficient amount to redeem the mortgage.

Now for the biggest variable of all: what the Government might or might not do. As I have pointed out, there are a large number of variables in an individual's life which will determine whether or not he or she is able to achieve the optimal tax reliefs available when first taking out a mortgage linked to an endowment policy. As it happens, even though an individual's status remains such that he would ordinarily qualify for those tax reliefs during the life of the mortgage, there is no guarantee whatever that the tax reliefs will be available over such a long period. In fact, the likelihood is that they will not.

Using tax legislation to help fuel the housing boom of the 1980s was a terrific political ploy. On the one hand, the idea of home ownership appealed to an electorate with little understanding of its dark side. On the other, by encouraging home ownership among the masses, vast tracts of the electorate were immobilised, assuring the Government of a consistent regional voting pattern. **The last thing any government wants is a mobile electorate free to move from one area of the country to another at will, witnessing for itself the variations in economic activity.**

Circumstances have a way of changing. The immobilisation objective had already been achieved. The houses have been bought and the mortgages have been granted. At the same time, the British Government has been running a huge deficit, and has had to increase its tax revenues to keep the deficit under control. Who became the target for tax increases? You've guessed it! The home owners who were being rewarded so generously by way of tax benefits a few years back.

At its peak, mortgage interest relief coincided with the housing market boom of the 1980s and amounted to £8.5 billion at today's prices in revenues lost to the Government, greatly benefiting home owners. In April 1994, the blow came: mortgage interest tax relief was reduced to 20%. In April 1995, it was cut again to 15%. From the peak of £8.5 billion in the 1980s, the level of relief was scheduled to fall to under £3 billion in the 1995/1996 fiscal year. This means, in aggregate, that the tax relief granted on mortgage interest has been slashed by more than half. It also means that the very wonderful figures being quoted by insurance agents extolling the benefits of an endowment mortgage back in the 1980s, simply no longer apply.

There is an unwritten law that relates to all financial transactions which says: the number of variables should be kept to a minimum. Obviously, the greater the number of variables relating to any transaction, the greater will be the difficulties in anticipating the outcome. A home is a necessity of life. Gambling on an unquantifiable number of variables with a necessity of life does not appear to be a particularly prudent way of going about your financial planning. I really cannot think of any individual, regardless of his status, who can be certain that purchasing a home with an endowment mortgage is the best thing to do. Money talks! In the case of an endowment mortgage, it usually says "Goodbye!"

MORTGAGES A LA MODE

IN GENERAL, any form of mortgage other than the straightforward equal monthly repayments of principal with interest calculated on the regular reduction of the principal outstanding during the life of the mortgage must be treated with caution — if not suspicion. There are no free lunches in housing financing. Variations on the basic theme which may appear so attractive do not come without cost. They can subject the home owner to considerable expenditure, which might otherwise be unnecessary.

In recent years, certain lending institutions have been willing to grant what has become known as a "non-status" mortgage. In practice this has meant that the borrower would not need to produce evidence of income or credit references; might not be creditworthy; might even be an undischarged bankrupt. But, provided he or she was able to come up with a reasonable deposit on the property, a mortgage would be granted...albeit at a price. The interest charged on non-status mortgages was invariably much higher than a lending institution adopting the normal criteria would charge.

Obviously, the lender willing to grant a non-status mortgage has little interest in the future welfare of the borrower or his ability to make future repayments. Such a lender assumes the deposit paid on the property will offer a sufficient margin of equity in the event of default and foreclosure. So there will be a minimal risk of loss. Lenders of non-status mortgages rarely, if ever, consider the prospect of a fall in residential property values to the extent that we've seen. Many lenders of non-status mortgages are now in a position where the value of the property is less than the mortgage granted to individuals who offered the poorest prospect of being willing — or able — to make future repayments. Those individuals who have been granted non-status mortgages, have not only paid above the odds in interest charges. They also face a far greater risk than others of having their mortgages foreclosed if payments are late. This is due to the underlying vulnerability of the lending institution responsible for granting such a mortgage.

The non-status mortgage increases the cost of purchasing a home by introducing additional variables into the equation that house buyers would be best to avoid. If an individual does not qualify for a mortgage at the current rate of interest with one of the major, established lenders, house purchase should be postponed until the normal requirements can be met. This could be for an indefinite period. It might even be for the lifetime of that individual. If this is the message of the regular housing market, the potential house buyer would be well advised to heed that warning. Arranging housing finance on an unconventional basis through circuitous means will always be to the advantage of the lender; never to the advantage of the house buyer. It can easily lead to serious financial loss and dislocation.

Along similar lines to the non-status mortgage are mortgages seemingly designed to help the first-time buyer with little or no money to put down as a deposit. There are also mortgages which appear to assist the young house buyer by keeping the payments down in the early years when his income is low. The payments then escalate in the later years, when supposedly, his income will improve. Watch it! Especially if this generosity applies to the purchase of a new house. More often than not, 100% mortgages on a new house are based on deals between the developers and the building societies to help the developers dispose of properties that might otherwise be hard to sell; and to do so at prices that would be difficult to achieve were a 100% mortgage, or mortgage on special terms, not included in the deal.

Low, or no down-payment mortgages, in other words, are designed to exploit the ignorance and impatience of young couples anxious to buy a home and start a family so that developers can sell overpriced housing, and mortgagees can obtain an above-average return on the money they are lending. This heinous exploitation of human anxiety and the impetuosity of youth would be a criminal offence in a caring society. Unfortunately, this is not the age of the caring society. It is the age of an every-man-for-himself society, in which young people learn the hard way to be wary of Greeks — or anyone else — bearing gifts. Forewarned should be forearmed. Unfortunately, it rarely is.

Any form of mortgage payment structure other than one which entails a normal down-payment of at least 10% — preferably more — with a long-term amortization of equal monthly payments of principal and interest, needs to be examined carefully and in great detail. Such provision as balloon payments, delayed monthly payments, staggered down-payments, fixed interest mortgage, variable interest rate mortgages and so forth must be subjected to close scrutiny and comparison. **Each of these variations has a cost. That cost could be onerous.**

First, a comparison must be made between total repayments that would be made under a normal mortgage at market rates with that of the mortgage offer on "special terms". In that way, the prospective mortgagor can determine the additional costs involved and decide how far those costs are justifiable. But, even more importantly, a table must be constructed showing the year-by-year results of the "special term" mortgage. In that way, and that way alone, the house buyer can see exactly where he stands if he redeems his mortgage in one year, 3 years, 5 years, 10 years — or at any other time during the life of the mortgage.

What I have said until now really applies to the first mortgage on a property. For, there are also second mortgages, third mortgages and an intriguing device known as a rent charge. Whoever holds a first mortgage on a property has a claim over any other charges that may be levied against that property. Specifically, the first mortgage must be paid in full before any other claims on the property can be considered. This means that the lender on a second mortgage, third mortgage or rent charge, has far less security than the holder of the first mortgage — the degree of the security ranking in order of the charge.

The amount of interest charged by a lender will invariably be related to the security offered by the borrower. A second mortgage offers a lender very little security. The holder of a second mortgage can execute a foreclosure only by purchasing the first mortgage. The holder of a second mortgage is unlikely to be inhibited by the thought of throwing people out on the street; as would a major institution which lent on a first mortgage. So the individual who takes out a first and second mortgage to complete the financing of a house purchase, places himself in a highly vulnerable position.

Those who grant third mortgages and arrange rent charges are doing little more than issuing private loans, but at a far higher rate of interest than a bank would ever consider charging. I have seen documents where the borrower is committed to pay as much as 20% per month on a level balance until the charge is redeemed. This amounts to 360% per annum. It would be cheaper to borrow from your local Mafioso loan shark. Needless to say, borrowing of that kind must greatly increase the cost of purchasing a home, reducing the prospects of ever recovering the price paid for it; while increasing the risk for the borrower of losing his home.

Borrow on a first mortgage only. If you can't complete the purchase with the proceeds of the first mortgage, look for a cheaper house. If it is not possible for you to purchase a home without the aid of secondary borrowing, forget about the whole thing for the time being. You would be almost better off living on the street with the homeless. Through secondary borrowing, you could easily end-up that way.

Mortgage contracts are far from simple. They can contain provisions that are to the extreme disadvantage of the mortgagor — the borrower. There can be penalty provisions if the mortgage is redeemed in the early years. Disadvantageous terms can also apply if the repayment of the mortgage is merely accelerated over the years. Clauses which determine your ability to transfer your mortgage to someone else who may offer to purchase your property in the event of you wishing to sell, can act either to your advantage or disadvantage. It depends on the clause. There can also be penalties for late payments and special provisions for non-payment and foreclosure. There is an in-built conflict of interest between the lender and the borrower in all mortgage contracts. Sound legal advice is necessary to determine the extent to which this conflict of interest could affect you.

CREATIVE FINANCING — THEIR PRICE YOUR TERMS

THE VERY best way to buy a house is with cash. It's an unbeatable way to get the best possible value for your money; especially in a period of high interest rates. Unfortunately, this is not a practical proposition for most house buyers, particularly young couples. The majority must rely on house purchase finance. House purchase financing arrangements can be classified into two broad categories: institutional financing and what has come to be known as "creative financing". Institutional financing includes conventional mortgages from banks, building societies and insurance companies. The predominant form of creative financing is owner-financing. That is to say the owner of a property contracts with the purchaser of that property for future instalment payments to be made to the seller rather than a bank or other institution.

In effect, the seller lends the money to the buyer. The main difference for the seller is that when a buyer receives institutional financing, the seller receives the whole of the sale price from the lending institution at the time of sale. The buyer then pays the lending institution periodic instalments on the loan over a period of years. On the other hand, the seller of a property who finances the deal does not receive the total purchase price at the time of the sale. Instead, the sale price, and the interest, are received in agreed instalments. When financing has been arranged in this manner, the seller retains full title to the property until the contract is paid in full; while the buyer obtains possession of the property at the time of purchase (ie. ownership rights). The seller must repay any outstanding loans on the property before he can acquire a free and clear title to pass on to the purchaser. The amount of the loan required in both methods of financing — institutional or creative — is the price of the property less any down-payment.

Creative financing can be subject to a wide range of variations, all of which must be negotiated between buyer and seller. The extent to which either side may benefit is usually based on the level of creativity and imagination exercised by those negotiating the deal. Creative financing techniques have been a great help to buyers and sellers alike in tough property markets; the kind we're likely to see for many more years to come. Sellers will want to sell while conventional financing becomes increasingly more restrictive. This is due to the extremely sluggish reduction of the debt overhang, which shows no sign of accelerating. In the future, owner-financing methods will fill a need for both buyers and sellers by facilitating arrangements which otherwise would not be possible.

During the greedy, glitzy 1980s housing boom, many property market operators and developers devised ways of taking advantage of rising prices through the deployment of a number of configurations of the basic owner-financing contract. In all too many cases, some of the bright sparks of the property game took advantage of uninformed or unsuspecting buyers. But the situation has changed considerably. This is now a buyers', rather than a sellers' market. The potential buyer, armed with a basic knowledge of the principles involved in creative financing, will certainly have the edge on anyone restricted to the conventional financing route. In the right circumstances it might even give the buyer an advantage over someone buying for cash.

The cost of financing terms can vary enormously. There are direct costs and indirect costs. The direct cost is the "rental" paid for money in the form of interest. One of the most important indirect costs is known as "opportunity cost". The "opportunity cost" of owning a property is the difference in the rate of return that might be received if the property were rented and producing an income as opposed to what would be received were the capital employed elsewhere; as in, for example, risk-free money market instruments, Government Securities, or merely used to repay a debt. The "opportunity cost" of holding a property will often vary with the circumstances of the individual.

"Opportunity cost" is an effective tool in creative financing when negotiating owners' financing terms. For example, let's say the owner of a property has a 50% mortgage on his property on which he is paying 8% per annum, at a time when property values are falling at the rate of 4% per annum. In the case of a property worth £100,000, the owner of the property is losing £4,000 per annum in capital depreciation while mortgage interest is costing a further £4,000. If the owner were to sell that property, he would be relieved of the interest burden on that £50,000 loan. After repaying the mortgage, he could invest the remaining £50,000 in a 10-year UK Government bond which would give him an income of £4,100 per annum at current rates of return.

The "opportunity cost" to the owner is, to begin with, the £4,100 he could receive were the capital locked up in the home invested in an income-producing asset. Then there would be the £4,000 he is losing in capital depreciation, and the additional £4,000 in interest charges. For the sake of simplicity I haven't included the maintenance costs and other expenses associated with holding the property. All in all the "opportunity cost" totals £12,100 per annum. If, in these circumstances, the owner of the property were to allow a buyer to take over his mortgage and grant an interest-free loan for the remaining £50,000 — over, say, a five-year period — he would reduce his "opportunity cost" from £12,100 to nil.

When property prices are falling, as they are now — which is a phenomenon that is likely to continue — "opportunity cost" can have a debilitating effect on an individual's net assets over time. When negotiating the purchase of a property while property prices are falling, it is wise to begin by focusing on the "opportunity cost" to the vendor of an unsold property. Most vendors do not consider this element of financial depreciation for which there is no tax allowance. I have yet to come across a property agent who has ever discussed this angle with a prospective seller for the purpose of negotiating a sale.

If you decide to purchase a home for £100,000 making a £15,000 down-payment and financing the balance with a building society at 9% interest over 30 years, you would normally take out a conventional mortgage with a bank or building society. The seller would receive £100,000, that is £15,000 from you and £85,000 from the bank or building society when the transaction is completed. The distinguishing characteristic of conventional institutional financing is that the buyer makes phased payments directly to the bank or building society on an £85,000 mortgage, while the seller receives the total selling price on completion of the sale.

But, suppose you are able to contract a better deal with the seller of the property than the one you would be able to obtain through conventional means. Let's say you paid £15,000 directly to the seller of the property who owned the property free and clear and who, in order to give you an incentive to buy the property, was willing to offer you a mortgage for the balance of £85,000 at 8% over 25 years, rather than 9% over 30 years. This arrangement would fall into the category of a "contract sale".

Had the seller not owned the property free and clear, and was still paying a mortgage, the situation would have been more complex. But it would not have been intractable. As a buyer, you could assume the seller's loan; although you might not have to.

Let's say the seller still owes £45,000 on a mortgage on the property and is currently making payments of £400 a month. As a buyer, you might be willing to assume the £400 monthly payment to the institution granting the mortgage assuming that you were happy with the terms. You would then assume the £400 per month payment and the seller would be released form all further obligations on the property. You and the seller would then sign a separate contract for the remaining £40,000 which would be the balance outstanding after you had handed the £15,000 deposit directly to the seller. In addition to the £400 repayments on the sellers' mortgage, you would assume the responsibility of payments to the seller on the £40,000 mortgage repayable over 25 years at 8%.

The interest payments on the mortgage you have taken over from the seller may not be the same as the interest payments you agree with the seller on the balance outstanding once the down-payment has been made. You and the seller may negotiate an interest rate on mutually agreed terms where the interest on the amount owed the seller is well below that of the mortgage you are taking over. This is particularly so if the mortgage you are taking over is at a fixed-rate above the market rates prevailing at the time of purchase. Under this type of transaction, the initial mortgagee would have the first charge on the property, while the seller would have a second charge. Your equity would be equivalent to the down-payment that was made.

Now, let's look at an alternative to this arrangement. Suppose after making your down-payment of £15,000 either you or the seller is unwilling for you to take over the outstanding mortgage; and you contract with the seller to repay £85,000 at 8% interest over 25 years. Briefly, there has been a seller's "wrap-around contract"; with the seller still owing a mortgage on the property being sold and the buyer neither assuming nor paying off the balance of the seller's mortgage. The buyer is paying the seller for two things: the seller's equity in the property and the balance of the seller's loan. This contract between the buyer and the seller in effect covers (ie. wraps around) both the seller's loan and the equity on the property. The arrangement requires the buyer to repay the seller the whole amount outstanding on the sale price of the property; to agree interest over the specified period after the deposit has been paid. The seller remains liable for the £400 monthly payments on his mortgage; and would retain the difference between the monthly payments made by the buyer and whatever he continues to pay the initial mortgagee.

By now, I think, it is clear that creative financing can take many forms. The variations are only limited by the creative imagination of the buyers and sellers involved. Take the "balloon payment" mortgage, this is often utilised in many owner-financed contracts which can be convenient for both buyer and seller, depending on the terms. A balloon payment is any payment of principal on a loan in addition to the regular periodic payments of principal and interest. The balloon payment is applied directly to the capital outstanding and reduces the balance of the loan or mortgage.

Owners who provide financing for buyers will generally offer contracts that include balloon payments for the sole intent of receiving total payment for a property in a relatively short time. This type of contract helps achieve a two-fold objective for the seller:

1. The sale of the property is facilitated because it is a contract sale.
2. The seller receives the total proceeds of sale in a short period, often as brief as two years.

Balloon payment contracts are frequently offered when a buyer has high expectations although he may be low on cash at the time. Because the vendor is willing to sell on contract with a small down-payment, carrying the unpaid balance at a lower interest rate than with conventional financing, the seller will often assume that a buyer will be willing to pay an inflated price. The seller's objective is to achieve a quick sale at a high price by offering terms that appear easy and attractive.

To illustrate how a balloon payment might work in practice, let's assume you purchase a house for £50,000 with no down-payment; and let's say the seller agrees to carry a three-year contract with 36 monthly payments of £514.31. The payments are based upon 12% interest on a loan amortised over 30 years even though the contract calls for a total payment within three years. The three-year repayment is accomplished with a balloon payment at the end of the 36-month period. Since most of the monthly payments in the early years of a loan go to pay interest, a total of £49,383 in principal remains unpaid at the end of the contract period (three years). In order to repay the loan, £49,383 would be paid at one time in the form of a balloon payment.

Like other forms of creative owner-financed arrangements, balloon payment contracts can be negotiated to suit many different circumstances in a wide variety of ways. There have been contracts that call for balloon payments of less than a total unpaid balance. Suppose, for example, that the balloon payment were for £20,000 of the unpaid £49,383 balance. A total of £29,383 would remain unpaid at the end of the three years — payments to be negotiated. Two different arrangements can be made to pay this remaining balance:

1. You can keep the same payments (£514.31) as before and reduce the number of years left to pay. In this case it would be paid off in seven years.
2. You can reduce the monthly payments of interest and principal. In this case, if you continued to pay on a basis of 12% interest for 30 years, you would pay £306 per month for the next 27 years.

You want, by negotiating the purchase of a property on owner-financed terms, to add to the value of your purchase, not subtract from it; attractive financing terms can enhance the proposition if the price is close to fair value to begin with. If you can negotiate an owner-finance deal that places you in a position where your total repayments at the end of the day are less than would have been the case with institutional financing, you're adding to the value of your purchase of the property. If the financing terms are attractive enough, it may even be to your advantage to pay above fair value for the property, allowing the financing terms to offset the difference between the price and value, if the value is higher than the price. In other words, if your seller wants his price, you tell the seller he should accept your terms.

Unless they are very carefully negotiated, balloon payment contracts traditionally favour the seller and not the buyer. More often than not they are offered by sellers anxious to unload their properties as quickly as possible. Unsuspecting buyers often fail to realise how large those balloons might be. Many buyers will agree to balloon payments in 10, 15 or 20 years because they seem so far into the future. These buyers assume that most of the loan will be paid off by that time. This can happen if buyers fail to calculate the amount to be paid, and agree to a contract that does not specify the exact amount of the balloon, but states — rather simply, innocently and deceptively — that the "remaining unpaid balance will be due".

A balloon payment contract can turn into an open-ended commitment involving a loan on a property that is simply never repaid. Even in the case of a conventional mortgage, where interest is charged on a reducing amount of principal, most people fail to realise how much interest is being paid in the early years and how little the loan is being reduced. Suppose you borrow £75,000 for a house which is financed on a 30-year conventional mortgage attracting an interest rate of say, 14%. Your monthly payments will work out at £888.65. After making payments for 20 years involving 240 payments of £888.65 each for a total of £213,276 you would still have only repaid 24% of the principal outstanding and would still owe £57,234. **You don't have to be a mathematical genius to understand how financially treacherous balloon payment financing can be.**

So be extremely wary, because balloon payment mortgages are now being incorporated on both owner-financed and institutionally financed transactions. Insurance companies and mortgage brokers have discovered that by offering balloon payment mortgages they are able to seduce an even greater number of people with inadequate resources who shouldn't be purchasing a home to start with. There are not many occasions where balloon payment financing offered by a mortgagee or a vendor will act to the advantage of the house buyer. In some circumstances buyers may have a guaranteed income source at some future time. When this is the case, the initial small monthly payments may allow the buyers to acquire a property which might not otherwise be possible, with the assurance that they will be able to afford the balloon payments when they become due.

Unfortunately, in many cases, the expectation of being able to meet balloon payments when they become due represents the triumph of hope over reason, which is all too common in far too many cases of property transactions involving inexperienced buyers. Buyers should simply avoid balloon payment financing unless they are assured beyond any doubt that adequate resources will be available at the time balloon payments are due. In most instances, planning that far into the future is simply not a practical proposition.

A buyer who enters the area of creative financing and attempts to negotiate an owner-financed purchase of a property, creates a long-term business relationship with the owner of that property. If the benefits of the arrangement are too lopsided in favour of one of the parties, the other's financial risk may jeopardise both of them. The primary goal of buyer and seller alike should be an exchange that is equally fair to both parties.

The value of an owner-financing contract must be quantified. There are cases where a property might be offered for sale at one price if cash is paid and another if it is owner-financed. I know of one such case where a house was being offered at £90,000 under an owner-financed contract with a 20% discount for cash. Depending on the situation the buyer would contract to purchase the property at either £72,000 or £90,000. If the value of the property was £80,000, then a £90,000 purchase price wouldn't look so good; the £72,000 purchase price would look a lot better.

You must remember that regardless of how a transaction is presented, there is only one value for the property, that is the amount of cash a seller is willing to accept at the date of sale in full exchange for the property. If an owner is willing to finance a property but offers a discount for cash, the difference between the two prices often represents a charge the owner is making for financing the property. That might well be in addition to the normal interest that would be asked under the financing agreement, whatever that was.

In conclusion, let me say that purchasing a home is a major commitment, which can prove traumatic enough without any unnecessary hassle. That's why the sensible and reasonable seller will so handle the transaction that the buyer is — and feels — fairly treated. The reasonable buyer will want to see to it that the seller is — and feels — fairly and adequately compensated. Unhappily, in today's world of grab-it-and-run, both parties can end up feeling sore and resentful. In which case either or both of them may be damaged, though the damage may not show until later. Above all the buyer must forever protect his or her own interests — no one else is likely to do so. Except, perhaps, a good lawyer. But remember, lawyers good or bad have too much work anyway and can prove financially burdensome.

◆◆◆

CHAPTER ELEVEN

HOW TO SELL... AND WHY YOU SHOULD

"A cow wearing eyeglasses is no more unusual than a donkey with a necktie."

Woody Allen

I SWALLOWED it all: hook, line, sinker, bobbin and reel...the lot...you name it. I believed it. I believed my country was the good guy in every war in its history. I believed communists were descended from Hades and had long horns and a tail. I believed the men and women who governed a nation had the best interests of the people at heart. I believed in God's will.

I believed my pet ant had a soul. I believed the Rolling Stones were musicians. I believed that Andy Warhol was an artist. I believed that sex was a naughty thing and that sex before marriage was never to be remotely considered. When I was in the Army, I believed they were putting saltpetre in the mashed potatoes. When I got out of the Army, I believed that if I wore my hair long, grew a beard, smoked pot and wore old clothes with holes in the knees of the trousers, I would strike a blow against famine, pestilence, poverty, injustice, prejudice and ethnic persecution. I believed that all men were created equal in the eyes of the Lord. I believed in the Nation State and that one day I might become more equal than other men and make President of the United States — or at least land a good job.

I believed just about everything that everyone else believed with the exception of what my mother and father told me to believe; which was also just like everybody else! My paradigm for the world in which I lived was a near perfect stereotype of the consensus totally undeflected by thought or reason in any way whatever. I reckoned that if I questioned this belief system, I might become the only kid on the block who had to wear glasses, would be deemed a heretic and could be struck by lightning. It should come as no surprise that I also believed that buying a house and taking out a mortgage was a good idea; and that house prices would rise forever, if not even longer.

Imbued at a very early age, I continued to embrace this belief system during my youth and passed puberty. But, with the passage of time, the necessity to shave, the ability to avoid premature ejaculation, grey hair, and amyl nitrate, I began to wonder about beliefs; slowly at first, faster afterwards. I began to feel that my paradigm might be flawed, especially since all the others with whom I associated didn't really seem to be doing all that well. I decided to ignore the little voice within me saying that to nurture any contrarian thoughts would be sacrilegious; and that I might be struck by lightning. I chose to run the risk. It was around that time I stopped going to confession.

As a young stockbroker with a background in economics — the bottom line of economics deals with the way people behave in aggregate and little more — I had somewhat of an advantage. Financial markets are probably the best human laboratories man has ever devised. As an insider, exposed to the total irrationality and psychological inanities of the outsiders, I gained invaluable experience that could never have been acquired in any other way. Financial markets have a way of stripping a human being down to his bare soul. The manner in which the atmosphere of a gambling casino will distort the psyche of the players is not dissimilar. Individually, and collectively, the approach to financial markets and gambling casinos tells you a great deal about the way most people are likely to address most things in life. Attitudes and paradigms are frequently less than pragmatic.

In the case of residential housing, there's been an epidemic of psychosclerosis — hardening of the brain — that seems to have annihilated whatever reason might have existed in the brain cells devoted to that line of endeavour.

If you are confronted with the problem of selling a house, or feel you may soon be faced with this awesome task, you must, whether you like it or not, take remedial action to put those damaged brain cells into proper working order. A cold, dispassionate appraisal of the real world of residential property is essential if there is a property mess you're trying to scramble out of. While house prices do not rise in perpetuity, it is conceivable that a house may remain unsold in perpetuity unless it crumbles into dust first.

A house is an asset...I think! At least most houses were assets at the time I began writing this book. Buying or selling a house involves a financial transaction. The market for housing is a financial market and the rules that apply to all financial markets apply to residential property. Financial markets are essentially auction markets, where the end price is determined by the lowest price at which a vendor is willing to sell meets the highest price a purchaser is willing to pay for a marketable property. Obviously, this is a bit of an oversimplification since so many ramifications are involved in the residential property market. Allow me a degree of poetic licence for the purpose of illustration.

Not all buyers are serious. Not all houses are as marketable as they could be — or might have been earlier on. I can't imagine a more cruel situation than a well-meaning, but naive, individual trying to sell a house, which is difficult to market, to a non-serious buyer. Any property agent who finds himself in such a situation ends up feeling like a ping-pong ball with the would-be seller and non-serious buyer wielding the bat. If you've ever had a rough deal from an estate agent, and feel you need the occasional touch of sadism to add spice to your life, I suggest that you anonymously send the address of an unmarketable property for sale, along with the name of a non-serious buyer, to an estate agent you seriously dislike. The outcome should give you more pleasure than a leather jock-strap, high black boots and a bullwhip — if you are that way inclined.

DETERMINING AND AVOIDING NON-SERIOUS BUYERS

NEARLY all that I have outlined until now has highlighted the problems home owners and house buyers are likely to face as difficulties in the housing market intensify. I am attempting to provide insights to enable the house buyer to anticipate some of the complications that could arise, while suggesting ways to help remove some of the obstacles to a sound proposition. For sure, the seller of a house is going to be in a similar quandary, faced possibly with even greater difficulties than a buyer; especially if he urgently needs to sell. It is therefore critical to any treatise on housing to address the problems likely to confront the seller of a property proposing a course of action that might help to solve a dilemma that could otherwise become critical as the spiralling decline in house prices reaches its imminent conclusion. Be warned. Conditions in the housing market are likely to get worse before they get better.

One of the biggest problems facing the seller of a property will be the amount of time lost, heartache suffered and aggravation aroused by the preponderance of non-serious buyers. Spending time with non-serious buyers can often mean the difference between getting a desirable or an undesirable price. It could reduce the prospect of a property ever being sold. If my projections are correct, selling a home will become increasingly problematical for the remainder of this decade.

Every seller must realise — and accept the fact — that it is to the advantage of the astute buyer to look at as many properties as possible after the initial decision to purchase a property has been made. If you are a seller, you may automatically assume that your potential buyer has seen a large number of homes before he came to your home; and he is likely to see several more after he's walked away from your door. Buying a home is not a matter that any responsible individual will treat lightly; particularly in current market conditions.

Exacerbating the unavoidable problems for a seller is the fact that many "buyers" aren't really buyers at all. Any estate agent can tell you — after years of wasting time, effort and money — most people who claim to be property buyers (or buyers of any "big ticket" item for that matter) seldom, if ever, complete the transaction. If you've been to an auction of "big ticket" items, you'll find that in a full auction room, less than 10% of those present will ever make a bid for anything. The rest have nothing better to do than "window shopping". Just as sellers appear to suck estate agents into deals that only a fool would consider, estate agents are repeatedly lured into wasting a great deal of time and effort talking to "buyers" who never actually buy anything. This, I may say, is to the grave disadvantage of anyone who needs to sell his home.

How do you neutralise the non-serious buyer? Begin with a mind-set. Accept from the beginning that the introduction of someone as a buyer does not mean he or she is serious. That's your point of departure. Once you have accepted that more often than not, you, or your agent will be dealing with a non-serious buyer, your antenna will have been extended. You can now set about the task of qualifying these "buyers". Non-serious buyers tend to talk and behave in the same manner, regardless of the business they're in. In the case of a home, if a non-serious buyer is asked about his guidelines, he'll most likely say that he "has no guidelines" — that he is "interested in looking at anything". When you hear that, the amber light should begin flashing. Most serious buyers have very clear guidelines, because they know exactly what they're looking for, and how much they are willing to pay.

Whenever possible, the seller should make direct contact with the prospective "buyer" and attempt to ascertain his intentions from the buyer himself, rather than relying on the agent. Another reliable tip-off is that when the seller begins to discuss the serious aspects of the proposition (such as amenities and prices), the non-serious buyer will tend to raise questions of secondary importance; such as those pertaining to location, construction, the size of the chimney and whether he is likely to get planning permission for an outside toilet. Although a number of these questions may be reasonable and normal, it is the sequence that should concern the prospective seller. A serious buyer will not normally show his concern over secondary matters until he is satisfied with the price and has a definite interest in actually purchasing the property. Serious buyers get down to the nuts and bolts right away; they've done their homework on values in the locality and will be keen to get down to the price, rather than raise a series of secondary issues.

At this stage, you may wonder why a non-serious buyer would be willing to spend so much of his own time — and waste the time of others — over a "phantom" transaction that will never come to fruition. There are, first, the "curiosity seekers" who have a passion for looking at other peoples' homes. Curiosity seekers crop up in every business and every walk of life. To make headway in a serious undertaking such as selling a house, you must weed them out; and avoid being impressed with their wide variety of intimidating ruses and disguises.

Non-serious buyers will often feel that they have "everything to gain and nothing to lose". Even though not seriously interested in purchasing a property, they figure that it's always a good idea to know what deals are floating around. Also, there's no telling when they might accidentally run across a "steal"; a property that is so good, at a price so low, that no one can pass it up. Obviously, they are looking for a virtually non-existent needle in the haystack: since there are more than sufficient serious buyers around to snap up any properties that really are such "steal".

The non-serious buyer is the counterpart of the not-really-serious seller who will put his property on the market for far more than it's worth, hoping a super-sucker will come along. A non-serious buyer keeps on looking and hoping that he too will meet the super-sucker who's placed his property on the market for far less than its worth out of sheer desperation due to personal circumstances. The unfortunate suckers do appear from time to time; but not all that frequently. Buyers and sellers alike who are serious players should not waste time waiting for the super-sucker to appear.

Any serious buyer will want to know how long a property has been on the market; the reason for the sale and whether it might not be a forced sale. He'll want to know the number of offers that have been made on the property and the reason the previous offers were refused; the price the vendor paid for the property or the cost of building, if the property was built to order. Obviously, there are other pertinent pieces of information which can help determine whether the seller is serious, or simply on a fishing expedition, trying to get an over-inflated price.

On the other side of the divide, there will be a number of items that the vendor of a property should want to know about his prospective purchaser to make sure he is not a time-waster. This information can be compiled with the assistance of an estate agent, but will nearly always have to be augmented with a face-to-face, heart-to-heart talk between the two parties.

For example, the vendor will want to know if the would-be owner is a cash buyer or whether he will need a mortgage. If a mortgage is required, is his status such that he will be able to borrow sufficient to purchase the property at the price offered? The vendor will also want to know if the would-be buyer has a property he is trying to sell, and how far the purchase is contingent upon the sale of that property. If so, it becomes necessary to discover whether or not the would-be buyer is realistic when it comes to the sale of his existing property. If he is not, he will remain in the category of a "would-be...subject to" after wasting a considerable amount of time.

A serious buyer, if he has a property to sell, will almost certainly have all but concluded the sale of his existing property before he starts looking for another. In the case of a "first-time" buyer, or a buyer who needs a mortgage, the serious individual will have a fairly good idea of the size of mortgage he can obtain. He will only view homes within his price range; based on the mortgage he can obtain plus his deposit.

Basically, non-serious buyers fall into two categories: the type that are looking for a fantastically undervalued deal but do not really expect to find one; and the type that are utterly unrealistic. In both cases, a little interrogation and information-gathering by an astute vendor can serve to reduce the time that would otherwise be wasted.

CREATIVE FINANCING AS A SELLING TOOL

AS I have mentioned previously, offering a prospective buyer a financing package can often make all the difference in securing a successful purchase or sale. Such a package can also enable the seller to obtain a price that he might not otherwise obtain if he didn't provide a financing incentive. As discussed, there are many variations, ranging from a balloon payment financing package, where the buyer doesn't even give the seller a deposit; to a package where the seller finances a relatively small percentage of the purchase price over a comparatively short period. Creative financing in the final analysis will depend on the bargaining skills and creativity of the seller, prepared to use this particular selling aid. The keynote is "creativity" and goodwill on both sides.

In any type of property transaction, it is vitally important for the seller to check out the would-be buyer. When a seller offers a financing package as an incentive to a prospective buyer, the qualification of the buyer becomes even more important. Of all the things that can go wrong with the sale of a property, the one that can end up costing a seller the most is when a financing package is extended to an unqualified or a dishonest buyer. The residential property market is replete with a history of buyers who have taken advantage of sellers, offering to pay a high price for a property provided that a creative financing package was offered. Some of these buyers entered into such arrangements with the knowledge that the seller would have a very difficult time collecting that element of the package that he financed. Invariably the costs to the sellers have been great. Those costs represent a grave injustice. But, in most cases, the seller must share the blame; because of his over-eagerness to sell and his willingness to make a sale as "convenient" and easy as possible for the buyer. By failing to take the simple precautions that any commercial lender would consider fundamental to any credit arrangement, the seller has virtually "asked" to be robbed.

When a commercial lender or an institutional lender considers an application for credit, the first consideration will be the buyer rather than the collateral offered as a security. The first question any commercial lender will ask will be, "Can he and will he pay back?" Short of clairvoyance, this question can usually be answered in a relatively simple three-stage process:

1. Requiring the borrower to complete a credit application.
2. Conducting a commercial credit check.
3. Evaluating the information collected in the first two steps.

Certainly, even if the buyer is willing to provide this information, the seller still has no iron-clad guarantee that the amount he has financed in order to assist with the sale of his property will be repaid. Yet, by evaluating the buyer's current financial position and past credit performance, the seller has a better chance of assessing the probability or receiving contracted payments.

Initially, any seller intending to offer a financial package to expedite the sale of a property should prepare his own credit evaluation questionnaire. On the questionnaire, the buyer should be identified along with his income, assets and liabilities. Buyer identification should include the buyer's name and address, family information (such as dependants), occupation, and employer — or details of business activities if self-employed. There should be an income statement that lists wages and income from all sources. Assets should include: cash in hand, securities, personal property such as automobiles, expensive equipment like computers, sound and video apparatus and sports equipment. The asset listing should also include the personal home, any other property investment and the value of these property assets. Liabilities should be listed and include: any consumer debt, such as credit car obligations; instalment debt and automobile loans; along with any major indebtedness such as a home mortgage, mortgages on other property owned, business loans (if self-employed) and any personal loans.

There should be a notation on this credit form which the buyer signs committing him to truthfulness, while giving the seller permission to contact the various sources listed on the form in order to verify the accuracy of the information provided. The credit form should be completed by the buyer after the offer to purchase has been negotiated and agreed. The seller should include in the offer-to-purchase contract a provision that acceptance of the offer is contingent upon buyer qualification. Only after the investigations have been completed to the satisfaction of the seller, should the final contract be entered into.

The process of verifying the information which the buyer has supplied on the credit form is relatively simple. An easy method of verifying the buyer's personal information and incomes is to request a copy of the buyer's tax returns for the past three years. Current income can be verified by recent pay-slips and current statements from a stockbroker, where part of the income comes from a securities portfolio. If the buyer is self-employed, balance sheets of his company for the past three years is a normal request. It is not unusual for commercial lenders to require tax returns from employed persons and balance sheets from individuals who are self-employed.

In verifying the buyer's liabilities with creditors, it is necessary to determine the accuracy of the amount of the liability stated, the monthly payment and whether or not the buyer is up-to-date on payments. It is less important in most cases to verify the assets listed on the credit form. If the personal information on income and liabilities is correct, it is highly likely that the information relative to assets is correct... since it is less sensitive. The asset information may be less sensitive than the other data supplied, but it is quite important since it tells the seller about the ability of the buyer to manage his or her financial resources.

The credit form which the seller asks the buyer to complete should be supplemented with a credit bureau check. This can often be done through the seller's bankers, who will contact one of the credit investigation agencies such as Dun & Bradstreet. A credit bureau provides a good source of information about personal histories of persons likely to buy a property. These credit bureaux have a co-operative working relationship with others throughout the country.

The information a seller will receive from a credit bureau consists primarily of bad news. Credit bureaux generally report when people are seriously behind in their debt repayments and when legal judgements have been entered for non-payment of debt. While the information from a credit bureau may be more limited than that on the credit form, it does represent an independent source revealing how well the potential buyer honours his financial commitments. But it is not safe to use credit bureau information alone. The seller must also take into account the information provided by the buyer on the credit form.

When evaluating the result of the effort that has been made to qualify the buyer as a candidate for a creative financing package to facilitate a sale, the seller may come across certain pieces of information that fall into the category of "red flags". If this type of information appears, it would be wise for the seller to cease negotiations until the problems have been resolved. In some instances, there are problems which simply cannot be resolved. Then the seller has no option but to find another buyer, unless he is prepared to run the risk of facing considerable difficulties later on.

Among such "red flags" would be any untrue statement on the credit form. Bankruptcies and legal actions are also a serious "red flag". The worst problem arises over current or pending bankruptcies and legal actions, because the property which you have sold, and on which you have extended credit, could be entangled in a web of legal proceedings that might take months — or years — to conclude. If the seller has also to repossess the property, a severe loss and heavy costs might well be involved.

Garnishment of wages, repossession of property, foreclosures or deficiency judgements are also "red flags". Any one of these items indicates a degree of irresponsibility in meeting financial obligations which might be congenital. A history of late or delinquent accounts with other creditors is a warning to proceed with caution when engaging in any kind of financial transaction with an individual.

There are also positive factors of an anecdotal nature that will help a seller to qualify a buyer. The buyer's age is a consideration. Normally, the older the buyer, the better in terms of potential credit worthiness. Generally, a married person is a better credit risk than a single person, all things being equal. The length of time at the buyer's present address is also a guide — the longer the better. Similarly, the period of current employment (or the length of time in business when the buyer is self-employed) provides a further clue to the stability of the buyer.

Some sellers feel unable or unwilling to embark on the task of qualifying a buyer. In that case, it is often possible to hire a commercial lender to evaluate the viability of the loan and the creditworthiness of the buyer. If you are extending credit to a buyer, a commercial lender can also arrange for mortgage insurance on the payments contracted for you. In addition, a commercial lender can arrange for an appraisal of the property to establish the amount of insurance required, and to confirm the fairness of the price of the property on offer.

The way this is done is to complete the negotiations with the prospective buyer, then take the buyer's offer-to-purchase, along with the financing agreed, to a commercial lender — such as a private bank or issuer of credit. The commercial lender is then requested to complete a properly documented loan package for you; and, in some cases, actually collect the loan payments on your behalf. This is likely to cost what might seem a considerable sum. But it is better than the alternative, which could result from failing to qualify the buyer.

In the financial world, there are not many guarantees that anyone can genuinely rely on. We live in a world that offers only possibilities and probabilities, but nothing more. In qualifying a prospective purchaser, the seller is quantifying the odds for and against receiving full payment for what will have been contracted. In any financial transaction, even though the odds of success may be 100 to 1 in your favour, there always remains that "damned 1".

COMING TO TERMS WITH SALEABILITY

LET'S suppose the worst. You own a property, and want to sell it. However you have realised there are some problems, aside from the state of the housing market, that make selling difficult, if not close to impossible. Perhaps the problems existed when you bought the property, perhaps not. Perhaps you knew about them, but did not anticipate any need to sell your property; or did not appreciate the devastating effect those problems would have on trying to resell. Maybe you bought a "handyman special", intending to do it up and turn it into the palace of your dreams, but due to financial circumstances beyond your control, it is still a "handyman special". In recent years some buyers have been in such a rush to become owners that their better judgement was left behind when they finally did buy. Others, because of inexperience and a failure to recognise the responsibilities of home ownership, simply never envisaged the problems they were taking on. Whatever the reason, some previous buyers are now sellers of properties which are failing to attract a buyer as quickly as they would like and expect.

The factors which influence the relative desirability of a home in order of importance are: (1) neighbourhood, (2) specific location, (3) exterior design, (4) interior design and floor plan, and (5) structural damage to the property.

While an ugly duckling building, impossible floor plan, or structural damage can be very expensive to put right, they can be fixed. Or, at least, the effect can be minimised with some careful redecorating and/or remodelling; sometimes at very little expense. On the other hand, if a property is in an undesirable neighbourhood, like close to an airport, or if it is located across the street from an open-air disco accommodating 10,000 bikers, bordered by a 24-hour, self-service filling station on one-side, and a round-the-clock Indian take-away on the other, there isn't much you can do about it. Although a psychiatric investigation into why you bought it might be in order.

Back to the point. The point is that you can't change the address or location of property. Often, because of where a property is, you may not be able to find a ready buyer very easily, if at all. Even if the property is in a good state of repair and tastefully decorated, you may find that few, if any prospects will view your property simply because of their limited tolerance of low flying aircraft, the incessant smell of curry and onion, or a distinct prejudice against 200 decibel disco music at 3 o'clock in the morning; not to mention the petrol fumes, which people can also find disconcerting.

So, what are you going to do with that property that no one seems to want because of the neighbourhood or its specific street location? You really don't have many choices. This you must accept from the outset. Essentially, all you have to work with are three other factors, affecting the saleability of a property: condition, price, and exposure. I will assume the condition of the property is as good, if not better, than those in the surrounding area. If it's not, you're going to have to do some work on the property if you intend to sell it at all. You really have no choice. Otherwise you could be sitting with that property for a long, long time, during which it will continue to lose value.

Even if the property is in good, or even superlative condition, you will want to be certain it is priced at or below other comparable properties in the area that do not suffer the same location problems. You may take a loss... maybe a big loss. This is the real world. It happens. The quick loss is the easiest. The loss will always be less if you sell than if you don't. So, lower your price. If you realised at the time you bought it, that the property had problems, and you were able to get a really low price yourself, you may be able to carry out some decorative improvements at a low cost, set a low price, and still come out on the right side of the deal. The way the property market is now, and given my projection of the manner in which the price cycle of residential property is going to unfold over the next five to ten years, the best advice I can possibly give you is that you do whatever you have to do to encourage a quick sale. If you didn't get such a good deal when you bought the property and you find you're going to suffer a bigger loss than people in the same boat as you are, grit your teeth, bite the bullet, and move on. **The lesson you will have learned is: either consider your future house purchase as a home — and only a home — that you will live in permanently; or, if you want to be certain that a home will hold its value, or not deteriorate in price faster than similar homes, make sure you give location a suitable priority in any future transactions you get involved in.**

Now let's suppose your property is in good condition and your price is right, but you still can't sell it because no one will come and look at it; or, having looked at the Chinese takeaway one side and the self-service petrol station on the other, they refuse to go any further. This may be the toughest of all problems to solve. Even so, it is not insurmountable. You're going to have to don your thinking cap and use a bit of creativity and ingenuity. You may also have to play a long shot, where you could end up throwing good money after bad. It is certain that you will have to engage the services of your local friendly vulture, the property agent. It's a tough road to travel, but it could make the difference between ending up with a worthless asset or a saleable property. Have no doubt! Regardless of what you paid for that property, if it is unsaleable, it is worthless, valueless.

There is one situation I know of where the seller owned a flat in a building a reasonable neighbourhood, but in a poor location in that neighbourhood. To add to his problems, the flat was not purpose-built. It was a conversion in a building of flats which were not converted to a particularly high standard. Now there's a property basket case if there ever was one.

The first thing this enterprising and desperate seller did was to organise an owners' association with the others who owned flats in the same building. The object was to put together a pressure group that would compel the superior landlord to improve the communal parts of the building and bring the conversions up to an acceptable standard specification. Having done that, the same resourceful flat-owner proceeded to spend £3,000 remodelling his flat. The result was a high-quality, fashionable apartment comparable to those in the smarter areas of the city. Next, he priced the property at £1,000 less than other units in the same area without the same improvements.

The next problem was to get people to view the flat and gain exposure. His strategy was unique. He advertised in the local newspaper for a property agent, which is almost unheard of. His advertisement read as follows: Wanted — Estate Agent. I am ready to sell my flat. I need your help now. (Telephone number)

When the various agents telephoned, the owner of the flat insisted they must see the property before they decided if they wanted to act for him. He showed the property to four agents out of the seven who called. Each said how unusually attractive the flat was and what a bargain it presented. As a result of his strategy, the agents went back to their offices, telling others what a great buy the flat would be. After all, where else could anyone buy a luxury apartment for so much less than the price for a similar apartment elsewhere. What made the property even more attractive was the fact that others in the same building began carrying out similar improvements, thereby up-grading the tone of the entire complex.

Enthusiasm for the property spread among agents. By the time the seller finally chose an agent to whom he was prepared to grant exclusivity, 25 different agents had toured the property. All the responses were highly favourable, because of its condition and price; even though the property had an undesirable location. The key to this success story is exposure. Of course, there is no guarantee the strategy will work every time. But it makes sense that if you can offer a better product for significantly less money — and people know about it — you are more likely to sell than if your product is undistinguished, overpriced, and no one either knows or cares...except you!

A SOW'S EAR INTO A SILK PURSE

SINCE the area and specific location are the biggest problems of all when it comes to selling a house, I have deliberately dealt with those two first. The other three determinants of saleability; exterior design, interior design, and structural defects, are problems which can be addressed more easily. If your property has a bad interior or exterior design or is in bad condition, you have a choice — fix it, or eat it! No good will come of doing nothing at all, unless you are willing to accept a knock-down price for the property and offer it as a "handyman-special". If you do nothing at all, and still prefer not to offer your property as a "handyman special", the likely result will be that no one will buy it all.

Realistically, it is generally much wiser to repair, remodel, or cover the problem, or sell the property at a give-away price, than hold on hoping for miracle. If the problem is one of run-down condition, you probably will be able to sell the property more easily if you repair it. In fact, you are likely to minimise the loss on a property in poor condition, if you attend to relatively expensive problems, like faulty plumbing, a bad roof, or cracked or slipping foundations.

If the problem is one of exterior design, you may want to remodel. For example, some older homes do not have driveways, carports or garages. If the other houses in the area have these amenities, you will probably want to install a driveway and carport or garage, providing of course that the cost of the carport, driveway or garage is less than the likely increase in the price you will be asking for the property.

At the same time, you must estimate how the addition of these amenities will improve the marketability of the property. Even if all you are able to achieve is to recoup your costs, the addition of these amenities is still advisable if it means the difference between a quick sale and a property that just sits on the market, continuing to lose value.

How would you like a rock garden instead of a grass lawn? Rock gardens were quite fashionable a while back. "Beckman, you must have rocks in your head," you're probably saying to yourself. I haven't but a few gardens and a few heads might. Grass lawns are still the thing for most houses. Some of these rock gardens that have been strewn about do not seem to appeal to anyone other than the owners who built them. Their appearance can limit the marketability of what otherwise might have been an attractive property, one that would have been easy to sell.

I knew of a property on the Cote D'Azure in France in a very desirable location that had been up for sale for quite a while. Yet, in spite of the ideal views and superb specific location, there had been no takers, or even bidders. The house appeared almost normal in most respects, except that on four outer corners castle turrets stood high above the roof line of the house. The problem for the owner was that few people shared his idiosyncratic taste and would want to live with these turrets. The first consideration of most potential buyers would have been likely to be whether or not the turrets could be removed and the cost of doing so, which would then be added to the cost of the house. The owner of the house actually believed he had improved the property by adding these turrets and had therefore priced the property above similar houses in the area. If the owner had faced reality, he might have had a very marketable property. The turrets could have been eliminated and the little rooms at each corner used productively in various ways. But reality has never been an attribute of idiosyncratic property owners.

To many people a home represents far more than just shelter and a roof to sleep under. To many individuals a home represents a lifestyle; a place to engage in personal indulgence and delights, displaying their tastes and preferences. There are those who like farming, plants, vegetables, flowers and farm animals. There are others who like swimming, tennis, gymnastics, weightlifting, hang gliding, arts and crafts, carpentry, repairing autos, light engineering, hoarding and a wide variety of activities that they consider contribute to the lifestyle they wish to adopt. Architectural tastes run from rural thatched cottages to pre-cast cement structures that resemble a sterile clinic in the Swiss mountains. There are some people who like all the things I've mentioned, and their preferences are reflected in the style of their home and the amenities they have added.

If you happen to own a thatched cottage with two up and two down, no bathroom and an outside toilet, and if the house stands on the edge of a cliff so you can indulge in hang gliding — when you're not training horses in the dressage circle that used to be a garage it is pretty obvious that it won't be all that easy to sell. Make it really 'unique', by having a swimming pool leading onto a tennis court from which you have immediate access to a small holding, where various domestic animals frolic and fertilise the soil, then you really do have something! You are probably going to sit there waiting for the one person in 200,000 whose tastes are similar to yours. Until then, believe me, that property is going to remain totally unmarketable; regardless of what it cost to buy and add all the "special features". The really hard fact for the genuine eccentric to grasp is that a property that is not saleable, and for which no market exists, is worth nothing whatsoever. Maybe someone might buy it for the site value. But that will be out of the question if the location is all wrong. So what does the owner do? Go on day-dreaming? That can be a very costly occupation; and an utterly futile one.

In my exemplary description of a property that might be unmarketable due to the eccentricities of the owners and their somewhat unusual preferences, I jocularly created an extreme case. Yet, there are situations that do not fall very far short of that extreme. If the same elements that add to the marketability of a property and make it easy to sell are conspicuous by their absence, the property will be difficult to sell. The amount an owner can do to improve the marketability of a property in a poor neighbourhood or a poor specific location is very limited. When these are not the major problems, there are many things an owner can do towards improving the chances of getting a sale. Conditions, conformity and 'best use' are three distinct features of a property that any owner can control and adjust to varying degrees, in order to execute a more favourable and speedy sale.

"Highest and best use" is a term used to describe the most commercial and suitable use for a property, given the planning and other restrictions on the land and location. The seller who has lived in house for a time and is about to put the house on the market should give careful consideration to the "highest and best use" of the property, in the way the phrase was intended. Marketability and values will vary according to whether the property is being put to "highest and best use", exploiting to the full the commercial potential, given the neighbourhood and planning restrictions. If other houses in the neighbourhood have swimming pools, and the house offered for sale does not, simply obtaining planning permission, without building the pool, can improve the property at little expense. If the property offered for sale has three bedrooms and most of the other properties on the same road have four bedrooms, obtaining planning permission for an extension and another bedroom is also a step towards improving the marketability of the property.

At the opposite end of the spectrum, if the homes in the neighbourhood are generally on plots about 1600 square feet and the home offered for sale is on a plot double that size, it could be to the advantage of the seller to obtain planning permission for a second house; selling of the extra plot separately, or offering the combination as a residential and "development package" to the seller. Conformity is another important item that determines the marketability of a home. Conformity is the tendency for houses in one area to be similar to other houses in the same area, with comparable or identical features and uniform size. Conformity in residential property is nearly always a good thing and will have a considerable influence on saleability. A non-conforming property will almost always present a problem to its owner because it will be difficult to obtain the full value for the property. The degree of non-conformity could reduce the value proportionately. This is especially true when non-conformity is the consequence of over-improvement.

For example, if in one neighbourhood, the majority of homes have three bedrooms and two bathrooms. You might come up with the idea that you will increase the value of your property, and make it easier to sell, by adding another bath, another bedroom, a swimming pool, as well as a nursery, office, den, outside toilet and gazebo. In terms of marketability and saleability, you wouldn't be doing yourself a favour. If the typical three-up and two-down house in the neighbourhood is selling in the region of £90,000 when the "improved" house goes on the market, the typical price of other homes will hold down the added-value feature of the non-conforming home; while the addition feature could limit rather than enhance marketability. There is very little chance that you will be able to come even close to getting a full return on the value of the improvements.

Non-conforming houses are difficult to appraise because it is hard to find truly comparable houses in the same or similar neighbourhoods. A valuer will have to make "adjustments for the non-conforming house based on the "typical" house in the same area which will mean there will always be a ceiling on the appraised value that will not compensate for the gold-plated taps. However, if making improvements to the property brings it up to the standard of the others in the neighbourhood, then the expense is justifiable.

TO FIX OR NOT TO FIX?

I HAVE chosen to deal first with the more difficult problems associated with selling a home, leaving the easier tasks for last. Let's say you have a normal home whose amenities are consistent with those of the other homes in the neighbourhood, and the house is in a reasonably desirable area and with a good specific location. The next thing to deal with is the condition of the property, inside and out. The condition of a home can influence marketability to a considerable degree. Improving the condition of a home can be achieved at a comparatively low cost if a few simple guidelines are followed. To some house buyers, even minor cosmetic repairs are overwhelming and unacceptable — even though very little time and money might be involved. It is far better that the seller of the property carries out those minor cosmetic repairs before the house is put on the market. At the other extreme, among some house buyers, the need for minor repairs and cosmetic problems are sought and even welcomed. Many house seekers will look for problems, feeling they can use the defects as a lever to get the price down. In this instance, the seller certainly wants to avoid having his property fall into the "fixer-upper" category, warranting a reduction in the purchase price when no more than a bit of elbow grease and few hundred pounds could make all the difference. Before any action on home improvement is entertained, the point of departure should be cleaning.

It is astonishing how much of a face-lift a house can get with some simple cleaning. Depending on the structure and finish of the house, cleaning stone work and paint work can often nearly accomplish what might otherwise mean an expensive paint job. The results that can be achieved by simply undertaking a total cleaning blitz can add value to a house in a relatively short time and at comparatively low cost. It can also be a do-it-yourself project or a family undertaking, since no special skill or expertise is required to give a house a good clean.

Second in line to cleaning, in adding value out of all proportion to the cost, is work on the garden. A bit of pruning, digging and planting along with guidance from your local garden centre can work wonders, and probably produce a one-hundred-to-one ratio on the money spent as a function of the increase in value. I doubt if there is one prospective house buyer that doesn't love an attractive garden. The garden alone, if it's nice enough, could swing a sale. An untidy overgrown garden will have the opposite effect and could knock several thousand pounds from the value of the house. A garden in keeping with those in the rest of the neighbourhood, or maybe a tiny bit more lush, could add several thousand pounds to the value of a house at the cost of a few hundred; maybe less. Remember, when it comes to offering your house for sale, presentation is extremely important.

At the bottom line, the ultimate objective for making improvements to your home before offering it for sale, should be that you increase its saleability; and that you enjoy a reasonable return for the time and energy spent to do the work which, hopefully, will be paid by the buyer. If your property requires more than cleaning, garden maintenance, a coat of paint, some new carpet and handy work that you can do yourself, think hard before spending money on items which require expensive materials and skilled craftsmen.

There is no question that home improvements above and beyond the basics I have outlined can be a very profitable undertaking prior to selling a home for certain home owners — that is the home owner experienced in carpentry, plumbing, decorating and the like. There are many home owners who delude themselves with respect to their actual abilities. This can be dangerous when tackling home improvements prior to sale. If you are a professional, the work done on the home will look like a professional job. On the other hand, if you are a do-it-yourself handyman without training, experience or the requisite skills, the job will look like a do-it-yourself job. This is often counter-productive and can actually detract form the value and saleability of a property, costing far more to undo than the work itself.

When work is required and you do not have the necessary skills, always try to hire professionals for renovations and repairs, alterations to design and general advice. If you hire skilled craftsmen, you must be certain that what is required will be cost-effective both on a monetary and a time-value basis. If you have a property that you think is worth, say, £100,000 now, but with some renovation and design changes, could be worth more and be more saleable, you must make some careful calculations. If, for example, the changes that have been recommended are going to cost £10,000 and take six months to complete, while property values are falling at the rate of 10% per annum with saleability contracting accordingly, you will end up worse than you started if £10,000 worth of renovation only adds about £10,000 to the value of the property. It should come as no surprise that when employing professional craftsmen a good deal of the benefit to be gained is going to end up in the professional craftsman's pocket rather than yours.

OFFERING A "HANDYMAN SPECIAL"

WHEN do you draw the line and say you just can't afford to fix whatever it is? This depends on your economic circumstances and the price you feel fairly certain will be realised. Remember, in a falling property market, you are trying to minimise your losses. If you have to spend too much on repairs or improvements, you may find it would have been cheaper to have done nothing at all. Of course, this is a matter of judgement. A current rule of thumb among experienced property renovators is that if a problem costs more than about 10% of the home's value without the problem, consider it unfixable and slash the price to get rid of the property. If it is decided that you are not going to involve yourself in lengthy and expensive repairs, you can call the property a "handyman special" and emphasise "how much fun" it will be to fix it up. This may appeal to a potential buyer looking for a bargain.

The same rule of thumb applies to interior design problems that are peculiar to an individual property. When it comes to interior design problems, professional advice is usually money well spent. There are many things that can be done cheaply by experts which otherwise might seem to be unfixable. Creative interior decorators can do wonders too in drawing attention away from floor plan problems; and in some cases, they can even convert some of the problems into unique pluses. I am reminded of a home with an unbearably small bedroom and a very small closet. The owner hired an artist to paint a rainbow across the wall opposite the entry. Not one person interested in the house commented on how small the room was. Everyone commented on the beautiful rainbow. If your property has a design problem, consult a professional interior designer to determine whether the problem can be mitigated with some inexpensive design alterations rather than renovation. If this is not possible, and there are other problems too, you're back to offering your property as a "handyman special".

There are a number of instances where offering a property as a "handyman special" can be a more viable proposition than going to the time, effort and expense of redesign, decoration, reparation and renovation. Here again the seller must always think in cost-effective terms...factoring in the time element. By allowing your potential buyer to assume that you are offering the property as a "handyman special" at a bargain price — the worst house in the neighbourhood could be turned into the best house in the area with a bit of ingenuity, and do-it-yourself skills. So the seller can often find himself in a far better position than if he had got involved in decorations and repairs. "Handyman specials" actually seem to have a kind of value of their own with certain buyers, especially those with carpentry, plumbing, electrical and decorative skills...real or imagined.

A word of caution. If you are offering your property as a "handyman special" for a quick sale with financing terms as part of the package, it is imperative that you check out the buyer to a reasonable extent. When selling to an uninformed and unprepared buyer who may have delusions of grandeur about his skills in the art of building and decoration, there is the threat that the buyer will run out of money, or be hit with costs he never envisaged, leaving him unable to fulfil his contractual obligations.

What may have appeared as a certain sale at the beginning can turn into a repossession, foreclosure and the necessity of a renewed effort to sell the property. By then the work that is being done on the property may have only been partially completed; and may also not suit the taste of any new prospective buyer. The upshot is that you could find the property back in your lap again, in worse condition, and more difficult to sell than it was when you originally offered the property as a "handyman special".

If you are selling a property in a poor state of repair as a "handyman special", subject to financing that you are providing, it will be to your advantage to determine the buyer's ability to follow-through on the contract and successfully renovate the property so it is brought up to a normally habitable state, in keeping with the other properties in the area. You can be sure that if an institution were granting a mortgage on this type of property, it would seek such an assurance. If you are financing all or part of the purchase, you should seek exactly the same assurances as any institutional lender.

Perhaps with the information I have provided in this section of the book, you may be able to turn a sow's ear into a silk purse; and you may be lucky enough to see your property as the maturing ugly duckling which becomes a beautiful swan. Regardless of how you see it, I hope I have contributed in some way to help you sell your property, and make this whole difficult process a little easier. At the very least, I trust I've managed to impress on you the need to avoid either taking chances or wasting precious time.

◆◆◆

CHAPTER TWELVE

THE NEXT BOOM IN HOUSE PRICES

"Winning isn't everything, but losing isn't anything."

Groucho Marx

IT STANDS to reason that if you don't know where you are — or where you've been — you're going to have a tough time working out how to get to where you want to go. If you're travelling along the path towards wealth creation and retirement, it is more than likely that you would prefer your hard-earned savings to make a detour at the Pearly Gates of money heaven and provide for you and your family when playtime arrives. If you have too much of your savings tied up in your home or housing, at the wrong time, "playtime" could involve virtually begging from friends and relatives; while you — metaphorically — stand on the street corner, with a long white stick, tin cup and dark glasses, in the hope of supplementing your state handout. That's not such a terrific way to spend those autumn years.

In order to avoid this you have several options, depending on your present age, on whether or not you own a home and the extent to which you will be depending on the value accumulated in your home to provide for you and yours in later years. If you have a home free and clear of any debt, and intend merely to use it as a shelter, because you have already made adequate provision for your retirement, then you're likely to be in pretty good shape. What's more, the future value of your home is irrelevant. On the other hand, you may have nearly all of your assets tied up in your home which is mortgaged. Servicing that mortgage may represent such a heavy charge on your income so as to impede your accumulating sufficient assets aside from your home for you to make adequate provision for retirement. You might plan to borrow against the future value of that home to provide for your declining years; or purchase a retirement plan from the proceeds of the sale of that home. Which means you are convinced that property must rise in value over the next 10 or 15 years. If that is your plan, your best course of action could well be to invest in that long white stick, tin cup and dark glasses right now...while you can still afford them!

If you do not yet own a home, you could — if practical — postpone purchasing a home until the beginning of the next boom in housing. Housing booms are long-term affairs, lasting from 30 to 40 years or more. So if you buy at the start, even when your mortgage has been paid off, you'll still have a nice nest-egg to play with when you need it most. Your retirement could actually coincide with the peak of the next boom. Sell at the peak and switch to rented accommodation and you will have beaten the housing cycle.

Obviously, there is a contingency involved. If you're going to rent a home now, and postpone purchasing a property until the next boom in the housing market begins, you're going to have to accept the realities of the housing market as it exists at this time. Then you have to work out when the next housing boom is going to start. This will require an appreciation of the forces that determine why house prices rise and why they fall; along with a recognition of the factors that must be in place before the next residential housing boom can take place. Unfortunately, you won't get much help on that score from the various vested-interest parties involved in the residential housing market. They will be free with their advice on when you should buy a home...which is essentially anytime...all the time! Now! **It is my contention that the only helpful, impartial advice you're likely to get on when you should buy a house is right here — in these pages, OK!**

BARBARIANS AT THE GATES

ACCORDING to several newspaper reports during the early summer of 1996, house prices had started booming again in Britain. *The Sun* newspaper said it was a great time to buy your own home with some of the best mortgage deals ever, along with the benefits of tax cuts in everyone's pockets. This was said to be the view of Sue Anderson, spokeswoman for the Building Societies Association in the UK, a group that has never been known to discourage mortgage lending among its members.

It would seem that the comments of Sue Anderson and others like her, employed in a similar or allied capacity, arose as a consequence of a report from the Halifax Building Society in early May 1996. The Halifax claimed that the value of the average house in Britain had risen by 1.5% during the first three months of the year. This was immediately taken up in several quarters.

"Whether you are buying for the first time, moving, or simply looking to re-mortgage, the lower interest rate means great deals can be found", said *The Sun* newspaper on April 25th 1996. "The Nationwide Building Society's basic mortgage rate is 6.74% — the cheapest it has been since 1965. And there are other deals which offer discounts for certain periods of a guaranteed rate for a set term. It means," *The Sun* added, "that you can now buy a home for the same — or less — than you would pay in rent".

Joining Sue Anderson of the Building Societies Association and *The Sun* newspaper in their enthusiastic appraisal of the outlook for house prices was the Trustee Savings Bank. By mid-1996, it would seem, the TSB had finally solved the mystery behind the fall in house prices. It was fear of redundancy that had deterred home purchasers in previous years. Suggesting that the problem had come to pass, Alan Dodds, mortgage marketing manager of the TSB said, "There are more jobs around now and a greater feeling of security for those already employed". This gave grounds for hope that the nasty, and seemingly endless, fall in the price of UK residential property was finally over. It wasn't the first time during this decade that such hopes had been raised. It certainly won't be the last.

If you're to avoid making an anal trough of yourself in your dealings with the residential housing market, the first thing you must do is to familiarise yourself with the anatomy of bullshit. Bullshit is O.K. Everybody employs it now and then. But when too many people start doing it to you, it could become a hazard and a danger to your wealth. I'm not suggesting that all the people making these optimistic projections of the fantastic benefits of home ownership and taking out a mortgage are deliberately lying. It would be absurd to imagine people going into their offices in the morning and saying to themselves, "What cock and bull story can I invent to sell some houses or push some mortgages today?" I truly believe their motives are far more innocent. At the same time, I do genuinely feel that some of these people want very badly to convince themselves that what they claim is indeed the truth. Unfortunately, they succeed in doing just that...convincing themselves very badly.

In the years ahead, existing home owners and potential house buyers are going to be bombarded with a whole host of reasons for believing the decline in house prices to be over and a new boom about to begin. Very little of what will be offered in evidence has ever been, or ever will be, a determinant of house prices. It will, therefore, be totally irrelevant and misleading. Nevertheless, the outcome will be a seemingly endless series of false dawns in the residential property market. They will encourage people to act prematurely, much to their disadvantage and will represent a real threat to their savings.

Should you require advice on how to drive fast on drugs and not spill your drink, you might ask any one of the many individuals involved in the residential housing market; and they might come up with a comparatively constructive and practical reply. Don't expect the same if you ask them when you should buy a house, whether it's a good or bad investment, or which way house prices are likely to move.

WHEN BLACK AND WHITE ARE SKY-BLUE PINK

LET'S examine a specimen of the reasoning behind some of the so-called evidence offered as proof that we were seeing an end to the fall in house prices in mid-1996; a time when the long-term secular decline in the residential property market was still in full swing. It was intimated by one notable that the reason for the decline in house prices over the years was rooted in a fear of losing their jobs felt by many workers. Ergo! If people start to feel secure in their jobs, house prices will rise again and another boom will get underway! That sounds reasonable enough. But so do all the other arguments behind the promise of a boom in house prices. There's only one problem; that argument, like most of the others, is pediculous, pusillanimous piffle.

If job security could be guaranteed for the whole life of a 30-year mortgage, this factor would still not be a determinant of house price movements. Job security may influence individual, would-be house purchasers. But, it was never a major determinant of housing trends, or a disincentive for the buyers who were blinded by the media hype for ownership during the 1980s. The boom in the demand for non-status mortgages at the time — granted to people who were unemployed and had dubious prospects for ever becoming employed — clearly shows the extent to which a lack of job security might have been a disincentive to those who were desperate to buy a house. And why? Because they were told they should be desperate to buy a house. In most cases, during the height of the house buying boom, job security was no more a consideration than whether the house would survive for the duration of the mortgage. To understand the sequences of booms and busts you must recognise and acquiesce to the forces of unreason. There can be no rational explanation for an irrational environment.

The point to be made is that lack of job security was only a minor factor in the decline in house prices. Job security should therefore be only a minor influence on any major recovery in house prices. There is a plethora of ancillary conditions exerting a far greater influence on price levels, which will have to be in place before the next boom in residential housing can begin.

For example, the availability and cost of financing have a far greater influence on the level of house prices than job security. However, to reach a reasonably reliable outlook for the future of house prices in that context calls for a detailed and precise examination of current and prospective monetary conditions. Simplistic assessments can lead to false and costly conclusions. So let's first take a look at what were regarded as the "great deals" in mortgage financing supposedly available to prospective house buyers in Britain circa mid-1996.

At the time, the Nationwide Building Society was charging a rate of 6.74% on mortgages; described by the media as "the cheapest since 1965". "Cheap" is a relative term dealing only with comparisons based on previous experience. The nominal level of interest rates, such as the 6.74% offered by the Nationwide Building Society circa 1996, may have appeared "cheap" compared with nominal interest rates charged in the past. But that's only part of the story. Nominal interest rates can be highly misleading. "Real" interest rates are the only true measure of actual borrowing costs; and whether borrowing is a viable proposition.

"Real" interest rates deal with the prevailing level of interest charged, adjusted for the rate of inflation. Since we live in a world of inflation, all expenditure must be adjusted for inflation. When house prices were rising at the rate of 12% per annum and interest on a mortgage was 10%, financing costs were cheap, rewarding the house buyer with a 2% positive return on the money borrowed. During the one year when house prices grew at a rate of 28% per annum, with mortgage interest at 14%, the cost of home ownership was dirt cheap. It rewarded the home buyer with a 14% positive return on the money borrowed. During both these periods, rising inflation was indeed a force driving house prices upwards. When the rate of interest charged on a mortgage was adjusted for the rate of inflation, borrowers received the benefit of negative interest rates.

In mid-1996, the absolute "best-case scenario" for the growth in house prices was an annualised growth rate of 6.0%. This was based only on the first quarter's stated rise of 1.5% in house prices. This might, or might not be sustained for any appreciable period. At the time, inflation in the UK was running at an annualised rate of 2.4%. So interest rates were not negative, as was the case when inflation was rising and house prices were keeping up with inflation. Real interest rates in mid-1996 were a positive 4.34%; and there was no guarantee that house prices would not begin once more to lag the rate of inflation, falling in both nominal and real terms. At a positive rate of 4.34% in real terms, mortgage rates were certainly not cheap in mid-1996. In fact, on an historical basis, they were very expensive indeed, and likely to impede any rise in house prices.

In the residential property world, where the purveyors of housing-related services make the black and white world look sky-blue pink, real interest rates are conveniently ignored. In the real world, real interest rates should be a quintessential consideration for anyone hoping to achieve a positive rate of return on the capital payments being made. In nominal terms, mortgage rates by 1996 may have returned to where they stood back in 1965 as the newspapers claim. But it was certainly not the case in real terms. In 1965, the rate of inflation in the UK was growing at an annualised rate of 5.6%, with house prices moving higher accordingly. At 6.74%, the mortgage rate charged by the Nationwide Building Society in 1965, real interest charges worked out at 1.14%. In other words, real interest charges at 4.34% in 1996 were nearly four times what they had been in 1965. Therefore to suggest that mortgage rates in 1996 were "the cheapest since 1965", is just not true...not in real terms.

I genuinely feel for the large numbers of people about to enter the minefield of home ownership without the vaguest notion of what may be in store. In mid-1996 the presentation of the interest rate equation was only one of the half-truths likely to mislead prospective home buyers for the duration of the fall in house prices. Another was the suggestion that mortgage lenders had given up the role of money-lenders to become philanthropic organisations, designing schemes that would act to the benefit of borrowers.

In the sky-blue pink world of Santa Claus, the Easter Bunny, the Great Pumpkin and the Tooth Fairy, the good people always help each other; and provided for, live happily ever after. Meanwhile the villains are seized and sent to the dungeon. Pooh Bear chuckles and Charlie Brown smiles...sometimes. Alas, in the black and white world, there is no Pooh Bear. Charlie Brown never smiles. And there are no free lunches. What were presented as "great mortgage deals" during the rise in house prices during early 1996 (and are likely to be presented in exactly the same manner as the continuing decline in house prices unfolds) is the same old wine in new bottles.

"GOOD" MORTGAGE DEALS?

YOU CAN be absolutely certain that any mortgage deal offering a discount for a certain period, a balloon repayment schedule, a guaranteed rate for a set term, or some other form of convoluted repayment mathemagic, will be at additional cost; but will rarely, if ever, be of advantage to the borrower. Schemes such as these tend to serve the best interests of the lender. That's the real black and white world, folks! So don't complain. Just learn to accept it — especially when making a financial commitment.

A mortgage is a loan. It is not a grant unless you happen to be a Third World country or a Russian borrower. If you are not a Russian borrower, or a Third World country, you must recognise that your mortgage is a debt that has to be repaid when you promise to repay it. Your house is the security for that debt. If you don't repay it, you lose your security. That's the black and white world. I admit I am appalled by some of the marketing tactics deployed by mortgage lenders, and disgusted by some of the propaganda some mortgage lenders encourage. But I find the bleeding hearts, who condemn mortgage lenders for realising their security when this becomes necessary, even more contemptible. Mortgage lenders are in business to make a profit. Mortgage lenders are commercial institutions. They are not subsidised by the Government or taxpayers. If the mortgages granted by mortgage lenders are not repaid, the mortgage lender will go out of business. This is not good news for those who have deposited their savings with mortgage lenders; and galling for those who always meet their loan obligations.

From time to time, mortgage lenders will experience losses as a consequence of mortgage defaulters. These losses will be compounded by the existing and prospective level of negative equity suffered by the property of the offending borrower. If a mortgage lender is to make a profit, and stay in business, gross revenues — which come from interest, charges, commissions on insurance contracts and income and charges from other sources — must be sufficient to meet the costs of running the business. That includes making provision for bad debts and allowing a reasonable margin for profits.

During a period of falling house prices, lenders have no option but to call in a mortgage if default looks likely, since the negative equity element will exacerbate losses with the passage of time. In order to survive, mortgage lenders must offer deals that serve the dual purpose of increasing market share and widening margins as conditions prevailing in the housing market make profits more difficult to come by. The pressures on mortgage lenders are unlikely to be to the advantage of the borrower until such time as there is a major recovery in house prices. So long as the disintegration of the residential property market continues unabated, mortgage lenders will simply not be in a position to offer any borrower a "good deal". This, after all, would be difficult to quantify at the best of times. So individuals contemplating a mortgage in the near future must accept this as an inescapable fact of life. You might say there's no such thing as a bad orgasm or a good mortgage. It's all relative. It just has to be taken aboard.

Residential property has traditionally been the most debt-leveraged of all markets. Few people can purchase a home unless they borrow money. Few people can sell a home unless the prospective purchaser is able to borrow money. Except for the very rich, obtaining a mortgage has been integral to buying a house. The easy availability of cheap after-tax mortgages was the most important single reason that residential property prices rose faster than consumer prices from the 1960s through the 1980s. It will be a major prerequisite for the next boom in the residential property market.

Another important feature in any comparison between today's mortgage rates and those available in 1965 is tax. The tax benefits of home ownership have now been slashed. Even if real interest rates were at the same level as in 1965, after-tax costs are much higher. Those cheap after-tax mortgages that fuelled the housing boom are a thing of the past, unlikely to re-appear for quite some time, if ever. One reason is the overwhelming size of Government deficits in the UK and elsewhere. Cheap after-tax mortgages were subsidised by tax revenues. Now, and for the foreseeable future, tax revenues can no longer be used to subsidise the housing industry. Tax revenues must be used to repay deficits.

It is likely to be quite some time before financing costs and the availability of funds will be at a level conducive to generating a new boom in house prices, or even to mitigate the continuing fall in house prices. Economic activity must show a sustainable improvement, and there must be a sharp reduction in Government deficits before we see a significant after-tax reduction in financing costs.

As we approach the year 2000, the existing and prospective levels of house purchase financing costs are completely out of line with conditions even remotely conducive to a boom in house prices; or even to an end to the unrelenting decline in residential property values. Interest rates will have to fall much further and the rate of inflation begin to rise again, before we could expect the next house boom.

There are, of course, important considerations apart from financing costs which will have to be right before any boom in house prices can begin. A major consideration is the balance between the supply and demand for houses.

MORE HOUSES "AT THE MARGIN"

HOUSING market followers were up in arms in May 1996 when it was reported that house prices were rising again. One month later, in June 1996, the arms dropped. According to the Nationwide Building Society, house prices stopped rising in May of 1996 and actually fell. Specifically, the house prices index dropped from 104.6 in April to 104.5 in May. This process of fits and starts, drives and dips, should be recognised as a continuing feature of the long-term secular decline in house prices. They should not be expected to move up and down in a straight line. In fact they will fluctuate from month to month. One month's rise is meaningless. Indeed, a rise of two, three or four months in house prices will be equally meaningless. These rises will not be sustained until the forces required to build a solid foundation that would encourage the next long-term boom are in place.

On the same day that the fall in house prices was announced, it was revealed that the number of homes being repossessed in the UK were on the rise again, reversing three years of decline. In the year to March 31st 1996, 46,290 homes in Britain were repossessed compared with 45,800 in the previous year. According to a survey taken during the first quarter of 1996, 338,434 homes occupied by more than 800,000 individuals — and several thousand animals — had been repossessed since the housing slump began.

Several building societies in Britain were believed to be on the point of more than doubling their forecast for the rise in house prices to 5% before the bulge in repossessions was revealed. This had led to hopes that repossessions would begin to slow significantly, as home owners in general (and the million-plus people caught in the negative equity trap in particular) could now think of moving and paying off some, or all, of their outstanding bad debts. Once again, we find a false premise wrongly influencing the judgement of those who should really know better. To suggest that one quarter's rise in house prices would lead to a lower level of repossessions reflects a surprising ignorance of the workings of the property market.

During a rising market, the trend in house prices feeds on itself. One month's rise breeds another. When there is a dip in house prices in any one month, potential house buyers will treat the dip as an opportunity to pick up a bargain. So the fall will be brief and shallow, tending to intensify rises in subsequent months. When the secular trend in property prices is downwards, as has been the case in recent years, the phenomenon becomes inverted. Any rise in house prices brings out the sellers, who have been waiting in the wings for the slightest indication that they might be able to lighten their burden. The rise in house prices, by seducing potential sellers, adds to the floating supply of houses in the market, thus intensifying the downturn in subsequent months. When the overriding trend is down, price rises will attract sellers, rather than buyers.

It is the size of the floating supply of houses that determines the price level of all houses. A minor change in that floating supply of houses will alter the price structure of the entire market. In other words, prices are not determined by the majority of the houses in existence. Prices are determined "at the margin."

Even in a market as liquid as the stockmarket, the maximum percentage of the entire stockmarket changing hands during the course of a month is likely to be no more than 2% to 4%. This 2% to 4% can result in share price movements of 20% to 30%, up or down, depending on the balance between supply and demand within that 2% to 4% margin. The attitude predictions — or perceptions — of those who hold the remaining 96% to 98% of the shares listed on a liquid stockmarket have absolutely no influence whatsoever on the prices. These holders are neither buyers making bids for stocks, or sellers offering stock at a specific level. Instead, it is what the "margin" — that active 2% - 4% — are doing that determines the price level of these financial assets.

It is vital to understand the forces which determine price levels in the residential housing market in order to anticipate the way in which prices are likely to behave in the future. The residential housing market is an auction market just like other financial markets. The supply of houses balanced against existing demand is what finally determines the price. The marginal influence on the price is even more pronounced in residential property than most other markets. That's because of its lack of transparency and illiquidity. To ascertain the price of a commodity, stock, bond — or even an automobile — is a fairly simple matter. Usually, all you have to do is consult a newspaper. In the case of financial markets, with the number of financial programmes that have invaded the boob tube, It Is difficult to avoid being reminded of what the value of investments are likely to be...hour-by-hour. This is certainly not the case when it comes to a house.

Since each piece of property is unique, prices are estimated on the basis of "comparables" and then "at the margin". There is only one way anyone can get a vague idea — and that idea is likely to be notably vague — of what a house might be worth in a given area. That is on the basis of the last price received by the seller of another house in that area, allowing for an adjustment in the value of its amenities. For example, if a two-bedroomed house were sold down the road for £65,000, £72,000 might perhaps be the price expected for a three-bedroomed house close by. Of course, the price at which the last property in a specific area was sold might be vastly different from the original asking price of that property. It could be oceans apart from the price that a similar property in the same area might fetch in today's market.

To say that residential property is one of the most illiquid of all markets means that to find a buyer almost always requires an active and prolonged effort. When a market is slow or depressed, prices are set by those who must to sell. It is pretty rare that someone must buy. Unlike selling, buying is purely a discretionary activity. The illiquidity of housing can look like manna from heaven to home owners when house prices are rising. But when property prices turn down and begin to fall over a protracted period, it can be very distressing for sellers. Once the residential property market turns sour, the difference between what people might be asking for their houses and the prices others are willing to pay can often be light years apart; with the gap getting wider all the time. For those with negative equity who cannot repay their mortgages and are forced to sell, owning a home becomes their worst nightmare.

These forced sellers must sell "at the margin". If a mere 1.0% of home owners are having difficulty with their mortgages and are forced to sell, this will have a devastating impact on price levels. In Britain during mid-1996, about 1,000,000 people were trapped with negative equity and 211,000 borrowers were over six months behind in their mortgage payments. Then repossessions began to increase again, tipping the balance of properties for sale "at the margin.". It is perceived that repossessions will only fall significantly when house prices start to rise and people are in a position to trade down or rent, which is the traditional way of solving the repossession problem.

What is regarded by some as a self-regulating process to help ease the repossession problem, is yet another delusion among many engaged in the residential property market. Rising house prices will not have a major influence on the repossession problem in any way at all. Repossession in itself will prevent house prices from enjoying a sustainable rise. The repossession problem can be eradicated only through the self-liquidation of debt. Repossessions must rise — and continue to rise — until debt levels and potential defaulters have been brought down to a point at which neither poses a threat to the housing market as potentially a major source of supply.

Before the next boom in house prices can get underway, a great deal more blood-letting will be necessary in the residential property market. More people must lose their homes and those homes must be sold at whatever price they fetch. That is the only way the debt is going to be reduced. The same holds true for homes subject to mortgage arrears, a latent source of supply in the event of repossession. As we approach the millennium, the residential property market remains in such a condition as to preclude the start of a sustainable rise in house prices for quite some time.

THE ULTIMATE SIGNAL

HAVING collectively written-off billions of pounds of bad housing debts, mortgage lenders have tightened their loan books and will continue to do so. In my estimation, debt write-offs in the residential housing market are still far from their peak. Always present is the threat of a return of the "red-lining" system, when whole areas of the country were unable to obtain mortgages. This, of course, would deepen the existing catastrophe, bringing the housing market to a standstill. It would make most houses unsaleable, while intensifying the bad-debt problem.

No longer a threat but a stark reality is the fact that certain types of property — such as one-bedroom houses, apartments in high rise blocks, many classes of leasehold properties and properties with a limited market, generally — are no longer able to secure a mortgage. Buyers of such properties will have to pay cash. It is likely that those in a position to pay cash for this class of property would not be owner-occupiers, but investors looking for an above-average return on their capital; a return commensurate with the risks involved in the residential property market. In order to secure an adequate return, which must be in excess of borrowing costs and well above the risk-free rate of return, these potential investors will inevitably buy cheaply.

At one time, the expectation of rising residential property values in perpetuity was built into the total return projected on a residential investment property. Say the property was producing an income of 2.0% per annum, while house prices were expected to rise 15% per annum; and the risk-free rate of return was 7% per annum. Say also that costs were 12% per annum. Then the 17% total return on a residential investment property looked like a pretty good deal. So it was, until prices began falling. The fall in residential property prices has turned such calculations upside down.

To date, the residential investment property market — the market for rented accommodation — has yet to factor a fall in house prices into projected total returns on the investment. Yet this will come. The practice of projecting rising values into projected total returns is certainly not likely to appear again for quite some time. That is another item with a potential for depressing property values, in aggregate, for quite some time. **Rental values and the market for rented accommodation are likely to prove the single most important factor in determining when the fall in house prices has actually ended and the next boom in house prices is about to begin.** First, it must become cheaper to buy than to rent by a significant margin. This will come about when property investment again attracts the mega-money investor whose sole interest is in investment returns regardless of the source. It is then the seeds of the next housing boom will have been sown.

Bear in mind the mega-money operators can go the other way. And they have done. For example, Trammel Crow, the legendary property developer, aged 71 at the peak of the residential property boom circa 1985, began selling property not to a partnership (his usual outlet) but to the public. Mark Progue, another mega-money operator in shipping, hotels, conglomerates and property, also reduced his property investments near the peak of the boom. It was reported that the Rockefellers too were lightening up at the time when there was a succession of offerings of property assets by developers and syndicators who presumably knew their business. Those who were among the most successful entrepreneurs in the property market were selling — and the public were scrambling to buy!

There is always the chance that the public knows more about buying property than Messrs. Progue, Crow and the Rockefellers. But it is most improbable. For sure, that was not the case in 1985 when the change in the character of those desirous of owning property marked a turning point in the market. Property values peaked. The risk associated with property ownership ostentatiously outweighed the potential rewards for serious investors. Crow, Progue and the Rockefellers, the best people in the field, saw some great prices and took them. It was an opportunity to build liquidity in order to take advantage of bargains in the future. They had done this so many times in the past. When investors of this calibre are afforded once again the chance of undervalued, fortune-making opportunities in the residential investment property market, you can be fairly sure they'll be buying with hands, feet and eyeballs. Unfortunately, the residential housing investment market has a long way to go before reaching that idyllic state. But attracting serious investment will mark the next turning point in the market.

THE NUMBERS RACKET

ONE problem with the residential property market is that the numbers are all wrong. They've all been wrong for years. Even when they looked right, they were all wrong. They're still all wrong.

Approaching the peak of the residential property market, one firm issued a prospectus presenting a series of "growth" or inflation assumptions, along with the projected annual rates of return that they would yield. This is the standard, one-way trip to mathemagic land, provided for the purpose of separating the prospective property investor from both his right mind and his cash. Here are the numbers. If property values, rents and lease rates increase by 6% a year, then the stockholders would enjoy an average return of 13.08%. At 4% inflation, the return would be 11.42%. At 8% inflation the return would be 15.07%.

Woweeeee! And a bowl of reachey peacheys, O'Rooney! Isn't that a super-slick return? It is if you want to believe it is. But the numbers raise some very provocative questions. In the first place, is 13% to 13.25% (to take the rates of return associated with a 6% inflation assumption) enough? Do they really compensate the investor for his risks? Are the inflation assumptions realistic? Then, too, there are the secular or cosmic questions. Why should property values always increase? Why can't they decrease? As this prospectus was making the rounds everybody, except the sellers of property investments who helped put together and approve the prospectus, thought property values would rise forever. Everybody — except the sellers — was wrong. It wasn't because the numbers were wrong. It was because the conceptual approach to the presentation of those numbers was wrong.

During the mid-1980s inflation was falling. There was a hidden agenda in the presentation of numbers, pre-supposing the fall in inflation was a short-term phenomenon. The mind-set of the average property punter at the time called for rising inflation in perpetuity along with rising house prices. So the presenters of the numbers obviously saw little need to extend their calculations to include falling inflation. Anyway, if they had, the numbers would have look lousy and detracted from the rest of the fairy story. Ten years later, inflation was still falling.

Even if inflation had returned, as most thought it would a decade ago, one might still question numbers that treated inflation as having an impregnable link with property prices. This assumption was based on anecdotal evidence rather than long-term historical precedents offering a high probability of recurrence. Back in the mid-1980s, when it would seem that most property players had already positioned themselves for inflation, there was every chance that the property market might not have responded. There was every likelihood that the property markets had discounted the prevailing level of inflation, prospective levels of inflation and rising inflation into the hereafter. That is surmise. But the fact is that nobody ever had the benefit of the returns on property that were being projected circa 1985.

When unrealistic and unreliable assumptions are used as the basis for projections, the results will be unrealistic and unreliable. It was an unbiased, unfailingly realistic recognition of "the numbers", ie. investment returns, that put the Rockefellers where they are today. It certainly encouraged them, and others like them, to start bailing out of the property mirage near the peak of the last boom. Those same "numbers" will be telling them when to get back in again.

An astute property investor, whose investment principles have not been polluted by the inanities of the asset mania we've just witnessed, will judge the value of an investment property on the basis of the discounted value of the income stream it can generate. Fortunes may have been made in the property market by inarticulate individuals who could hardly read or write, much less understand the intricacies of the discounted value of an income stream. But they belong to a bygone era, and are unlikely to return for many decades, if ever. In the future, serious investors will be demanding a risk-evaluated return on property investment that covers all contingencies. Until they are able to achieve such a return, residential property market investment will be dead in the water — with the residential property market floating belly-up alongside.

The late 1960s were the last time that residential investment properties appear to have been offered at price levels representing sound value. Then the rule of thumb for rentals was 1% of market value per month. At that time, rental yields were greater than those of competitive investments, because it was perceived that the risks of investing in property were greater. And they were. As late as the 1960s, most people could still remember the debacle of the 1930s, when house prices plunged and — contrary to expectations — failed to recover. They fell in value, year after year, in a seemingly endless decline, until a house was generally considered a depreciating asset. During the 1960s investors required a large yield to compensate them for the risk. Currently, the inherent risk is not fully recognised. But it will be, as house prices continue to fall.

I am a professional investor. I have been for 40 years. I am also a professional investment adviser, and have been for a corresponding period. At the top of the housing mania, one of my clients came to me for advice. His plan was to retire abroad. He wasn't quite sure whether he should sell his London West-End property, or keep it as an investment, renting it out while he was abroad. He told me he had been offered £1,000,000 for the property. Its rental value was £2,500 per month. He was more concerned about losing the "future potential capital gain" if he sold the property than the rental. His priorities were misplaced. The low rental value was screaming at him.

I told him to take the £1,000,000, invest the proceeds, and run. Then he wouldn't have to worry about the cost of the upkeep on the property and could improve his cash flow quite substantially, given the difference between the return on the property if he rented it and the return he would receive if the proceeds were invested elsewhere. Moreover it could be invested in an area that would entail far less potential risk to capital. My client couldn't shake off the paradigm of future capital gain potential, so he didn't take my advice. He's living in France, renting his London property for £2,500 per month. The house is now worth £500,000, and on its way to £250,000, which is about its correct value, given the current rent.

Rentals are not going to rise under the influence of some mysterious force, reaching a level which will satisfy the demands of investors in the residential property market. Those requirements will be met as a consequence of a fall in capital values. Residential property had investment potential when home ownership was restricted to those who could afford a substantial deposit; and who purchased a house for its utility value, not its perceived investment value. Then unemployed, itinerant dog-walkers began purchasing houses as an investment. They obtained 100% plus mortgages which provided for legal fees, a bit of capital repayment, with some eating money left over. Prices rose and yields fell, leaving property as a very poor investment. Markets typically have the greatest capital gain potential when they offer high current yields. When the yield becomes derisory, the "grim reaper" is too close for comfort.

The number of residential properties that can now be purchased and then rented for a positive cash flow is virtually non-existent; perhaps totally non-existent. The average house rents (or earns) only about 5% per annum of its market value. This is roughly equivalent to a business selling at 20 times earnings. Only paper-pushers in the stockmarket would ever seriously consider paying 20 times earnings for a business! It would only be under very special circumstances that any serious property investor would pay 20 times earnings for a property. Were inflation, say, zero, and borrowing costs around the 1% mark, then a 5.0% return might be viable. That could well be!

What will happen is that property values will reach a level where the return becomes attractive to the same type of investor who moved out of the property market during the late 1980s. When that happens, the serious mega-money operators with an eye for value, wherever the value appears — in property or in second-hand car horns — will start to move in again. Just as the continuing slide in residential investment property values will impact on the whole of the residential property market, serious long-term investment buyers will be absorbing supply at such a rate as to lift the whole of the market in a sustained ongoing rise, similar to the last housing boom.

I expect returns to reach a level of 6% above borrowing costs plus an overshoot. Then serious investors should be attracted to the residential property market and house owners and house buyers may be able to look forward to a steady appreciation in the value of their property. Until that stage is reached, individuals must regard their home as a depreciating asset.

Among the dung heaps and other mountains of fertiliser that ne'er-do-wells keep on shovelling on to the residential property market in the hope that it will grow, is the notion that certain nouveau riche ethnic groups will begin buying and supporting the market. Maybe they'll turn it around. From time to time, the media have pedalled stories of Middle-East potentates purchasing vast tracts of property in the West End of London. The intent was presumably to convince intellectually underprivileged, prospective house buyers that foreign buying was going to mark the start of a nationwide property boom.

In recent years, similar reports have appeared, signalling the appearance of "Japanese buying". Because of the strength of the Yen (which has since weakened) the Japanese supposedly had found British property dirt cheap and were proceeding to buy all they could. Inadvertently, just as the "discovery" of the Japanese myth was beginning to penetrate, it was realised that Japanese property investors had a proclivity for making fools of themselves in the property market even when able to maintain a false market and manipulate prices. The myth imploded. The evaporation of the Japanese property buying spree was followed by reports of heavy buying of residential property by Hong Kong refugees, as well as Chinese buyers emigrating from that vast, newly-emerging country where the per capita income isn't enough to feed a Western-owned Chihuahua. The contemporary conundrum also details big...really, really big....buying from "Russian sources". I am told these Cosa Nostra-insky deals are all in unmarked bills of small denominations.

To date, this "gold-rush" of foreign buyers hasn't helped the British or any other property market, in any corner of the planet, one little bit.

It is anathema to assume that foreigners are going to know any more about a domestic property market, or be more aware of its opportunities than those who have previously made fortunes there over many, many decades. And, regardless of the ineptitude exhibited by foreign buyers of residential property, only a idiot would be dumb enough to see the weight of foreign buying as ever offsetting the force of domestic selling during a period of declining residential property values.

THE FINAL EPISODE

FEW people seem to remember that a house is no more than an expensive consumer item, like a boat, an automobile, or the latest multi-media computer outfit that performs on voice command. It can compute, calculate, play CDs and video discs, and might eventually take you into a world of Virtual Reality from which you may never wish to return. But each of these items has a service life, after which they must be scrapped, or subjected to extensive and costly renovation and repairs. In the case of a house, the only residual value will be in the land. The house itself is a wasting asset.

Of course, most people don't see it that way...yet. The mind-set of the average house owner is linked to fond, recent memories of a house as a "no-lose" investment. A feature of the final episode of the decline in house prices and a precursor to the next housing boom will be a shift in this mind-set. When buying and owning a home seems like the most foolish and hazardous undertaking anyone could possibly make — and this view is shared by all and sundry — you can be fairly certain that another housing boom is looming large.

The bad news is that it is going to take a long, long, time, for all the pieces to fall into place. So the next boom in house prices can get underway. My reckoning is that it won't happen much before the year 2005. It might take longer. People must learn to accept this. A realistic assumption of what house prices are likely to do — and what they are most unlikely to do — becomes a lot easier when the responsibility of home ownership is assumed for the right reasons.

A home is a nest. It is not a nest-egg. Residential housing has proved a good investment for only relatively brief segments of history. Any long-term perspective will show that it was on brief and sporadic occasions alone that owning a home was considered an investment, producing profits worthy of incorporation in a wealth-building programme. If you sit down and really think about it, it shouldn't make any difference at all to the house-owner-in-residence whether prices rise or fall. Whatever the direction or level of house prices in the future, the house will still be in the same place, the walls won't have moved, the roof won't have changed and the amenities will remain relatively constant. If prices rise, the home owner may get more for the house he sells, but he's going to face a corresponding price rise if he buys another house offering similar amenities. If prices fall the home owner may end up getting less than he paid for the house he is selling. But he will be able to purchase a house with similar amenities at an equivalent lower price.

When I forecast the collapse in house prices in my book *The Downwave*, I said the plunge in house prices would be "a crash that wouldn't look like a crash". When I published the details of what I considered to be the likely course of action the residential property market would follow during "the crash that wouldn't look like a crash", I emphasised that property prices would not move in a straight line downwards any more than they had risen straight upwards. I expected prices to fluctuate for the duration of the long-term decline in property values.

It was my prediction that prices would go down quite a bit, then rise a little, and then go down quite a bit again, before rising a bit once more. It would repeat this process over and over, taking prices far lower — and for much longer — than anybody believed possible. It was also my prediction that each time there was a temporary rise in house prices, the consensus would lose no time in jumping to the conclusion that the fall in house prices was over, while making every effort to spread the "good news". I cautioned that minor interruptions in the decline in house prices posed the greatest threat to potential house buyers. They might well be tempted to buy homes prematurely, on less than favourable terms, continuing to pay prices based on the perceived investment potential of residential property. I also forecast that the consensus would be wrong for a long, long time, before they suddenly got it right.

The cycle of ups and downs in the property market is far different from that of the business or stockmarket cycle. Financial markets have cycles that look like a hyperactive yo-yo with a tribe of Mexican jumping beans for innards. The property market cycle spans an entire generation, and more, from peak to trough. Property values can rise, encompassing only minor interruptions on the way, for as long as 40 to 50 years. They can also fall for as long as 20 to 25 years — and possibly longer — encountering peripheral interruptions. **The laws of physics dictate the duration of the angle of incidence will govern the angle of reflection. This law applies to the property market cycle as well as many other natural and man-made phenomena.**

My forecast for the demise of the residential housing market called for a fall in house prices in real terms rather than absolute terms at the beginning. As the trend of property values continued along the preordained cycle of financial excess, it was my subsequent proposition that prices would then begin to fall in absolute terms and continue to do so. As time passed and prices dipped lower, I feared that the risk to the individual would steadily increase as each and every brief counter-trend rise in house prices would be accompanied by a growing bevy of unrelenting housing desperates. They would insist the decline in house prices was over...over and over and over and over again...for the duration of the declines which I believe would last two decades from the 1980s peak, possibly more. The persuasive hype that I am certain will be the response to each and every modicum of improvement in house prices, whether it be for a day, a month, a week, or a few months, during the long and tenuous decline in house prices, will remain a feature of "the crash that doesn't look like a crash". It would be much to the detriment of those who succumb to the erroneous conclusions based on the same familiar false premises, claiming that eventually — and inevitably — house prices will rise in perpetuity.

Due to the length of the residential property market cycle, there are only a few sequences from which we are able to establish precedents. It would appear that these sequences are peculiar to property trends in most countries, which does augment the material available for study. If the empirical evidence of these sequences is to serve as a useful guide — essentially we have no other — it would not be unreasonable to assume that the decline in residential property values in the US, Canada, UK, France, Germany, Italy, Hong Kong, Japan and other areas, are still in their early stages.

Home owners holding property surplus to their needs, who have decided to maintain their holdings on the premise that prices may have fallen as far as they are likely to go, should consider the possibility, the very strong possibility, that house prices have now moved toward another precipice. It is no less foreboding than the peak reached during the 1980s. House prices have been trending downwards during what most economists consider to be a major expansion in global economic activity. That period of expansion has now reached a state of over-maturity. During the latter part of 1995, the French economy moved into recession. During the early part of 1996, the German economy had suffered two consecutive quarters of declining GDP, the standard definition of recession. In June 1996, the British Chancellor of the Exchequer cut interest rates, claiming it was needed because economic growth had not reached previous expectations. If the global economy now contracts and moves into recession, the downturn in house prices is going to accelerate with a ferocity not seen since the 1990-1992 recession. Those who have been postponing sales of property may suddenly find a new dearth of buyers in the period ahead. With very few exceptions, homes may soon become the financial graveyard of all over-extended households. If you are thinking of selling, my suggestion is to stop thinking and start acting. You may still beat the last-minute rush.

However, the outlook is not totally black. It all depends on your circumstances and perspective. Property buffs have been claiming for decades that you can't go wrong if you buy a house at the right price. I would certainly agree with that. Populations are going to continue to expand, real wealth will continue to increase and wealthy individuals from emerging nations will continue to choose countries such as the US, UK, France, Germany and Italy as their playgrounds. In addition, a bit further down the road, there will be a period of long-term, sustainable economic growth that will rival the post-war boom in intensity and duration. In other words, the forces that are needed to power the next boom in residential property prices will fall into place before long. But, I suspect, it's not going to come until we move into the next millennium. While you're waiting, there are a few things you should keep in mind.

If you must buy a house in the near-term for reasons relevant to your circumstances, and have a choice of location, stay away from traditional urban and suburban areas. Regardless of whether or not the global economy or domestic economies move into recession over the near-term — or long-term — there are going to be further advances in telecommunications — satellites, High Definition TV, cellular telephones, faxes, personal computers, fibre optics and multi-media, to name just a few. It could become far less important to have your body in a particular place to do your work or conduct your business. Traffic congestion and air pollution are making it increasingly difficult and inconvenient for people to get where they want to go in town and suburb. The city, and areas in close proximity to cities, will steadily decline as centres of economic activity. Wealthy, independent, productive people will increasingly abandon the city to the masses. I made the decision to do just that several years ago, and I remain as productive as ever...in certain ways, more productive.

Several factors will influence the saleability of specific classes of property and property in certain areas. Residential property in areas where local governments are known to be high spenders are likely to be vulnerable to prospective tax increases. Try to avoid housing in areas that may be subject to high taxation. Properties that showed the greatest increase in value during the boom, but have yet to fall substantially, are also among the most vulnerable. Expensive property still has a lot further to go on the downside than property which reflects quality, but has not been the jewel in the property market's crown. Keep away from properties that have shown the biggest price increases during the 1970s and 1980s, unless they have suffered the sharpest decline since then.

If you have property surplus to your needs, and are tempted to let pending the return of the boom in house prices, there is a specific formula to follow if the decision is to be a viable one. The return you receive should — after all costs — exceed the risk-free rate of return on a bank deposit by a reasonable margin. 6.0% in real terms would be a fair return. During the 1960s, before the great boom got underway in earnest, 12% was a normal cash-on-cash return. Some multiple dwelling units consisting of "bed-sits" produced 20% returns.

As the drama unfolds and the decline in property prices accelerates, property values will hit bottom in certain areas before others. The residential property market in any individual country will not "bottom" everywhere, all at once. The bottoming process will be fragmented and regional. There will be many bargains on offer in certain areas while prices in a broad front are declining. A second-hand home should not be considered a bargain unless it is selling considerably below replacement cost. For properties in Britain, 50 pence in the pound is a good working hypothesis. That number was typical of what properties were going for after areas such as the South West of England and the Midlands experienced regional recession in the mid-1970s and mid-1980s. Generally, if you're out there trying to find a "bargain", the market for property shouldn't be just "soft" it should be absolutely rotten, so much so that you expect *The News of the World* to run *The Death of Home Ownership* as a cover feature.

In the period ahead, the best deals for the home buyer are going to be at the top end of the market. There are some rules of the property game that will remain inviolate. "Location, location, location", are the three factors seen as the best determinant of value. Everything else being equal, the home buyer — if he can afford it — should restrict his interest to the most unique and upmarket properties. To do so in future will probably be even more important than it has been in the past. If profit remains the motive, the surest and largest profit from a home as an investment will be made by owning a home that well-to-do-people would like to have. In other words, you don't want the kind of property the "average" person is likely to buy. Because the average individual is likely to be losing what he has and not buying any more. The type of monetary and economic turbulence we now have — and which shows every sign of continuing — has always tended to destroy the middle-class and to increase small the upper and large lower strata: a spectacle known as polarisation. So, if you must buy a house, look upmarket. A smaller house in a good location is always a better bet than a larger house with larger grounds in a poor location. In short, there are going to be some tremendous upmarket bargains in the years ahead.

I would point out that my forecast for the future of property prices is not an absolute set in stone. I consider such forecasts to be absolutely useless in every respect. My forecasts are based on the manner in which existing economic trends are likely to develop, all things being equal. My forecasting work is based on the possibilities and probabilities of conditions that are likely to unfold under the outlined scenario. I consider that the scenario I have constructed, which empirical evidence and the lessons of history have helped me compile, is the most probable for the residential property market, given the global economic trends I foresee over the next decade.

I repeat: I would advise all who may be contemplating purchasing a property to examine the possibilities and probabilities inherent in my scenario prior to making any move. Housequakes of one sort or another are bound to recur from time to time. When? By now your guess should be as good as mine.

◆◆◆

When it comes to dealing with future events that are likely to unfold, no editorial matter can be considered timeless nor the view set in stone. In the preparation and updating of my manuscript, in many cases I have had to use generalities when considering the lead time for publication and the likely period of distribution. I feel that what I have created is sufficiently ahead of events to provide most readers with the type of information they will need to make prudent decisions in the residential housing market, all things being equal. Unfortunately, in the real world, all things do not remain equal for very long. Conditions can, and often do change quite rapidly and without prior notice. It is the function of my weekly publication **Investors Bulletin** *to monitor these changes and make adjustments to any forecasts that have been made accordingly. In* **Investors Bulletin**, *property and property related matters are covered on a regular basis in addition to the regular economic and investment commentary.* **Investors Bulletin** *is now in its 50th year of publication. During the past 28 years,* **Investors Bulletin** *has been under my editorial stewardship. If any reader feels he or she might be interested in reading a copy of* **Investors Bulletin,** *send your name and address to Investors Bulletin, 2 Bedale Street, London, SE1 9AL, England. Other comments and questions anyone might have can be sent to the same address.*

"Shelter would like to thank Robert Beckman who kindly agreed to donate 10 pence per copy sold to Shelter, the National Campaign for Homeless People, a registered charity (No. 263710) of 88 Old Street, London EC1V 9HU

The content of Robert Beckman's book does not necessarily represent Shelter's views"

INDEX

Rushmere Wynne

are publishers of finance, investment and management books.

If you would like a copy of our current catalogue

Please write to:

Rushmere Wynne
4-5 Harmill
Grovebury Road
Leighton Buzzard
Bedfordshire
LU7 8FF

or fax: 01525 852037 or phone: 01525 853726